Adventures in

Adventures in Prayer

Reflections on St Teresa of Avila, St John of the
Cross and St Thérèse of Lisieux

NOEL O'DONOGHUE

BURNS & OATES
A Continuum imprint
LONDON • NEW YORK

BURNS AND OATES
Burns & Oates
A Continuum imprint

The Tower Building
11 York Road
London SE1 7NX, UK

15 East 26th Street
New York, NY 10010
USA

www.continuumbooks.com

Copyright © Noel O'Donoghue

British Library Cataloguing-in-Publication Data
A catalogue record for this book is available from the British Library

ISBN 0 8601 2348 0 (Paperback)

Typeset by BookEns Limited
Printed and bound in Great Britain by Cromwell Press, Trowbridge, Wilts.

CONTENTS

ACKNOWLEDGEMENTS

The illustration on p. 145 is taken from *The Collected Works of St John of the Cross,* translated by Kieran Kavanaugh and Otilio Rodriguez, © copyright 1964, 1979, 1991 by Washington Province of Discalced Carmelites, ICS Publications, 2131 Lincoln Road, N.E. Washington, DC 20002–1199, USA. *www.icspublications.org*

Chapter 3 was originally published as *With Inward Glory Crowned: A Guide to St Teresa's Interior Castle* by Carmelite Centre of Spirituality (Dublin), 1981.

The poem by Gerard Manley Hopkins on pp. 172–3 is taken from *The Poems of Gerard Manley Hopkins* published by Oxford University Press, 1982.

I would like to thank John Bate for kindly allowing me to print his poem 'Whose Frailty', and Susan Cammack who helped to finalize this manuscript.

FOREWORD

One of the most lucid and lyrical of modern writers on prayer, Noel O'Donoghue has spent a lifetime weaving together the Carmelite mystical tradition with that of his Celtic and Irish Christian heritage, locating both of these traditions in the broader Platonic or Neoplatonic stream that irrigates our civilization. Both in his teaching and in his writing, certain key insights recur, but they are insights capable of endless development. Two of these insights are the central importance in the soul of the Imagination (understood as a faculty of perception or cognition), and the intimate relationship between love and suffering. Out of these profound themes Father O'Donoghue develops a form of Christian Gnosis (*not* 'Gnosticism'), turning the Catholic faith towards the light that it carries within itself, so that it can no longer be called 'blind' but becomes an actual seeing of God, a journeying into him.

In this bold enterprise Father O'Donoghue is linked to St Paul and St Augustine, to the great Alexandrian Church Fathers Clement and Origen, to the Christian Platonist John Scotus Eriugena (an Irishman!), to the medieval mystics (including Julian of Norwich), to the saints of the Catholic Reformation (from Ignatius to Teresa), and – closer to our own time – to the 'little' Thérèse, to Maurice Blondel, Henri de Lubac and Hans Urs von Balthasar, inspirers of the *ressourcement*. He is in tune, too, with the English-speaking Romantics from William Blake to George MacDonald and Kathleen Raine, not forgetting G.K. Chesterton and the Inklings. At the same time, his writing opens up a way for Christians to understand better the Islamic Sufis, who place a similar emphasis on Love and the Imagination, and the Jewish Kabbalistic tradition, which are both similarly entangled with Neoplatonism. There are many differences of emphasis here, but these are undoubtedly some of the sources and influences inspiring our author – or helping him to find the words for his own religious experience as a Celtic Christian.

Unlike many younger writers on Christian spirituality, Father O'Donoghue was rigorously trained in the old school, and if he has fought free to some extent of what he felt as its deadening hold on his imagination, he owes a great deal to that training and the deep formation it implanted. In this book we have what may be his most complete study of the Carmelite tradition of prayer, the origins of which are lost in the mists of time on the slopes of Mount Carmel. Behind it stands perhaps Elijah; in the foreground the three great saints and doctors of the Church who are the focus of this volume, the saints he describes in terms of Vision, of Fire, and of Childhood. As its title suggests, the book is about *adventures* in prayer, and therefore not about the mere academic study of prayer, or the typology of prayer. The interior life to which he invites us is the biggest adventure there can be.

We embark on this adventure, if we are wise, with our hand held firmly by one of the masters of the interior life who have gone before us, and in that of the Master who lives in them and lives too in the deep levels of ourselves, through the grace of the sacraments. Baptism plunges us into the cold waters of death, but only so that a light and a fire can kindle and heal us in the land that awaits us on the other side. There Jesus himself welcomes us with a charcoal fire, fish and bread (John 21: 9). Or on the Mountain of Transfiguration we see the glory attained through sacrifice that cannot be glimpsed from the valleys. In the revelations that await us, whether on the shore, in the depths of our own Interior Castle, or in the hill country, each person has a unique place, but the Journey is one we take with others, in a *communion*, rather than alone.

An important theme of this book is the nature of mystical love. The three great Carmelites are very different in style and tone, in personality and mission, but they are united in knowing God as the Bridegroom of the Soul, and the mysteries of marriage hinted at by Saint Paul in his Letter to the Ephesians are luminously present in their poetry and prose alike. The love of beauty, assumed into a love of divine glory, the spiritual *eros* at its most intense and hertfelt, is an experience that transcends sexuality but at the same time validates it, as grace builds upon and validates the created nature that yearns for God. The divine marriage is never far away in this book, and with that is implicit the goal of our Journey, the deification of which the Church Fathers speak, the 'union with God in the Spirit', the coming of God's kingdom into the heart of the one who seeks it.

Stratford Caldecott
Chesterton Institute for Faith & Culture, Oxford

PART ONE

ST TERESA OF AVILA: WOMAN OF VISION

CHAPTER 1

A JOURNEY THROUGH THE LIFE

Teresa Reads a Dangerous Book

At first it might seem that prayer is a most peaceful and harmless occupation, and that a person who chooses prayer as the first and greatest occupation of life will be left in peace to get on with it, whatever the inner difficulties that may be encountered. Yet, if we look back on the history of the Christian Church or indeed of any of the great religions what we find is that prayer is the most dangerous and delicate way of being and acting that anyone can undertake, and that the lives of the great masters of prayer were hemmed in by oppositions and misunderstandings and a very real danger of being imprisoned, tortured and burned at the stake. The two great Carmelite mystics of sixteenth–century Spain, Teresa of Jesus and John of the Cross, were no exceptions to this and we shall try to look carefully at some of the dangerous and complicated adventures in which they found themselves. I begin with the discovery by Teresa of a certain book which, though she did not know it in the least, was to bring a great deal of trouble and anxiety into her life.

Teresa de Cepeda y Ahumada was already a nun in the Carmelite Convent of the Incarnation outside the walls of Avila when in her twenty-third year she went for treatment for a breakdown of health to a place called Becedas and stayed for a while en route with her uncle Don Pedro, a very pious but somewhat depressive man, who gave her the book which all Spain was talking about, the *Tercer Abecedario* or *Third Spiritual Alphabet*[1] of a Franciscan preacher

---

1. An 'Alphabet' was a kind of device for dealing with a variety of related topics: A kind of *dictionnaire* or encyclopaedia.

3

called Francisco de Osuna, or simply Osuna. Uncle Pedro asked
his niece to read for him, and she gives us a charming description
of the relationship between the lively young nun and this rather
daunting man whose conversation 'was ordinarily about God and
the vanity of the world' (*Life* 3.4).[2]

The *Third Alphabet* of Osuna is a treatise of the kind of prayer
which is an inner focusing of the mind and heart on God as source
and creator of our being and especially as revealed in Jesus of Nazareth
as Messiah, Saviour and truly God as well as man. Osuna was a
Franciscan with the true Franciscan centring on the affectivity and
the natural world as showing forth God's glory. But above all he
taught recollection, *recogimiento*, a kind of silent inner attention
to God which ascended upwards on the two wings of self-knowledge
and knowledge of God in Christ. Augustine with his unique gift
for profound and pithy phrases had put it all long ago in four words:
noverim me, noverim te (that I may know myself, that I may know
thyself). Sometimes recollection has been called mental prayer as
contrasted with vocal prayer; thus it came to be named in Catholic
seminaries such as Maynooth and Saint-Sulpice, and a period of
time was devoted to it each morning, usually half an hour. It was
also named meditation, or (sometimes) simply prayer or silent
prayer. As Osuna and the Franciscans conceived it, this way of relating
to the Source was given a central place in the spiritual life and a
man like Francis Borgia gave five or six hours a day to it. Prayer
in the sense of silent or 'mental' prayer was seen as the centre of
life and even as the whole of life; thus the Christian was fulfilling
quite literally (too literally perhaps?) Christ's own command or counsel
that we should always pray.

Like almost all Christian traditions and forms of activity, the
way of recollection had its special key texts from Scripture among
which one text had a special place, namely Luke 10.38–42 where
Mary, who simply sits at the feet of Jesus and 'listened to His teaching',

---

2. E. Allison Peers, tr., *The Complete Works of St Teresa*, Vol. I (London: Sheed
   & Ward, 1957), p. 18.

is commended for having chosen the 'good' or 'better' part (the original can bear either translation), which shall not be taken from her by her sister of the 'active' life who is 'anxious and troubled about many things'. It is hardly possible to exaggerate the influence of this one text of that tradition of recollection, going back to the Rhineland and Northern European mystics, which Teresa encountered in one of its most inspired exponents in the *Third Alphabet* of Francisco de Osuna.

It must be noted, however, that the Mary and Martha text attained such central importance in the theory and practice of recollection or silent prayer only because it was felt to express clearly and graphically something at the heart of the Christian gospel, absolutely central to the life and teaching of Jesus the Redeemer, teacher and model of the true relationship with God. The youthful Teresa knew enough of the Christian gospel to see and feel that all that Osuna was doing was to express this gospel powerfully as a personal call to close union with the source of her being. This call came to her loudly and clearly in this book that she was forced to read because (shrewdly, one suspects) her pious uncle, Don Pedro, asked her to read it to him.

In responding however reluctantly to the way of interior silent prayer advocated by Osuna and by a whole spiritual movement in those days (the first half of the sixteenth century) Teresa was, without knowing it, playing with fire. By 1559 Osuna's latest book was to be condemned and the whole movement to which he belonged was to be regarded with deep and continuing suspicion by the agents of the Spanish Inquisition, who saw it as their duty to seek out and destroy every sign of heterodox spirituality which included not only Erastianism and Lutheranism but also what was called *Alumbrismo* or Illuminism. On the whole, Spanish Catholic writers try to make a sharp distinction between Illuminism and orthodox Christian mysticism, but the Anglican writer Allison Peers tends to find Spanish Illuminism and Christian mysticism inextricably mingled or intertwined in their origins and roots, somewhat as today we find that New Age Christians may belong within the mainline churches or very far outside them on some eccentric or original path.[3]

When, however, Teresa at the age of 23 received Osuna's *Third Spiritual Alphabet* from her Uncle Pedro it was a book highly regarded by all spiritually inclined persons, and Teresa read it avidly; it was to be her guide on the way of prayer, as for many years she could find no confessor to guide her. By 1959 when Osuna came to be treated as suspect by the Inquisition, Teresa was established in her own way of interior prayer with reliable guides to help her. Yet the watchdogs of the Inquisition prowled around, and it had been noised abroad that she was a woman of visions and strange experiences, which tended to place her within the camp of the Illuminists. It was because of this that one of her confessors asked her to write down her experiences and her way of prayer. The result was the *Vida* or *Life*, one of the great spiritual classics of the Christian West. So it is that we are indebted to the Inquisition for this quite priceless book.

But the writing of the *Life* did not suffice to put Teresa beyond the reach of the Inquisition; on the contrary, it came to be used against her by her critics and her enemies. Indeed the book did not come to be published in any real sense until after her death and then only because the powerful Philip II made it known that he favoured her. Indeed, the first edition of her main works was dedicated to the Queen and Empress; otherwise it might have been publicly burnt as dangerous and heretical, as indeed Teresa herself might have been burned or cast into prison. It would seem that this deep shadow of the Inquisition lay over Teresa all her life long. The way of interior prayer was seen as a threat to the Established Church of word and sacrament as was the case with the Quaker movement in eighteenth-century England: indeed there is a real sense in which the Discalced Carmelite movement that swept across the religious life of Spain in the sixteenth century was then,

---

3. For the Catholic Spanish approach at its most scholarly see M. A. Martin, *Los Recogidos* (Madrid: Fundacion Universitaria Espanola, 1976); see also E. Allison Peers, *Studies of the Spanish Mystics,* 2 vols (London: SPCK, 1951).

and still is from an English perspective, a kind of Catholic Quakerism and no less open to misunderstanding and persecution. The woman or man of prayer has found a personal direct line to God and that must always pose a profound threat to the established order – ecclesiastical and, where there is an Established Church, political as well. In sixteenth-century Spain the Established Church was extremely powerful and extremely present by way of inquisitors and the Inquisition, which was only loosely connected with Rome. By her personal, direct, unmediated approach to the divinity, Teresa (and indeed Osuna before her) was posing a dangerous threat to this awe-inspiring juggernaut, no less dangerous than that posed by a certain Augustinian friar in Saxony named Martin Luther. Teresa had been brought up to detest Luther and Lutheranism and indeed founded her new Carmelite Order partly as a bulwark against the inroads of Lutheranism. She and her followers rightly resented accusations of being close to Luther and Erasmus, yet by her way of prayer she was affirming the central Protestant principle of that personal, immediate link with God and Christ which Luther found in St Paul's Epistle to the Galatians.[4]

El Demonio

But more than any inquisitor, Teresa as a woman of her time felt she was in danger from that enemy within herself which she named *El Demonio,* the devil or Satan, that adversary who is a central negative presence in the New Testament. We need only read Chapter 13 of the *Life* to see how much the constant deceiving presence of Satan was taken for granted. Satan is very subtle in the work of turning good into evil, even sometimes causing us to exaggerate what is good so that we come to reject it. Thus, too many penances can lead us to reject all penance so that we end up by becoming far too concerned about rest and bodily infirmities.

---

4. See N. D. O'Donoghue, 'The Cloister and the Tower', *Carmel* (Sept.–Oct. 1982) pp. 14–18.

Or the devil may persuade us that we are superior to others, and so we lose the most precious gift of humility; the temptations which the old devil, Screwtape, advises in order to capture the newly converted Christian, in C. S. Lewis's *Screwtape Letters* have a curious resemblance to the stratagems which Teresa attributes to *El Demonio*: they are seen as the stock-in-trade of the tempter at all times.

It is quite clear that Lewis's Screwtape and Wormwood, uncle and nephew, are fictitious characters used by the author to make some moral and religious points, though it is interesting that Lewis found himself, as he wrote, being taken into a strangely real and frightening world. It seems likely that *El Demonio* was for Teresa sometimes a kind of shorthand for ordinary human weakness and self-deceit. It seems, however, that both for Teresa and for sixteenth-century Spain, *El Demonio* was very real and very personal, as in the writings of the New Testament, and that one had to take account of Him (or *Her*, for the masculine pronoun had no gender significance) at all times and especially in matters of prayer and the spiritual journey. Satan's dark kingdom was constantly threatened by prayer and spiritual progress, he could not prevent this, or rather he could counteract it only by twisting human freewill in his direction, by subtly sowing seeds of pride or self-indulgence or timidity. It was understood that Satan attained special power over those who gave themselves up to softness and love of comfort, and so it was that an ascetic lifestyle became connected with the spiritual journey, and this sometimes went to extremes of vigils and fasting and a kind of hair-shirt existence, so much so that spiritual progress was seen as almost impossible without it. It must be said, however, that the physical hair shirt, and all it means in terms of vigils and fasting, was seen as a way for novices; the more mature spiritual athlete was given a far more interior and 'spiritual' hair shirt. Opposition from without and anxieties from within were no small part of the texture of this hair shirt.

In the face of this fearsome and ever-present adversary, Teresa had one important help and protection, that of those men, nearly all monks or friars, whom she herself chose as confessors or spiritual directors. They were many and various and Teresa managed them all with enormous charm and skill, yet she was ready to accept what they said, and this saved her from many worries, inner tensions and fears. It is doubtful whether she could have survived the perils and terrors of her way of prayer and inner journeyings without them. Certainly we owe her writings to them and to that genial use of obedience by which they insisted on keeping her at her writing when she begged to be allowed to get on with her spinning and her work in the kitchen.

The Four Waterings

In the *Third Alphabet* of Osuna, Teresa read that there were levels of prayer beyond that vocal prayer used largely in the recitation of the Divine Office and other prayers recited in community. Osuna saw a second level of prayer as an opening up of the *corazón* or heart by which he seems to have meant the affective level of the soul or psyche, in so far as it tried to reach beyond all human loves and delights to the source of our being, which was named God and which had become a living man in Jesus Christ. Incidents and images and imaginative projections of the human Jesus of Nazareth abounded at this level and it has indeed always been central to the Franciscan 'way' to which Osuna belonged. Osuna had deep respect for this way of the heart, yet he felt that there is a form of prayer that goes beyond this realm of images and affectivity to a purely mental and spiritual realm where the humanity of Christ merged and lost itself in the eternal Godhead. It must be noted here that Osuna tends to identify the mental or intellectual with the spiritual, and indeed we find Teresa rather petulantly saying that she fails to see any distinction between mind, soul and spirit. This was how she avoided trying to make distinctions which were beyond her – one of her strengths as a writer is that she never sets down what she does not fully understand without admitting the fact – yet in practice she is very clear that the kind of ascent that Osuna advises is not something she can follow. She sees the stages of prayer in her own way; however, it may be well to look at the famous traditional distinction of the three ways of the spiritual life that goes back to the early Greek fathers of the second and third centuries and appears constantly in the later Latin patristic and medieval writers: the Purgative, Illuminative and Unitive ways which can be best understood as stages in spiritual growth to which prayer is of central importance.

The first way is the stage of turning away firmly from the allurements and involvements in the world, the flesh and the devil: all that pulls the spirit back and holds it down. In the Illuminative way the person who has managed to achieve such a degree of purification as rules out grave faults and failings and tendencies is gifted with a new understanding of the sacred Scriptures and the things of the Spirit and, though encountering times of darkness, is finding comfort and joy in a new lightsome world. This leads on to the way of Union in which the spirit is deeply and constantly immersed in the presence and love of God. These ways, though they represent a journey from one level to the next, can nevertheless reappear within these levels, and also from time to time, later ones can appear unexpectedly and briefly at earlier levels; for example touches of the prayer of Union can come at both the first and second levels.

Not the least of the hazards attending Teresa's adventures in prayer was her ignorance of the theological vocabulary and that world of metaphor which had grown up over the centuries. She met this hazard triumphantly by discovering within herself a rare, perhaps unique, gift of shaping her own metaphors from the simple universal facts of life and her limited reading. She seems to have found Osuna's three levels of prayer as confusing as does the modern reader, and it seems that she never quite felt at home in the spirituality of the three ways. So in one of those moments of insight which seem to have come to her as she wrote and tried to explain herself, Teresa saw her soul (or mind or spirit) as a garden, according, it would seem, to the imagery of the Song of Songs, and she reflected that as a garden it needs regular watering. Then in a flash she saw that the whole process or set of processes used in watering a garden could be used to explain, in a way everybody could understand, the development of the life of prayer from its first plodding steps or green shoots to its full flowering in the experience of total absorption in God. So it is that in Chapters 11 to 22 of the *Life* we have the statement and explication of the Four Waterings of the garden of the soul. The passage is characteristically sharp and clear and even simple, yet it should be reflected on again and again. Perhaps, at the end of reading it and reflecting on it, the modern reader may be led to pray with Hopkins: *Lord, send my roots rain.*[5]

The metaphor is easily stated; it is the 'carrying across' or application of the metaphor that can be demanding and even tantalizing. One should note the remarkable way in which the human effort and labour passes over into a deep passivity or receptivity of the soul as the divine source takes over in what is strictly mystical, or in Teresa's terms 'supernatural' prayer. This may be the place to note that the modern student of the ways of prayer is well advised to avoid the word 'mysticism', for it has become a kind of debased currency, and should speak rather of *mystical prayer* as an experience that may come to those, and only to those, who give themselves to prayer as the most important activity in life, as Teresa did and John of the Cross and Osuna and the Spanish, Rhineland and English mystics from Eckhart onwards.

Here in the Kavanaugh–Rodriguez[6] version is Teresa's account of the metaphor of the Four Waterings and of the application of the basic, all-important first mode of watering the garden. It must be noted that in the order of activity it is by far the most difficult of the Four Waterings or stages of prayer and that here the basic will and willingness is all-important, not only as stable and courageous, but also as a kind of conversion of the affectivity by which the 'heart' is set on God beyond all human affections. Teresa tends to take this for granted, though for many people it is the

5. Gerard Manley Hopkins, 'Thou art indeed just, Lord' (written 1889).
6. Kieran Kavanaugh and Otilio Rodriguez, tr., *The Collected Works of Saint Teresa of Avila*, Vol. I (Washington, DC: Institute of Carmelite Studies, 1976), pp. 80–7.

rubicon that they have to cross on the journey of prayer. Here, then, is the key passage from Chapter 11 of the *Life*.

> (7) It seems to me the garden can be watered in four ways. You may draw water from a well and aqueducts in such a way that it is obtained by turning the crank of the water well (which is for us a lot of work). Or you may get it by means of a water wheel (I have drawn it this way sometimes – the method involves less work than the other, and you get more water). Or it may flow from a river or a stream. (The garden is watered much better by this means because the ground is more fully soaked, and there is no need to water so frequently – and much less work for the gardener.) Or the water may be provided by a great deal of rain. (For the Lord waters the garden without any work on our part – and this way is incomparably better than all the others mentioned.)
>
> (9) Beginners in prayer, we can say, are those who draw water from the well. This involves a lot of work on their own part, as I have said. They must tire themselves in trying to recollect their senses. Since they are accustomed to being distracted, this recollection requires much effort. They need to get accustomed to caring nothing at all about seeing or hearing, to practicing the hours of prayer, and thus to solitude and withdrawal – and to thinking on their past life. Although these beginners and the others as well must often reflect upon their past, the extent to which they must do so varies, as I shall say afterward. In the beginning such reflection is even painful, for they do not fully understand whether or not they are repentant of their sins. If they are, they are then determined to serve God earnestly. They must strive to consider the life of Christ – and the intellect grows weary in doing this.
>
> These are the things we can do of ourselves, with the understanding that we do so by the help of God, for without this help as is already known we cannot have so much as a good thought. These things make up the beginning of fetching water from the well, and please God that it may be found. At least we are doing our part, for we are already drawing it out and doing what we can to water these flowers. God is so good that when for reasons His Majesty knows – perhaps for our greater benefit – the well is dry and we, like good gardeners, do what lies in our power, He sustains the garden without water and makes the virtues grow. Here by 'water' I am referring to

tears and when there are no tears to interior tenderness and feelings of devotion.

(10) But what will he do here who sees that after many days there is nothing but dryness, distaste, vapidness, and very little desire to come to draw water? So little is the desire to do this that if he doesn't recall that doing so serves and gives pleasure to the Lord of the garden, and if he isn't careful to preserve the merits acquired in this service (and even what he hopes to gain from the tedious work of often letting the pail down into the well and pulling it back up without any water), he will abandon everything. It will frequently happen to him that he will even be unable to lift his arms for this work and unable to get a good thought. This discursive work with the intellect is what is meant by fetching water from the well.

(11) These labours take their toll. Being myself one who endured them for many years (for when I got a drop of water from this sacred well I thought God was granting me a favour), I know that they are extraordinary. It seems to me more courage is necessary for them than for many other labours of this world. But I have seen clearly that God does not leave one, even in this life, without a large reward; because it is certainly true that one of those hours in which the Lord afterward bestowed on me a taste of Himself repaid, it seems to me, all the anguish I suffered in persevering for a long time in prayer.

In the first stage of prayer the pray-er or suppliant is active, engaging deliberately and resolutely in what can only be seen as hard work. The suppliant has, of course, felt a kind of drawing towards this way of prayer and has esteemed it as the most important or indeed the only important thing in life. At first this drawing may be attended with a kind of delight and inner sweetness which some writers call 'first favours'. Teresa does not mention these first favours directly but a careful reading of what she says makes it clear that they are taken for granted as well as the resolute approach to the labour involved. Indeed she comes near to equating the water of this First Watering with 'interior tenderness' and 'feelings of devotion' (end of para 9). The work is not simply undertaken as a matter of pure, cold willingness or decision but has a deep presence in the heart or affectivity thus drawing on that eros or sexual drive without which men and women are more dead than alive. Teresa did not address herself to this kind of personality, which she tended to place under the general heading of *Melancolia*.

Yet – and this is her main concern here – this vitalizing sense of devotion soon gives way to distractions and aridity in which prayer and meditation become a daily burden, a kind of 'journey through the desert' or 'journey in the dark' attended by weariness and dullness and (though Teresa touches on the matter very lightly here) what Francis Thompson calls 'the searing ploughshares of scrupulosity'. At such times, in Teresa's imagery, there is no water in the well and yet the suppliant must keep up his journeys to and fro assiduously. At such times praying, and meditation too – Teresa assumes that what she calls discursive meditation is going on at this time – seems the most pointless and fruitless of occupations. With her characteristic motherly tact Teresa has some welcome words of consolation to say to the wilting suppliant (para 10B). She goes on to say (para 11) that this great trial of aridity which may go on for years is necessary if the original willing and decisional strength of the suppliant is to be made strong enough to receive the tremendous awe-inspiring experiences that God has in store for it. And of course great trials await it as it follows the way of the cross and of the imitation of Christ.

It is especially when she talks about the Cross and the trials that attend the ways of mystical prayer, that we must listen carefully for the tone or accent behind the text, which is always vital and positive and nearly always full of a deep joy, always wanting to express itself in lively and homely metaphors. Here, especially, as she talks of the trials that await the suppliant who is determined to travel all the way, one feels that if we have the companionship of this cheerful maternal voice the journey ahead may be possible. Yet we are being explicitly asked to walk the way of the imitation of Christ rather than the substitutional road that Luther found. Luther will have the Christian hold on firmly to Christ by faith, not looking to any works of his own. He tells us how he strove to be a good monk in the traditional way and only fell deeper and deeper into despair, until he suddenly realized that it was by pure unconditional faith in Christ that the presence and power of God came to him. Teresa will admit this in the sense that 'without God's help we cannot have so much as a good thought'. But her approach is totally synergic or co-operative, so that it is only if the suppliant works hard at drawing buckets of water from a well that may at times be almost dry that we can ever hope to travel the way of mystical or 'supernatural' prayer. As time goes on, God begins to 'take over' and has taken over entirely in the Fourth Watering, but this happens only because the suppliant has worked hard, perhaps indeed *long* and hard, in carrying out the First Watering as described in Chapters 11, 12 and 13 of the *Life*, especially in Chapter 11.

The Spark from Above

Part of the adventuresome nature of the way of prayer is that ordinary logic and consistency has to be sometimes left behind. For instance, in ordinary logical discourse a human enterprise that involves a series of stages will be seen as a journey from one stage to the next and a metaphor such as that of the Four Waterings, or the Seven Mansions, will be seen in a serial fashion, so that if a person has anything like full experience of the Fourth Watering in which the heavenly rain falls abundantly, he/she will no longer have to contend with those periods of dryness and lack of all devotion that form part of the way of the First Watering. That is not the case. A person may have had abundant experience of the inundation and transformative power of the Fourth Watering or the state of deep union of the Seventh Mansions and may still find themselves quite unable to pray, quite surrounded by faults and failings. The most precious fruit of mystical prayer at its highest is a certain substantial joy and peace which can descend so deep into the soul that it becomes unconscious of itself as in the 'old people' of the Celtic tradition as described by Alexander Carmichael and the Irish writers of the Blasket Islands. This is the world of mystical prayer as 'heaven in ordinarie' in George Herbert's phrase.[7]

---

7. George Herbert, 'Prayer: Prayer the Church's Banquet' (1633).

So it is that the wrong way to benefit from St Teresa's schema of the Four Waterings is to pass on quickly from the first laborious phase of the buckets and the uncertain spring to the later phases of more and more abundance. Teresa is at pains to counter this attitude. She writes (*Life* 13.16). 'No soul on this road is such a giant that it does not often need to become a child at the breast again. (This must never be forgotten: I may repeat it again and again, for it is of great importance.)'[8] The childhood metaphor is not used here quite in the sense of 'spiritual childhood', which can be a very exalted state, but simply as a metaphor to state vividly that we are all beginners all the time in the spiritual journey even when we have reached the highest prayer of Union. Here we are dealing with the strange paradoxical upside-down logic of the spiritual journey. It can make sense only if we reflect that all is gift and that a gift can be withdrawn for a time at any moment so that we realize that it *is* a gift. The truly humble suppliant rejoices in this.

In the metaphor of the Four Waterings of the garden, the First Watering is the work of the suppliants themselves, though the hidden help of divine grace must be assumed; at least it is very firmly assumed by Teresa. This is the level of active or ordinary prayer. It is with the metaphor of the windlass that the way begins to open up to mystical prayer, which Teresa calls 'supernatural' prayer and which, after Osuna and rather confusingly, she calls the Prayer of Quiet because the understanding (as well as the memory) is now at rest, though the will, or 'heart' in Osuna's terminology, is active in loving God with a deep fervour as if it had become ignited by a divine 'spark'. This spark is a gift which the soul simply receives into itself. This it seems is more deep and enduring than those first favours that helped to keep the soul going in the strenuous labours of the First Watering. It is nevertheless quite different, for it is *lasting* and is independent of moods and all kinds of natural drynesses and vicissitudes, as it is also independent of passing thoughts and memories and the vagaries of the imagination. It is of the same kind as the spark spoken of by Meister Eckhart and the Rhineland

---

8. Peers, *Complete Works of St Teresa*, p. 80.

mystics and perhaps also that 'naked intent of the will' of the author of the fourteenth-century *Cloud of Unknowing.* By its presence all worldy interests and desires are placed under a 'cloud of forgetting'.

We are in fact, Teresa tells us, crossing the threshold of 'supernatural' or mystical prayer. It is pure gift and by it God is 'taking over'. Mystical gifts of this kind always percolate deeper and deeper into the spirit and here we are not far from the level of the 'unconscious' of Nicolai von Hartmann and certain nineteenth-century philosophers, which was taken up by Freud and his disciples, though they are not dealing with the world of mystical prayer. This 'little spark of true love for the Lord which He begins to enkindle in the soul' (*Life* 15.4)[9] is a phenomenon common to the personal phenomenology of all the great mystics within and outside Christianity and it echoes not only the tender profound agape of the Christian New Testament (as in 1 Corinthians 13) but also that intellectual *eros* of which Plato speaks in the two great dialogues devoted to human love and loving, the *Symposium* and the *Phaedrus,* and that deeply Platonic passage in which Aristotle speaks of the contemplation of the truth as the highest function and purpose of the human soul (*Nicomachean Ethics,* Book 10, ch. 7). Those *letrados* or learned men who formed a little group around Teresa when she wrote the *Vida* would have some knowledge of this background in the great tradition and the Christian *Holy Book* or Bible in its Latin (Vulgate) version.

That stage of prayer which Teresa names the Prayer of Quiet and the coming of the 'little spark' of Divine Love is roughly that which in her figure of the Mansions she calls the Fourth Mansions; it marks the passage from ordinary laborious prayer to the way of mystical prayer. It involves a high degree of detachment from possessions of all kinds, including one's own pride and wilfulness, yet not that *total* detachment of the self *from* the self which can only be done by God through a great inner darkness and letting go of one's own-most self. It is in a sense a less than total dying of the natural self, yet it is for all that a very precious and elevated

---

9. Ibid., p. 90.

experience which, St Teresa believes, can come to many people who have given themselves to the way of prayer. In Teresa's tradition it is the fruit of meditation especially by way of considering the life of Christ, His teachings, His 'mysteries' and especially His sufferings, all this against the background of one's own sins and failings and coldness of heart without, however, indulging in anxious self-examination but rather looking outward and upward to Christ and His mysteries. It is here that the Ignatian Spiritual Exercises may be used or various forms of mantra (e.g. the *Maranatha* of John Main), or what is called 'the prayer of the heart' as expounded in *The Way of the Pilgrim* by an unknown Russian writer[10]. There is also, for Catholics especially, the Marian Rosary which can be used by any Christian (or indeed anybody), since it is firmly and uniquely based on the words of the New Testament. People in the Reform tradition may find themselves more at home in the prayerful meditative reading of Scripture (including, especially, the Psalms) by which certain phrases can act as a sort of mantra to concentrate the mind on God. This is the recollection of which Osuna speaks, as do many others among the predecessors of Teresa and John of the Cross. All such exercises prepare the way for the coming of the presence of God into the soul, but only according to God's will and grace.

In her concluding chapter on the Second Watering, in which the spark from above begins to irrigate the garden and we are at the gateway of mystical prayer, St Teresa throws out a remark which it is well to reflect on. Here are her words in the Peers translation: 'In this life of ours the soul does not grow in the way the body does, though we speak of it as if it did, and growth does in fact occur' (*Life* 15.12).[11] Teresa is here directly concerned with her favourite theme of the need for humility at all times, but it is possible to generalize this principle in a helpful way, as has been done by the late Winifred Rushforth in her talks on psyche and physique in which she claimed that there is a law by which the soul gets stronger or is somehow meant to get stronger as the physical body

---

10. R. M. French, tr., (London: SPCK, 1942)
11. Ibid., p. 94.

weakens and disintegrates in old age; she herself died at 97 years of age, and the week she died was running several dream groups; and people from all over the world came to consult her.[12] It is in their later years that many people come to the ways of mystical prayer very quietly without anybody noticing. But those who really have understanding that this is so do notice it, and far from despising the old woman or old man clutching rosary beads or crucifix or book of prayers, will be alerted to the possibility that they are in the presence of that most precious force that elevates the whole world: genuine mystical prayer. If ever this were realized there would be an end to that *ageism* which is a most destructive inflection in Western society.

From this point of view it is worth looking carefully at the *Carmina Gadelica* of Alexander Carmichael, that uniquely beautiful and profound collection of prayers and songs made in the Western Isles of Scotland about a hundred years ago and representing a folk tradition that goes very far back towards the world of the Celtic monks and missionaries. These prayers and hymns represent a Christian and pre-Christian religious consciousness that went its own way, independently of priest or minister, towards the heights and depths of mystical prayer. To anyone who reads Carmichael's account of where and from whom he collected these prayers, it will soon become clear that he is calling not only on the memory of old people but on their present living experience of a kind of prayer that flows from sources beyond the words and incantations and will perhaps realize how much a certain asceticism of life and close contact with nature opens the way to the God of creation *Ri na ndúl.*

Contact with the *Carmina* and the tradition which it represents may well awaken us to the riches, from the point of view of mystical prayer, of our own old age and of old age generally.[13]

Those who want to look for a scriptural warrant for this prayer-mysticism of old age will find it vividly and carefully presented in

---

12. See Winifred Rushforth, *Something is Happening* (Wellingborough: Turnstone Press, 1981), ch. 14.
13. See N. D. O'Donoghue, *The Angels Keep Their Ancient Places* (Edinburgh: T & T Clark, 2001), ch. 7.

the second chapter of the Gospel according to Luke, in the carefully balanced man–woman diptych of Simeon and Anna and their reception of the divine child of promise into the depths of hearts prepared for him.

The Sleep of the Faculties

In the Third Watering, the suppliant is brought fully within the world of mystical or 'supernatural' prayer, in which the Divine Presence takes over all the powers or faculties of the soul: the spark of the stage of the Second Watering has become a kind of conflagration setting the whole soul on fire (*Life* chs 16 and 17). Here the prayer adventure, unique though it is, connects with two other great human adventures: the adventure of artistic inspiration and the adventure of falling in love. In both of these adventures a man or woman is taken over and, as it were, lost to the world, becoming easily detached from everything else and becoming happily yet painfully immersed in the object of its inspiration or its infatuation. All the powers of the soul or psyche are taken up and taken over by the Divine Presence at this level of prayer, taken into a kind of madness that wants to burst forth in words or gestures like Michelangelo at work in the Sistine Chapel or Elizabeth Barrett Browning writing her *Sonnets from the Portuguese*. Such people are so totally led by their purpose and fascination that there is barely space to give attention to everyday necessities and commitments. But there *is* some room, and at this stage Mary and Martha can work together.

At this level of involvement with the Source, the human soul becomes beside itself and from sheer, almost painful, exuberance and overflowing, breaks forth in song and poetry and 'utters a thousand holy follies', ready indeed to run towards martyrdom in a kind of 'celestial holy madness' (*santa locura celestial, Life* 16.4). It must be borne in mind that this experience is merely a passing experience and not by any means a stable state. Nor does it remain clearly fixed in the memory, though it can recur as it did for Teresa when she was describing it in the *Life*. It is clear that she is striving in every way she can to give a clear and exact account of her experiences not for any other reason than that she was asked to do so by her confessors. She is at her best in describing her own experiences and at her most obscure in linking her experiences with the terminology provided by the writers on mystical prayer of her day. Thus it has happened that a certain technical terminology elaborated by writers with less clear and deep experience of the ways of prayer than Teresa had, have come to be associated with her doctrine and have served to veil it rather than clarify it.

So it is that as a general description of the Third Watering of the soul, in which God takes over in an abundant flowing of light and fire, Teresa uses the phrase which she took over from Bernardino de Laredo (and others) and speaks of 'the sleep of the faculties' (*un sueño de las potencias*). We must pause to ask what Teresa and the mystical tradition to which she belongs understands by 'faculties' or *potencias* and in what sense these faculties may be said to 'sleep' in such a way that they are 'neither wholly lost nor yet can understand how they work' (*Life* 16.1).[14]

For that great Western philosophical-theological tradition the soul or psyche was seen as common to all living things, animals and plants as well as men and women, and was a principle of life immersed in matter in such a way that it was seen as whole in the whole corporeal entity and whole in each part of it. It had powers or faculties at the various levels of life, sentiency and intelligence, for example the power of growth and reproduction belongs to trees as well as animals and men, the faculties of locomotion and perception belong to animals and men, while the power or faculty of forming ideas and judgements belongs among visible beings only to the level of the human.

It is the purely human powers that for the most part are given the name of *potencias* or faculties by Teresa and John of the Cross, that is to say powers not possessed by the non-human animal world. Now where Thomas Aquinas and the Dominican tradition quite firmly spoke of two, and only two, higher 'rational', exclusively human faculties: intellect or understanding (*ratio, intellectus*) and

---

14. Peers, *Complete Works of St Teresa*, p. 96.

will (*voluntas*), Teresa and John in the Franciscan–Augustinian tradition spoke of three higher rational faculties: intelect, will and memory (or memory-imagination – sometimes memory *and* imagination, making four rational faculties in all).

When in our present text (*Life* chs 16 and 17) Teresa talks of the sleep of the faculties, she means that in this state in which God seems to take over the soul in abundance of light and fire, all those rational faculties – intellect-understanding, will and memory-imagination – are so taken up, so inundated that they seem lost to the world, as artists of deep inspiration and people very deeply in love tend to be. The supplicant-lover is totally or almost totally absorbed in the presence of the Divine Lover as all-good, all-compassionate, all-beautiful, and while this condition lasts she/he is, as it were, 'lost to the world'.

It must be noted that Teresa arose within a long tradition of theological erudition and a critical understanding of the ways of prayer. All her life, she consulted the living masters of this tradition and always wanted to be guided not just by holy men but by *learned* men, that is to say men who carried the tradition along with them. It should be added that such guides did not have to be *men*, and indeed in a discreet way Teresa became learned in the tradition and a guide to others. But they *had* to be learned as knowing the tradition and its source in Scripture if Teresa was to feel safe in following them. All the better if they were holy as well, but it seems clear that she distrusted mere holiness and enthusiasm and could easily bear with faults in truly learned men and indeed was quick to defend them.

Besides, Teresa had the inestimable advantage of living with other women in community, and she saw that ultimately the real criterion of growth in prayer and union with God was not great experiences and inebriations but the simple devastating test behind the question: Is she (am I?) becoming more easy to live with? In other words the test set forth by St Paul in 1 Corinthians 13.

Sometimes the word ligature, from *ligare*, to bind, is used of the way in which the spirit or soul is bound into the Divine Source by mystical or receptive prayer. There is question of a kind of falling in love with the source of our being at once immeasurably deep and immeasurably transcendent, the only possible answer to the prayer of Augustine's *Soliloquia* (written in his Platonic period) *Noverim me, Noverim Te*: Let me know myself, let me know Thee. Thus it is that in her greatest treatise on mystical prayer, *The Interior Castle*, written in her later years, St Teresa sees the human soul as a great castle at the very deepest centre of which dwells the Lord of glory and goodness.

For Teresa and all the great mystics, humility is central and it is worth remembering that Teresa never chose to write about her experiences and that, of his own volition, John of the Cross simply wrote a few poems. This matter of humility is deep, paradoxical, and many-sided, and is in direct confrontation with that love of glamour and vulgar success which is the old Adam in all or most normal people.

Equally important as humility is detachment, which is both the condition and the fruit of the kind of mystical prayer St Teresa is describing in the Third and Fourth Watering. Mystical prayer brings with it a deep, all-absorbing attachment to the Source which involves radical detachment from every thing else. This detachment must be clearly distinguished from indifference or a lack of appreciation for life and the good things of life; rather does it imply a zest for life and a real taste for the things of the earth. The poet T. S. Eliot expresses this memorably in the third stanza of 'Little Gidding' which is the final part of his great poem on mystical prayer, *The Four Quartets*. (This poem shows how somebody can be open to the ways of mystical prayer without having the full experience of it: this is an important consideration.) The great master of detachment is, as we shall see later on, St John of the Cross; it is no less important for Teresa, though she does not give it the same kind of centrality as does John of the Cross.

Teresa's Eurydice Experience

In his book *Teresa of Avila*, Rowan Williams speaks of what he calls 'The pervasive problem of the *Life*', which is that 'it is brilliant and clear as individual phenomenology; strained and muddled as a structural map of Christian growth'.[15] In other words the *Life* reads easily as an account of Teresa's own experience of prayer but is much harder to follow when we try (or *she* tries) to make sense in an ordered schematic way of these experiences. But the main difficulty here is not so much that her head is addled or muddled, for she had in reserve a whole battalion of medieval logicians in the form of Dominican and Jesuit 'learned men' to sort out her 'muddles' for and with her when she needed this. No, the main difficulty for Teresa was that she never quite wanted to distil her feelings and depth experiences into clear, intellectual, logical terms, and this is true even when she herself has discovered a unifying and clarifying metaphor.

So it is that when we come to the Fourth Watering (chs 18 to 21), when the rain comes to water the garden of the soul abundantly, the clarity and finality that we naturally expect is almost totally denied us. Teresa seems to lose her nerve and to wander off into a kind of rhetoric of unworthiness. This would be rather tiresome were it not that it is trying to express a genuine personal crisis, indeed one of the most dangerous and dramatic of Teresa's adventures in prayer. Briefly, Teresa, having been given deep experiences of union with the Source of all goodness and glory, looks back on herself and the bondage of 'the world the flesh and the devil' from which she has escaped, and she feels totally confused and confounded. As a result she losses her nerve more than once, and decides to give up prayer altogether and, indeed, does so for over a year. Thus at the level of prayer, Teresa is living out the myth of Orpheus and Eurydice, in which Orpheus is Christ and Pluto is Satan. She looked back and she fell back; so she warns against this and tries to strengthen the resolve to look upwards to Christ, the Saviour, in whom her soul delights in the certain hope of *being* saved. Above all she strains every nerve to persuade us to keep *at* it, *at* the work of prayer, that is, not to fall into Satan's trap of looking back and comparing the graces we are receiving,

---

15. London: Geoffrey Chapman, 1991, p. 69.

not only with our own past failings and selfishness but with our
present human lack of perfection. She knows instinctively that a
certain kind of perfectionism is one of the greatest enemies we
can meet on the spiritual path. She knows, too, that the nearer
the soul comes to the great Divine Source of truth, purity and beauty
the more its defects will appear and the greater the danger of that
hopelessness which puts an end to all aspiration. She must keep
her gaze on her Orpheus-saviour who is Christ in his divine but
truly human humanity.

Teresa does not mention that *acedia* or tastelessness, even disgust,
in relation to the spiritual journey and the spiritual atmosphere
which many ancient writers speak about. Her temperament was
eager and ardent and the danger for her was not the negative attitude
of *acedia* but rather the positive attitude that loved life too much
and too passionately.

As well as these dangers and critical points within herself Teresa,
like all those who follow the way of mystical prayer, had to face
moreover the opposition and even the fury of those around her.
We must look at this; it was lifelong and relentless, as it is in some
form for all who devote themselves to the way of mystical prayer.

If we are to understand Teresa's experience in what she calls
the Fourth Watering of the garden of the soul, we need to read
the nineteenth chapter of the *Life* again and again. It is indeed in
Rowan Williams words 'strained and muddled' in terms of intellectual
logic, yet from the point of view of psychological logic it is a very
powerful piece of writing. One should note especially a new twist
in the use of the watering metaphor. She is speaking of the
impression made by the suppliant on those about her as she
advances into the stage of the Fourth Watering and the rain from
above.

Here is the passage in the Peers translation:[16]

The benefits thus achieved remain in the soul for some time; having
now a clear realization that the fruits of this prayer are not its own,

16. Peers, *Complete Works of St Teresa*, pp. 112–13.

it can start to share them and yet have no lack of them itself. It begins to show signs of being a soul that is guarding the treasures of Heaven and to be desirous of sharing them with others and to beseech God that it may not be alone in its riches. Almost without knowing it, and doing nothing consciously to that end, it begins to benefit its neighbours, and they become aware of this benefit because the flowers have now so powerful a fragrance as to make them desire to approach them. They realize that the soul has virtues, and, seeing how desirable the fruit is, would fain help it to partake of it. If the ground is well dug over by trials, persecutions, back-bitings and infirmities (for few can attain such a state without these), and if it is broken up by detachment from self-interest, the water will sink in so far that it will hardly ever grow dry again. But if it is just earth in the virgin state and as full of thorns as I was at first; if it is not yet free from occasions of sin and not so grateful as it should be after receiving such great favours: then it will once again become dry. If the gardener becomes careless, and the Lord is not pleased, out of His sheer goodness, to send rain upon it afresh, then you can set down the garden as ruined. This happened to me several times and I am really amazed at it: If I had not had personal experience of it, I could not believe it. I write this for the consolation of weak souls like myself, so that they may never despair or cease to trust in God's greatness. Even if, after reaching so high a point as this to which the Lord has brought them, they should fall, they must not be discouraged if they would not be utterly lost. For tears achieve everything: One kind of water attracts another.

There is a paradox typical of the way of mystical prayer at the centre of this passage. The formidable list of trials and so on, which serve to prepare the ground, is not seen negatively but very positively. One should worry if this harrowing at the hands of others does not come. Without these harrowings by severe opposition and rejection by those around, the soil of the garden begins to dry up and harden into a kind of common righteousness that is really self-righteousness, and the great adventure of mystical prayer is in danger of ceasing, and the inner glow of fading into the light of common day.

Teresa is by no means a scrupulous and simple-minded young

girl. She is a mature woman, who knows well when she is really at fault and really failing to respond to the call of the upward journey. She is by no means, never was, a saintly saint, totally lacking in guile, totally patient and forgiving, ready to be painted and framed as Santa Teresa de Jesus. She was just an ordinary woman, being drawn upwards by a great all-demanding, all-consuming love, breaking from time to time into song and rather hopeless poetry.

What arises here in all its ambiguity and confusion is the distinction between the activity of Martha whom Jesus loved in her busyness, and the receptivity of Mary as the pot boils over, unheeded (Luke 10.38). It should be noted that Teresa, as we know her, was extremely sharp with the kind of novice who would let pots boil over (yet might secretly be on her side). One might well find all this rather muddled; and so it is if one does not keep an eye on where Teresa is going – to a place of tears, when all is said. There is no place for the clever, dry-eyed 'performance' person along the path of mystical prayer. Neither can the logician traverse this path unless he or she is blessed with the gift and grace of intuitive imagination.

It has been said that in matters theological and mystical, women, on the whole, tend to follow the way of personal vision and visions and there is some truth in this as regards Teresa of Avila, though it must be said that these visions were backed by long and deep meditation as well as the receptive experiences of mystical prayer. Sometimes the question was not so much of visions as of hearings or 'locutions', and Teresa tells us it was when she was in that state of turmoil that seems to disturb the peace and clarity of the Fourth Watering that for the first time in her life she heard a clear word from the Source, 'the first word which I ever heard Thee speak to me'. While she was wondering and worrying why the graces and favours that she was receiving were not given to others better than herself she heard the words, 'Serve thou Me, and meddle not with this' (*Life* 19.8).[17]

---

17. Ibid., p. 115.

We have to move on to Chapter 25 to find a full presentation of Teresa's views on locutions. There she endeavours to distinguish between real locutions, from God, and those which merely come 'from the spirit conversing with itself' actively. Those words passively impressed on the spirit by God, produce a kind of clarity and 'clearance' and substantial peace, and, as it were, effect what they signify. These seem to accord well with the general receptivity of mystical or 'supernatural' prayer. This Chapter 25 of the *Life* is one of Teresa's most subtle and magisterial pieces of writing and demands several careful readings; it is full of the immediacy and urgency of personal experience. It is one of those passages which shows how important the presence of the adversary, Satan, *El Demonio,* was in Teresa's self-examination. Sooner or later in reading Teresa one has to ask how far this third persona (besides God and the self) was metaphorical (in some sense) or real, or psychological. One way or another the figure of Satan gives substance to the Eurydice aspect of Teresa's experience.

Teresa Refuses to Budge

The woman who speaks to us in Chapter 22 of the *Life* is self-confident, incisive and even aggressive–this in striking contrast to the tentative, pleading and tearful woman of the first twenty-one chapters. Here for the first time she firmly takes on the role of mentor and guide. Thus in para 7 she looks straight at her (then) confessor, giving him both his civic and ecclesiastical titles, and telling him what to do on a certain important matter in which she, Teresa, is going against a long tradition. 'Your Reverence and Lordship', she writes, 'should desire no other path even if you are at the summit of contemplation; on this road you walk safely.'[18] Yet both then and later Teresa is forced to admit the possibility of 'other paths', as we shall see.

The question at issue was that of the humanity of Jesus and its place in the various stages of prayer. In the Last Discourse, as we

---

18. Kavanaugh and Rodriguez, *Collected Works,* p. 147.

read it in the Fourth Gospel, we find that Jesus tells his apostles at 16.7: 'It is to your advantage that I go away, for if I do not go away, the Counseller [i.e. the Holy Spirit] will not come to you.' This has been taken to mean that there comes a time in the stages of prayer when the suppliant should go beyond all corporeal images, even that of the physical humanity of Jesus Christ. As we have no knowledge of what Jesus looked like, all images of his human physical presence can only be the work of imagination and have no more reality and truth than that. This is true at the purely physical level, yet at the personal level, the four Gospels provide us with a rich and varied portrait of Jesus according to which we can sit at his feet as a teacher and hear his words within us, see him in the epiphanies or appearings of his life, at his baptism, in his temptations and controversies, in his transfiguration and above all in his agony, passion and death. His resurrection body was always before the eyes of Teresa, and with it the wound of his glory. In her deepest prayer experiences she made connection with his presence in suffering and glory.

So when Teresa heard that she should go beyond all corporeal images in her prayer, she first accepted this but then deep down she rebelled against it, and at the time she wrote Chapter 22 of the *Life* she is in full rebellion against it, and against the whole Dionysian mystical tradition which we find in Pseudo-Denis and in many spiritual writers deriving from him, including the fourteenth-century author of *The Cloud of Unknowing*.

> If there had been no higher perfection in this life but in the beholding and the loving of the manhood of Christ, I know that He would not have ascended unto Heaven whiles this world had lasted, nor withdrawn His bodily presence from His special lovers on earth. But for there was a higher perfection the which a man may have in this life – that is to say, a pure spiritual feeling in the love of his Godhead – therefore He said to his disciples, that it was expedient for them that He went bodily from them (John 16.7).[19]

---

19. Abbot J. McCann, *The Epistle of Privy Counsel*, ed. (Wheathampstead: Anthony Clarke Books, 1964), p. 139.

The spiritual books that Teresa read were full of passages like this, which almost laid it down as a principle that the way of prayer should move 'upwards' beyond all such images. Indeed this was the teaching of the book that first opened up to her the world of prayer: the *Third Spiritual Alphabet* of Francisco de Osuna. This ascent was not leaving Christ behind but rather the human corporeal image of the humanity of Christ, with all its openness to sentimentality and self-deceit. It affirmed the divine nature of Christ as announced in terms of Platonic philosophy by the prologue of the Fourth Gospel. It went beyond all images and all clear concepts in the direction of God as totally hidden and mysterious, totally other.

Here we are in the world of Dionysian apophaticism brilliantly expressed in practical terms in *The Cloud of Unknowing*, one of the few really good treatises on mystical prayer to be found in the English language.

Dionysian mysticism takes its name from an early Christian writer who wrote under the name of St Paul's Athenian disciple Dionysius or Denis called the Areopagite or member of the ruling council before which Paul spoke (Acts 17). It was thought all through the Middle Ages that Denis was that disciple of St Paul which he claimed to be, and so his treatises on mystical theology were treated as quasi-canonical by St Thomas Aquinas and others, including St John of the Cross and Teresa's mentors, including outstandingly the unknown author of *The Cloud of Unknowing*. It was only in the nineteenth century that it was shown by scholars that Denis was a fifth or sixth-century Persian monk, deeply influenced by Neoplatonic ideas.

One of those ideas has to do with the hiddenness or unknowability of God, so that we may be said to know rather what God is not than what God is. We reach towards God in the midst of a great darkness and only (as *The Cloud* says) by 'a naked intent of the will', and by that hidden spark of love which Teresa accepts, following Osuna. Here we are very near to the passive dark night of John of the Cross. This is the way of negative or apophatic theology, negative in that we can only know God as a being beyond knowing and, as some modern theologians say, a being beyond being, that is, an unknowable being beyond all ways of knowing being. This is the way of Dionysian apophaticism which Teresa refuses to take. On this road she refused to budge and she stays at the level of the human Christ as he comes to us in the gospel and through our own meditations on the Gospels. She stays at the cataphatic level, that is to say, at the level of things that can be said and thus bring God down (*kata*) close to us, rather than seeing God, and the Logos-Christ as beyond or above (*apo*) all knowing and attainable only to the *will,* as seeking and loving.

This twenty-second chapter of the *Life,* together with a passage in *The Interior Castle* (VI. 7) where the need to stay with the human Christ is even more strongly affirmed, has been followed by all later Spanish mystics (see Peers footnote *in loco*) and has had the effect of causing a division between Teresa's Christocentric mysticism and that of John of the Cross, which seems to be rather in the tradition of the negative or 'dark' mysticism of Denis the Areopagite and the author of *The Cloud of Unknowing.*

Yet on closer examination, both ways, a different picture emerges.

On the side of Dionysian negative theology, it seems clear that the author of the Dionysian treatises fully accepts the Christian New Testament and its message as it is centred on Christ, though he would have found most modern Christian theologies lacking in the dimensions of mystery and symbolism. As regards *The Cloud of Unknowing,* recent scholarly work such as that of Dr Bruce Norquist at Aberdeen, has shown that the author of the *Cloud* is very Christocentric in his thinking and direction, as is clearly the case in St John of the Cross.

On the other hand a close textual analysis of Chapter 22 of the *Life* and of Chapter 7 of the Sixth Mansions of *The Interior Castle* can produce surprising results.[20] In the latter text from Teresa's most mature book we find that when Teresa insists on Christian prayer keeping close to Christ's humanity at all stages, she means that Christian prayer should begin with Christ and should never

---

20. See N. D. O'Donoghue, *Mystics for Our Time: Carmelite Meditations for a New Age* (Edinburgh: T & T Clark 1989), ch. 4.

lose touch with this beginning even though it ranges far and deep within the skies and deep dark oceans of the Divine mysteries. Teresa is in no way putting a *no road* sign across the vertiginous and awe-inspiring paths of the dark night and the light inaccessible. What she is saying, and this is the core of her originality in this matter, is that the Christian mystic must not lose touch with the companionship of Christ. Even here she is not absolute, and will allow that there may be times of deep darkness and dereliction such as Jesus himself underwent when all companionship is taken away and all that is left is the unprayable prayer of the Agony in the Garden and the *Lamma Sabacthani*. Teresa puts this vividly in *The Interior Castle* by saying that even in the Seventh Mansions there may be times when 'it seems as if all the devils in hell attacked the soul'. This is the time of the 'unprayable prayer' and the paradoxes of total dereliction expressed so powerfully by those poets who have glimpsed it, as in G. M. Hopkins' so-called 'terrible sonnets'.

Perhaps, when all is said, Teresa did not budge from her position, but she was, nevertheless, forced to refine and qualify it. The experience was possibly the most testing of her adventures in prayer. She would not budge, and yet she had to budge. Only those who have never experienced this kind of ambiguity, so typical of the maternal heart, can really understand or judge her. Perhaps we are nearer to something which Zen philosophy can deal with better than can the Aristotelian logic of the Great Tradition. Yet, again, it was Aristotle himself who said that in human matters absolute principles must not be understood absolutely.

Nee veeon see gan lockt. 'There is no (human) wisdom without a flaw', so says a wise Gaelic proverb. It is next to impossible to work out how far Teresa did budge in this matter and how far she is in deep disagreement with John of the Cross. The great Carmelite tradition certainly needs both of them for its fullness.

Teresa goes Looking for Trouble – and Finds it Again and Again

Teresa points out that growth in the ways of mystical prayer involves a deep, and ever more deeply tested, humility. Indeed she finds that the men who are going along this road of mystical prayer with her ('we five') are for the most part held back by their attachment to *honra* (their 'public' image) whereas, she seems to imply, women find the way of humility more easy to follow. One might say that the virtue of greatness of soul and all it entails of courage and self-assurance is more natural to men, and the virtue of humility with all it entails of patience and receptivity is more natural to women. To go any distance along the road of mystical prayer a man must develop that feminine side that can properly emerge only with full masculine maturity, and a woman must develop that masculine side which only develops with full feminine maturity. It was through the strengthening of her soul in its masculine side by way of mystical prayer that Teresa became in her own words 'a strong man' (*Way of Perfection*, VII), and thus able to face forward into what was, especially in sixteenth–century Spain, a 'man's world', i.e. that of ecclesiastical and secular politics.

So it was that at the age of 50 when she is established after many vicissitudes in a stable way of mystical prayer, she decides to lead an army of women and men against the advancing, seemingly irresistible tide of the Lutheran and Protestant Reformation. She stands with Ignatius of Loyola as one of the two great pillars of that Spanish Counter-Reformation, which was by no means an attack or counter-attack on the German and Swiss Protestant Reformation, but rather another kind of attack on a worldly and heavily politicized Established Church, Roman more in its arrogant imperialism than in its living connection with those humble martyrs Peter and Paul, with whom it claimed unbroken succession.

Where Luther said 'Here I stand' in his opposition to a Church that seemed to have betrayed the gospel of the cross of Christ, Teresa in effect said 'Here I pray' and collected around her an ever-growing constellation of women and men of prayer who followed Jesus Emmanuel on to Thabor and further on to Gethesmane and Calvary, towards the glory of the risen humanity in a transformed world.

Between the year 1558 when she was 43 and the year 1582 in which she died at the age of 67, Teresa founded 17 convents

throughout Spain, and after her death similar foundations came
to be made all over the Christian world and extended to 'missionary'
lands as well. Such foundations according to Teresa's rule are still
being made, and their numbers have included not only great
spiritual geniuses such as Thérèse of Lisieux, but also great
philosophers such as Edith Stein and genuine poets such as Jessica
Powers.

It was a chance remark by a bright schoolgirl named María de
Ocampo that served, as sometimes happens in great matters, as a
spark to ignite that great conflagration that became the world-
wide Carmelite sisterhood and brotherhood of prayer that is still
with us and still flourishing all over the Christian world. Maria
simply asked Teresa – they were cousins – why she did not set about
a reform among the Carmelites such as was happening among the
Franciscans. 'It would be possible', said this practical young woman,
'to find a way of establishing a convent.' But what really set Teresa
on her way was her several encounters with a certain Peter of Alcántara
(subsequently canonized) who was deeply involved in the renewal
of the Franciscans at that time. Teresa gives us a vivid description
of this ascetic who looked so weak and gaunt 'that he seemed to
be made of nothing but roots of trees'. Yet, for all his formidable
asceticism, Teresa found him 'affable' and 'extremely intelligent',
and they had many talks together, in the course of which he
persuaded her to found her convents in total poverty and let the
Lord provide. Sensible people, among them bishops and the civil
authorities, said that there were far too many convents already looking
for support and that Teresa was quite mad to found another chain
of convents, without money, and therefore simply a burden on the
people around. Indeed, there were those who said firmly that this
woman should be restrained and even put in prison. It was in the
context of this continuous opposition of good holy folk as well as
worldly and unbelieving people that Teresa made her foundations.
Truly, Teresa setting out to make one foundation after another,
was asking for trouble and always finding it in abundance, so much
so that the story of her foundations reads like a series of impossible
situations and nail-biting adventures. Dip into this story anywhere

and you will find the same scenario of hardship, hopeless situations and intolerable pressure. This is what Allison Peers, in what still remains the best short account of Teresa's life, has to say about one of these journeys:[21]

> The story of those last months need not be told in any detail. It is chiefly of journeys begun with great apprehensiveness, and punctuated by illnesses and fights against depression. First, in January 1582, to Medina, Valladolid (detained four days by illness), Palencia ('I am still pretty wretched' – *algo ruin*), and Burgos, for her seventeenth foundation – the last. How she survived the journey we may well wonder. January is at best a bitter month on the plateau ('it was so cold and the cold always affects me'), and this January chanced to be a month of snow and rain. 'The roads were frequently flooded'; and Gracián, who accompanied the party of eight nuns, had to go on ahead of it to find passable tracks 'and help drag the carriages out of the marshes'. It was quite usual for them to sink into the mud, when 'it would be necessary to take the animals from one carriage to drag out another'. Nor did it help matters to have 'drivers who were young and rather careless'. One episode of that nightmare-journey Teresa describes in detail. Near Burgos was a ford known locally as the Pontoons.

> > Here, in many places, the water had risen so high that it had submerged these pontoons to such an extent that they could not be seen; and we could not find any way of going on, for there was water everywhere, and on both sides it was very deep. In fact, it is very rash of anyone to go that way, especially with carriages, for, if they heeled slightly, all would be lost.

> Not knowing what to do, they hired a guide who lived there and 'knew the best way through, but it was certainly a very dangerous one'. Before long, to use her own vivid phrase, Teresa saw that they were entering a 'world of water'. There was 'no sign of a path or a boat,' and, she adds, 'even I was not without fear, despite all the strength Our Lord had given me. What then must my companions have been?'

> Eventually they won through; and only at this point does the

---

21. *Mother of Carmel* (London: Bloomsbury, 1979), pp. 160–1.

Saint remember to add that she was suffering all the time from a sore throat and a high temperature, which, as she puts it, surely in fun, 'prevented me from enjoying the incidents of the journey as much as I might'.

It is of this journey that the famous story is told of Teresa's complaint to Our Lord, of His reply: 'But that is how I treat My friends', and of her ready retort: 'Yes, my Lord, and that is why Thou hast so few of them.' Authentic or not it may be, but it is highly characteristic.

The Carmelite Order was initially a fraternity of hermits who lived in a little group of 'cells' or huts at the foot of Mount Carmel, not far from Jerusalem. From the beginning this fraternity combined the solitary or eremetical life by which each man had his own space within the community (usually a small room) with the common, communal or coenobitical life (from the Greek words '*koinos*' meaning common and '*bios*' meaning life). This first group of men under the leadership of a certain Berthold asked for a written 'rule of life' from Albert, the patriarch of nearby Jerusalem, and this simple document became known as the Primitive Rule. It was centred on the activity of prayer or meditation according to which each brother (father, friar) was to meditate day and night on the law of the Lord, that is to say, on the Scriptures, New and Old Testament.

By a kind of providential accident this original group of brothers or friars came to group their cells around an ancient chapel dedicated to the Virgin Mary of Mount Carmel, and so they came to be known as the brothers of the Holy Virgin Mary of Carmel. Mary's birthplace was in nearby Nazareth; she was symbolized by the little cloud that appeared long ago in the vision of Elias, the man of fire and abundant rain. It is easy to see how the metaphor of the Fourth Watering connected with the Elias vision of the little cloud that brought abundant rain, as Mary of Nazareth brought forth the Saviour from within a deep union with the Holy Spirit.

Now the Primitive Rule and the primitive austerity and poverty of the Carmelite way, which later became a sisterhood as well as a brotherhood, was in various ways softened or mitigated over the centuries, so much so that in Teresa's time it seemed as if the original spirit of austerity and total dedication had come to be lost. As in the case of other orders, such as the Franciscan, there were calls for reform and a return to the primitive spirit and the primitive rule, just as, far away in Saxony, an Augustinian friar named Martin Luther called for a return to the primitive spirit, not simply of the Augustinian Order, but of the whole Church *et in capite et in membris* (that is to say, from and including the Pope and Roman curia.) Even more truly than in the case of Teresa, Martin can have had no idea what troubles he was drawing on himself.

In any case there came a point in Teresa's adventures in prayer where she began to see that she was somehow being asked to draw the Carmelite sisterhood to which she belonged, and the Carmelite brotherhood too, within the mystical way which had been opened up to her with the advice and support of her Dominican, Jesuit and Franciscan mentors. She felt (and was assured) that she could achieve this best of all by a return beyond all its mitigations to the Primitive Rule and the primitive spirit of the Carmelite way.

Teresa's reform of the Carmelite life was a return to the Primitive Rule of the first hermits and it involved a good deal of poverty and hardship. The reformed Carmelite way of Teresa was named Discalced or barefoot because these women and men wore light sandals on their bare feet, but the title was used as denominative rather than definitive, that is to say as a sign of simplicity and austerity of life as in the case of the Discalced Franciscans of St Peter of Alcántara. Teresa was quite captivated by Peter's simplicity and austerity of life and it was largely because of his advice that she made that leap of faith that was involved in founding her convents in almost total poverty, in contrast with well-endowed convents such as the Incarnation in Avila to which Teresa originally belonged.

But Teresa, for all her admiration for ascetics and especially for Peter of Alcántara, was not herself primarily an ascetic. She was primarily and all the way a woman of prayer, and only an ascetic in so far as a simple, austere and penitential style of life made a total dedication to prayer possible or more achievable. She was concerned above all, as was John of the Cross, with detachment rather than feats of asceticism. She knew that a soul filled with other things than God is not open to that inflowing presence of

God that is at the core of supernatural or mystical prayer. The story is told that some people found that she was dining on partridge and were somewhat scandalized; Teresa told them, with typical tartness: 'There is a time for fasting and a time for partridge.'

In this and other matters her work as a foundress involved Teresa in almost daily complications and misunderstandings and this continued right up to her death. By taking on the work of founding convents and monasteries, Teresa was asking for trouble and it came her way abundantly. Any idea one may have that she found rest, peace and undisturbed joy in the prayer of the Seventh Mansions is totally untrue.

Teresa Visits Hell and is Visited by Heaven

We are now going on to look at an aspect or recurrent set of episodes in our heroine's adventures in prayer that are usually dealt with reductively or ignored altogether. A reductionist approach would explain Teresa's encounters with angels and demons by reducing them to medieval or Catholic superstition, which can be given a psychological explanation. Thus Rowan Williams, in his portrait of Teresa, avoids this aspect of her life and doctrine more or less completely. T. M. Cohen, in the introduction to his translation of the *Life* in the Penguin Classics, explains away her descent into Hell as a 'kafkaesque' storm in Teresa's unconscious, and even Allison Peers, most faithful of her English language commentators, tends to pass over this darker side of Teresa's adventures.

Although the University of Edinburgh began as a School of Theology fully accepting of the reality of the 'three-tiered' world of the Bible, it is fairly clear that all belief in angels and demons has almost vanished in what has become a complex of schools of professional studies, where hard factuality and exact measurements are king and queen. Imagination and what is above imagination, the real imaginal world of spiritual presences as well as the opposing world of the Adversary, all the more present because unrecognized – all this is denied or ignored; not worth discussion. In this ambience Teresa can be seen as a historical personage and a very interesting human being, but not to be taken seriously in her encounters with angels and demons any more than we are to take the ancient Celtic world of invocations and spells seriously.

It is mainly in Chapters 31 and 32 of the *Life* that Teresa writes fully and frankly about her encounters with the demonic world and describes very vividly her experience, as she saw it, of being taken into Hell and feeling the terrors and pains of damnation. To connect with these two chapters without being either dismissive, facile, naive or patronizing is the most difficult task facing us in providing a worthy account of our heroine's adventures in prayer.[22]

Teresa's description of her 'descent into Hell' is a very powerful and vivid piece of writing, and it helps us to understand that rather unfortunate distinction of form and content by which, in some centres of Hispanic Studies, Teresa the writer is almost totally separated from Teresa the mystic.

Here is a paragraph from the description in the Peers translation (*Life*, 32.2):[23]

> My feelings, I think, could not possibly be exaggerated, nor can anyone understand them. I felt a fire within my soul the nature of which I am utterly incapable of describing. My bodily sufferings were so intolerable that, though in my life I have endured the severest sufferings of this kind – the worst it is possible to endure, the doctors say, such as the shrinking of the nerves during my paralysis and many and divers more, some of them, as I have said, caused by the devil – none of them is of the smallest account by comparison with what I felt then, to say nothing of the knowledge that they would be endless and never-ceasing. And even these are nothing by comparison with the agony of my soul, an oppression, a suffocation and an affliction so deeply felt, and accompanied by such hopeless and distressing misery, that I cannot too forcibly describe it. To say that it is as if the soul were continually being torn from the body is very little, for that would mean that one's life was being taken by another; whereas in this case it is the soul itself that is

---

22. See O'Donoghue, *Mystics for Our Time*, ch. 3.
23. Peers, *Complete Works of St Teresa*, p. 216.

tearing itself to pieces. The fact is that I cannot find words to describe that interior fire and that despair, which is greater than the most grievous tortures and pains. I could not see who was the cause of them, but I felt, I think, as if I were being both burned and dismembered; and I repeat that that interior fire and despair are the worst things of all.

Two points must be noted. Teresa is not saying that she really visited that real Hell in which she really believed. What she says is 'I found myself *as I thought* plunged right into Hell (*me parecia*)' Teresa is making no claims to prove or show in any way what Hell is like or even that Hell exists as an actuality. Rather is it a possibility for the human spirit or personality that allows itself to be seduced by the Adversary, the terrible *ponaeros* that is constantly and inescapably present in the New Testament, and is indeed 'the Lord of the Cosmos.' For 'the whole world lies prone (*keitai*) in the power of the ponaeros' (1 John 5.19). It is deliverance from the *ponaeros* (evil, the evil one) that the Christian prays for in the final petition of the Lord's Prayer.

There is also the *peirasmos* or trial which is named in the penultimate petition of the Lord's Prayer. We ask not to be led (too far) into the terrible depths of the 'trial' or test, as Jesus prayed in Gethsemane; when he emerged from this terror according to St Luke's account he found his disciples asleep and upbraided them saying, 'Arise and pray lest you enter into the *peirasmos*.' Hell was near not because God created it but because the power (*exousia* – cosmic angel) of darkness stands in its own rebellious being, totally cruel and destructive over against God. Every true Christian mystic will experience the cold breath of this annihilating terror, as Teresa did, as John of the Cross did, as in the late nineteenth century Thérèse did in the mode of the total absence of God. This is the most terrible of all the adventures of prayer, so terrible that no other terror can really terrify the person who has had even a touch of it.

There is no doubt but that the *ponaeros* and the *peirasmos* were utterly real and totally terrifying realities for Teresa; there is no doubt also but that her experiences and beliefs were socially and historically conditioned, as when she sees 'the demon' as taking the shape of an 'ugly little negro'. What of her eulogy of 'Holy Water' which nowadays only the most traditional Catholic will feel comfortable with? Yet the modern Christian reader, whether Catholic or not, might well ponder on the ancient rite by which salt and water were exorcized and blessed and ponder on these prayers in relationship with the many references to Satan in the New Testament. Perhaps Christians today have lost touch with the reality of the 'spirits of wickedness in the high places' (Ephesians 6.13) or rather have ceased to be on guard against them and have become, as St Paul feared, vulnerable and unprotected in the face of them. This is perhaps one of the ways we can learn from the world-view of Celtic Christianity. Teresa was not obsessed by the demonic, yet its terrible presence and atmosphere was never far from her mind.

In Chapter 29 of the *Life*, Teresa relates an experience which is the polar opposite of that related in Chapter 32 and, since it *is* a polar opposite, has with its opposite a common ground or basis in a certain kind of transcendence or entry into regions other than that of everyday perception.

This is the experience of the Transverberation or 'piercing', which Teresa sets down vividly as follows:

> Sometimes I would see an angel near me, at my left side, in bodily shape . . . not great but quite small, and very beautiful, with such a glowing countenance that it seemed to be one of those very exalted angels that are all on fire . . . In his hands he held a great golden dart, and the tip of the metal seemed to be aflame. He penetrated my heart several times with this dart, and it seemed to search out my inmost depths. Indeed as he withdrew the dart it seemed as if my very entrails followed it, and I remained totally on fire with a great love of God. So great was the pain that I cried out several times, and so much greater was the sweetness which was the result of this pain that one could not take it away no matter how one tried; nor is one satisfied with aught less than God Himself. This

is not a physical pain but a spiritual one; yet the body does share it, and sometimes very strongly.[24]

There are at least two sculptural representations of the Trans-verberation: that of Bernini in a Roman chapel which called forth Richard Crashaw's poem 'The Flaming Heart', and that in Seville by an unknown artist, which Allison Peers uses as a frontispiece for his 'portrait' of Teresa, entitled *Mother of Carmel.* The Bernini sculpture shows a strongly physical, somewhat erotic experience of piercing (which is quite transcended in Crashaw's poem). The Seville portrait is full of quiet contemplative receptivity seeming to flow into the body in the eyes and the hands. Teresa's text can be seen to fit either representation, yet the Seville sculpture seems to fit the general visionary *persona* of Teresa, not only more exactly, but to the exclusion of the other, as a misrepresentation of the whole experience. Crashaw's poem speaks of Teresa's 'brim-filled bowls of fierce desire,' yet also and equally of her 'large draughts of intellectual day'. Indeed Crashaw's poem is essentially a prayer that we may die in order to live, as Teresa did, and it must not be forgotten that the poet's prayer was sparked off by Bernini's sculpture.

As in so much else, the Teresa of the descent into Hell and of the ascent into angelic regions of light and fire was, and is, a very human person, and her special individual voice sounds clearly in both narratives, so much so that the exact reality-status of what she encounteres becomes almost irrelevent. Those who can connect with these prayer-experiences are enriched by the connection; those who cannot do so are all the poorer for it.

---

24. My own translation using the Aguilar (Silverio) edition (Madrid, 1957).

CHAPTER 2

PRAYER AND VIRGINITY

Teresa Sings her Song of Songs

All writing about prayer in sixteenth-century Spain was a dangerous
occupation, a perilous adventure and this was especially dangerous
when the writing took the form of a commentary on the Song of
Songs or Canticle of Canticles, which Teresa wrote in 1574. Indeed
one of the most outstanding theological writers of the day, Luis
de Leon, an Augustinian priest, was suddenly seized by the servants
of the Inquisition and detained for a time in prison. For some reason
the idea that a woman should write such a commentary was
especially suspect, and Teresa's confessor at the time ordered that
her commentary be burnt at once, though he changed his mind
before it was disposed of.

The reason for this attitude to the Song of Songs was probably
the fear that its strong sexual imagery could be taken naturalistically
rather than anagogically or ascendingly, as expressing the union of
the human soul with God. From the anagogical point of view, human
sexuality in man and woman and *between* man and woman may be
called a holy force, which can express its sacredness in the ascending
scale or diapason of the spiritual senses as expressed in Book 10,
Chapter 6 of the *Confessions* of St Augustine, following Origen.[1]

Moreover, and this is a delicate and important point, something
of this holy loving normally arises in the relationship of men and
women who are bound together by a shared love of God in its
various levels. So it seems to have been with Francis and Claire in
the twelfth century, St Francis de Sales and St Jane Frances de Chantal
in the early seventeenth century, and many others.

---

1. R. S. Pine-Coffin, tr. (Penguin Books, 1987), pp. 211–12.

But we must avoid giving the impression of a single and exclusive man–woman relationship in these cases. In fact any kind of possessiveness would cloud and ultimately destroy this kind of relationship which can never be more than a mediation of something deeper, higher, and as wide as the virtualities of the heart of man and woman, in other words something that can only find its full meaning and its full completion in Divine Love and loving.

Neither is this love necessarily heterosexual. It can exist between man and man; it can exist between woman and woman. But in all cases it must be totally free of holdingness and possessiveness. Thinking of the *Symposium* and the *Phaedrus,* one may call it Socratic love.

This kind of love may be called the true flowering of celibacy and virginity, not rejecting of, but reaching far beyond the ways of physical union and physical procreation. It is the noble ancient Christian way of virginity and celibacy, always fathering and mothering the whole world. There is question of an option based on total dedication to God and it may be asked whether this is possible in its inception without the radical asceticism of a total commitment. Furthermore, it may be asked whether it is capable of flourishing beyond the tension of asceticism without the discovery and development of mystical prayer.

In Chapter 5 of the *Life,* Teresa gives a vivid and moving account of her encounter with a man from Becedas who stirred her feminine self very deeply and who clearly was much 'in love' with her. It is a rather tragic and moving story. She found that the man, a priest vowed to celibacy, had fallen under the spell of a woman among his parishioners who tried to bind him to her by a kind of talisman or charm (*idolillo*). Teresa, who had gone to him for spiritual direction, found herself directing him and forming a bond with him which could have ended up in a frankly sexual affair, for she became quite fond of him. She managed to resist this, and within a year of her first meeting with him the priest took ill and died. In retrospect she was quite happy about what happened between them, but she is conscious of having been deeply drawn towards this man and she is still drawn towards her memories of him when she is writing her *Life.*

Far different was her relationship with a man she met in the course of founding her first monastery for men. This was John of the Cross as he came to be called. As the Becedas priest met her in the lowlands of her feminine self, so John met her in the uplands of her being where she was no less a woman as he was no less a man. She found that John for all his modesty had a great power of summing up spiritual and philosophical matters in sharp and even piercing epigrams, and she called him her 'little Seneca' *Senequita*, recalling the Latin author who was famous for his epigrams. There is, it must be said, a slight distancing involved in this name; Teresa tended to find John rather too absolute and demanding in his spiritual teaching and maxims. Nevertheless, John shone like a star upon the uplands of her feminine consciousness and aspirations and it seems there was a deep understanding and even tenderness between them at this exalted level that was far beyond possessiveness, jealousy and sexual indulgence. So it was with all those men who played such a large role in Teresa's spiritual development. The relationship was always a woman–man relationship of high companionship bearing fruit in that motherhood by which Allison Peers very wisely defines Teresa when he names her 'Mother of Carmel' in his sketch of her life.

But Teresa did meet a man who was for her the complete man who made her feel a complete woman. This was Fr. Jerome Gracián. When they met he was a relatively young man moving into his prime while Teresa was moving into old age and was greatly rejuvenated by the encounter. He seems to have been all that Teresa admired in men: learned, of courtly manners, zealous for the things of God and the life of prayer, sensitive, lively, expansive. Also the kind of celibate priest who loved women religious and was loved by them: '*muy monjero*' in the Spanish phrase that still lives on, a phrase that cannot be translated simply by 'fond of nuns'. For Teresa, John of the Cross was 'a heavenly man', but Gracián was much more a human man, as Teresa was a human woman. What Teresa, who made so little of her own writings, did not quite realize was that John was a very great poet and master of mystical theology whose work was of the stuff of immortality, while Gracián, the man of charm and of action, could not be the father of Carmel as she was the mother of Carmel. It seems clear that Teresa saw Gracián rather than John as the 'man' of the Carmelite reform but history has obviously disagreed with her. If she was wrong it would seem that her heart led her astray.

Yet perhaps there is more to be said if we are to understand Teresa as a woman and as a very great guide in the ways of mystical prayer. It is true that John was her soul's consort in the uplands of her being but this relationship for all its reciprocity and fruitfulness was not the whole of Teresa or Teresa's immensely fruitful motherhood. That part of her that loved to dance and could not help laughing, and knew so well how to weep, could never find full partnership in John. She could not share with John as she did so easily with Jerome Gracián what may be called the everyday domesticities of Carmel and the all too human eccentricities of women, and of men, striving towards the spiritual heights and depths. John was by no means a cold man, but his warmth was that of the sun on the high mountains. Gracián could occasionally be somewhat ridiculous, as John never was, but Teresa always remained woman enough to take a man's limitations into her understanding heart.

Her love for Gracián was at times all too human in its everyday manifestations as is clear from those letters where she complains of his absence when she needed him. Part of Teresa's charm is that she never seems to have even thought of playing the saint; she was, right to the end, who and what she was before God and man, yet totally dedicated to that eternal adventure in which the human spirit from the depths of its bridal longing reaches towards the God of love and glory.

The Pierced Heart

For Teresa, this bridal longing involved a deep piercing of the heart, which culminated in the experience of the angel with the golden spear, commemorated by Bernini's famous statue and the verses written about the statue by Richard Crashaw, as we have seen.

We do not know – or at least *I* do not know – how this experience of the angelic piercing of the heart is related temporally to the pathway of transformation set forth in the *Mansions*, Teresa's fullest statement of her spiritual journey, but there is an obvious unity of experience between the two. Probably the piercing may be said to find a place amongst those ecstatic experiences described as belonging to the Sixth Mansions, the level of spiritual espousal rather than spiritual marriage.

The feminine as relational, as forming with the masculine a complete unit, is receptive, though by no means passive. Its deepest desire *as feminine* is to receive the masculine within it, as conversely the deepest emotional-instinctual desire of the masculine is to be taken into the feminine, and to be nourished and supported. We are here in the domain of Eros and of the language of Eros, but it is essential to distinguish clearly between the *descending* Eros which splits off from the spirit and dies into itself, and the *ascending* Eros which opens up to the love that is self-transcending and universal and energizes the spirit. Without this Eros-agape all transcendence loses its human colour and beauty and becomes purely intellectual. The ascending Eros opens up towards transcendental unity as one of the five illuminations of the human mind closely connected with transcendental beauty and its ascetical-mystical journey upwards from earthly and human beauty to Beauty itself, which is also Reality itself.

The piercing of the heart as vividly expressed in Bernini's sculpture expresses the joyful-mystical aspect of this experience which has an accompanying ascetical aspect. Without this the mystical aspect can only be seen – so some psychologists have seen it – as no more than an expression of the descending Eros in a woman starved of normal physical love. The asceticism of virginity and celibacy, however, is not the negation or denial of Eros and of the normal human thrust towards procreation and sexual partnership. The ancient Latin fathers defined virginity as *meditatio incorruptionis in carne corruptibili,* literally 'the meditation of what is beyond corruption while one is living in the corruptible body'. What seems to be in question here is the category of the physical incorruptible.

This region is not the region of the purely intellectual in any kind of Platonic sense; rather is it close to the region of the angelic persons or presences that is always present *near* to ordinary perception throughout the New Testament. If we do not take account of this category of the physical incorruptible we cannot understand either the Christian affirmation of the Resurrection of the Body nor the Christian affirmation of celibacy-virginity as a special flowering and glory of certain inner resources of men and women. There is question neither of eunuch-impotency nor of virginal barrenness but rather of a special potency and a special fruitfulness in men and women.

Now just as physical intercourse and procreation has its ecstasies and its travails at the corruptible level, so too, spiritual intercourse and procreation has its ecstasies and its travails at the physical-incorruptible level. Here it is necessary to draw a distinction between mind and spirit. Our intellect and our 'higher' willing belong to the mind and a world of crystalline clarity and transparency; the spirit, on the other hand, is a composite of pure mind and celestial or subtle matter. Thus the Holy Spirit is at once pure mind (the spirit of truth) and also an inner breath and breathing as is clearly shown when Jesus after the Resurrection breathes physically on his followers and says 'Receive ye the Holy Spirit' (John 20.22) This breathing is not merely a ritual, not merely a metaphor, any more than the risen body of Jesus is a mere apparition without substance or reality. This world of the physical-incorruptible also has its travails, the whole travail of the crucifixion as written on the Body of Christ and as shared by those who follow him. It is in this sense that virginity and martyrdom have been closely connected in Christian tradition. There is question not only of the martyrdom of physical pain and physical affliction but also of spiritual afflictions of various kinds as is abundantly clear in the life of St Teresa; this would have to include her deep attachment to Fr. Gracián through which she brought so much pain on herself in her later years. Yet it would seem that it was only because this pain, this piercing, was accepted as part of the total sacrifice of dedicated virginity that the experience of the angelic piercing of the heart was possible in the order of spiritual transformation.

There was nothing ecstatic or aspirational about that dull heartache by which Teresa, now an old woman, yet as young in heart as only a virginal being can be, awaited the comfort of Father Gracián's presence day after day in those last years of her life. But the piercing of the heart was real and deep, and in that reality and in those depths, the true work of transformation was achieved. It was achieved not only by virtue of the pain, which any woman or indeed any man can feel; it was achieved by virtue of that living receptive prayer by which the human piercing became filled with a divine presence, by the 'inarticulate sighings and groanings' – there is no other word – of the Holy Spirit. 'For we do not know how to pray as we ought, but the Spirit himself intercedes for us with sighs too deep for words.' So the RSV translates Romans 8.26, yet the *stenagma* of the original are 'groanings' rather than 'sighings' and are the inarticulate language of the pierced heart or psychic centre as it accepts, in that deepest activity of receptivity, that seeding in the depths from which a new world is born.

There is much more to be said on this, but we do not have the language in which to say it. Perhaps it can only attain a kind of prayer-speech in some of the depth-experiences of mystical women and men.

The Strong Woman

Teresa wanted herself and her spiritual daughters to be 'strong men' in their deep basic attachment to God, to the Source, and she put this image clearly before the young women who followed her into the convents of the Carmelite reform. The whole personality according to this image becomes an image of God and a mediator of the divine power and presence to others. This is a putting on of originative fatherhood that can be continuous with nurturing motherhood that has its own strength in its loyalty and endurance. So it was that in her maturer years Teresa was named The Mother *La Madre*, by both her women and men followers. Usually the name was amplified to *La Santa Madre*, The Holy Mother. This title was by no means perfunctory, by no means merely honorific. It was full of meaning, full of the sense of a very human and very genuine transformed humanity.

When St Teresa told her spiritual daughters that she wanted them to be 'strong men' she was, of course using a metaphor. But it was a very laden metaphor, a very highly-charged metaphor, a metaphor whose kernel was and is a most important truth at once literal and basic. Perhaps the best way to understand it is to say that her fellow Carmelite, John of the Cross could equally have said to his young men in the noviciate that each of them needed to find within them a woman's heart: indeed this is implicit in all his delicate and exalted imagery of the soul as bride in his three great mystical poems and commentaries: *The Dark Night,* the *Spiritual Canticle* and the *Living Flame of Love.*

Here we touch on a mystical truth which, as befits the very nature of the mystical, is a hidden truth about which little or nothing is to be found in the otherwise admirable treatises on mysticism which have appeared in the last century and which may by now be regarded as classical: those of Poulain, Farges, Saudreau, Brémond, Evelyn Underhill, Von Hügel and Butler. Neither is there anything to be found in the more recent treatises of Thomas Merton, Happold, Wood, McGinn and others.

This mystical truth is that in order to attain mystical maturity a man must become femininized in a very deep and all-pervasive way and a woman must become, in St Teresa's phrase, a 'strong man'. But let me hasten to add and to underline quite heavily that the man must first of all be a truly manly man and the woman a truly womanly woman: otherwise the man becomes effeminate and the woman a virago.

Moreover, there is an important place for what is called 'soul-friendship' across the sacred space between feminine and masculine. In concrete terms a woman needs the love and support of a man or men and a man needs the love and support of a woman or women. The word 'soul-friendship' is a literal translation of the Gaelic *anam-chara* (soul-friend) and *anam-chairdeas* (soul friendship).[2]

---

2. See John O'Donohue, *Anam Cara* (London/New York: Bantam, 1997).

Feminine and masculine are reciprocal and relational conditions and reveal themselves in this reciprocity and relationality. Teresa was a very feminine woman, not because she lived her life in convents surrounded by women but because of her deep, constant and centrally important relationships with men. So, too, St John of the Cross was a very masculine man, not because he lived his life in celibate monasteries of men but because of his deep friendship with those women, in the cloister and outside it, with whom he corresponded regularly and for whom in the first instance he wrote almost all his poems and all of his mystical treatises.

Teresa had a deep respect for those men in her life who were priests, theologians and/or spiritual directors. In her letters to them there is respect but no subservience, and she was quite capable of scolding them roundly as in the case of the unfortunate Jesuit prior whom she accused of parading his humility at her expense. (However, *he* had the humility to keep her letter as a treasure, whereas *she* destroyed his.) She wanted the men in her life to be holy and learned but if she had to choose between a holy man and a learned man she had no doubt whom she would choose: she would choose the learned man. It seems clear that she looked for a certain breadth and largeness of mind in a man and did not respond to that immature or sentimental piety not uncommonly found in 'pious' men, then and now. She did, however, see very clearly that flaw in the manly man which stood in the way of his becoming a mystic. Neither learning nor prudence nor firmness were lacking, but Teresa saw very shrewdly what was missing, or rather what was present that was a barrier. It was all summed up in one word: *Honra,* which, though untranslatable in all its nuances, may be sufficiently indicated by the phrase 'public opinion', what others think of us, having a place of honour among men and women. It is because they cannot let go of this that most men, for all their steadiness and wisdom, cannot enter into that way of transformation which may be called the mystical. They cannot get beyond the Third or Fourth Mansions in that greatest of journeys which is into one's own interior, the Seventh Mansions where God dwells. So, though Teresa exhorted her 'daughters' (for whom the Mansions was written) to be 'strong men,' she knew well that it is the strong man *within the true woman* that most commonly goes all the way.

All Teresa's writing is concerned with the training of the strong woman, a very feminine woman inasmuch as she is related to God through man as companion, guide and priest. It is doubtful whether Teresa saw the feminine as ever mediating the divine *actively* or could accept the priestly ordination of women; rather did woman mediate the divine receptively (though by no means passively) and overflow into men by a kind of persuasiveness and gentle sharing rather than directively and preceptively as by way of priestly ministry. Like Catherine of Siena, Teresa was surrounded by men who drew from her wisdom and who revered her, though she never saw herself as having authority over men but rather as variously receiving direction from the men whom she so deeply influenced, so much so that all her works without exception were written under obedience to some of them and submitted to them for correction. Yet even in contradiction to these men she always spoke up clearly for the truth as she saw it. So it is that for the Carmelite 'way' the writings of 'The Holy Mother' were treasured as equal to, if not even safer to follow than, those of John of the Cross.

John was a great poet, as Teresa was not; when somebody told her that her verses lacked 'feet' she replied that they had neither hands nor feet. But Teresa was a great writer of prose, as John was not; he admitted that his style was laboured and cumbersome, but his poetry shines across the centuries with unexampled brilliance and grace. That power of the creation of the right, uniquely right, image, which sparkles in the poetry of John, sparkles with equal brilliance, though innocent of 'hands or feet' in Teresa's prose.

Two images especially dominate Teresa's exposition of the journey towards the making of the 'strong woman': the image of the Four Waters or Four Waterings in the *Life,* which we have already explored, and the image of the Castle of Seven Mansions, which we will explore in the next chapter.

CHAPTER 3

A GUIDE TO *THE INTERIOR CASTLE*

The Figure of the Mansions

The Mansions are all found within every soul. It is therefore more correct to speak of the Mansions being in the soul rather than the soul being in the Mansions. It is because she realizes this that St Teresa says she seems 'to be talking nonsense' when she speaks of entering *into* the Castle. 'For the soul itself is this Castle, and it seems nonsense to tell a person to enter a place in which he already is' (I, i, par. 5).[1]

Her reply to this difficulty is simply that there are many ways of being *in* a place. She means that in a sense every soul is in the Castle or rather circumscribes it; yet in another sense each soul has to find its way into this Castle and come to possess its Mansions. There is question of the soul's journey into its own interior.

This is a very rich and beautiful conception. God dwells at the centre of the soul, and the great task of life is to travel inwards towards this centre, being guided by the light of the Divinity

---

1. I have followed the Allison Peers translation, *The Complete Works of St Teresa*, Vol. II (London: Sheed & Ward, 1957), but have consulted the Spanish texts all the way, using the Aguilar (Silverio) edition, (Madrid 1957). I have also consulted the more recent translation by Kieran Kavanaugh and Otilio Rodriguez, *The Collected Works of St Teresa of Avila*, Vol. II (Washington, DC: Institute of Carmelite Studies, 1980): it corrects Peers at certain points, but is in my opinion a less sensitive translation. It does not really matter what translation the reader of this guide uses, but it is essential to have some acquaintance with St Teresa's book in order to use this guide to the best advantage.

shining within us. Psychoanalysts speak of the unconscious depths of the soul (which they call the psyche) and tell us that all kinds of dangerous monsters dwell in these depths; St Teresa tells us that the monsters dwell on the outside, beyond the outer Mansions, while the God of all power and goodness dwells within. The soul that is in touch with God dwelling serenely in the depths need have no fear of the enemies that lurk in the shadows, and that find their way into the courtyard and the outer rooms of the Castle.[2]

The Idea of Spiritual Progress

The whole conception of *The Interior Castle* involves progression: the soul journeys from one Mansion to the next. The same notion of progression is involved in the figure of the Four Waters of prayer in the *Life*, and the figure of the Dark Night of St John of the Cross. The idea of the spiritual life as the ascent of a mountain was very common in the spiritual writing and discussion of sixteenth-century Spain. It suited well the optimism and sense of conquest of Spain's Golden Age. But it hardly appeals at all to our more chastened consciousness. Besides, the emphasis in present day spiritual writing is rather on the stripping of the soul, the return to childhood that is necessary for spiritual progress. This is not a change of doctrine but a change of emphasis; there are two sides to the process, the one breaking down and simplifying the soul, the other building it up. Those who emphasize the one do not in

---

2. By the soul (*alma*) St Teresa means the human person seen as related to God, as fearing him, as seeking him, above all as loving him. It is a very spiritual conception inasmuch as it places man face to face with God, who is pure spirit. It is also concrete and even physical in that, though it excludes the corruptible, it yet does not exclude that incorruptible corporeity which is the material of the glorified body. A modern reader has to be careful to avoid reading dualistic concepts of the soul into St Teresa's mind. Her concept of the soul is best understood as naming the bridal partner in the Spiritual Marriage.

theory rule out the other. But the practical result is that the person who tries to advance from one Mansion to the next receives nowadays very little help or encouragement from friends or directors, and may indeed be regarded as deluded or presumptuous.

We do not feel at home with a doctrine of measurable step-by-step spiritual progress. In order to meet this difficulty, we must note in the first place that the metaphor of the Castle is after all no more than a metaphor: the soul does not in fact journey from one Mansion to the next; what is true is that the soul's progress towards ever deeper union with God may be expressed under the guise of this figure.

It must be noted, further, that the seventh set of Mansions is in a place apart. Here at the soul's centre God dwells, and it is the light from this centre that radiates through all the other Mansions. Even in the outermost Mansions it is the light from the Seventh Mansions that is illuminating the soul and guiding it onwards: the other Mansions *participate* in the glory of the Seventh Mansions. If we are to speak of progress then, we can speak of progressive illumination just as truly as of progressive journeying from one Mansion to the next. Moreover it is the same Divine Light that shines all the way so that we can say that there is a sense in which all who seek God have experience of the Seventh Mansions. The soul's journey is simply the progress of learning to live with this marvellous light.

Finally, it is worth enquiring whether the modern antipathy to measurable progress may not contain as much prejudice as good sense. It is true that there is the danger of delusion and smugness; and yet one must surely pause in reflecting that St Teresa, for all her marvellous humility, could speak without the slightest apology or embarrassment of definite progress, a progress verified to the full in her own experience. Do we not discourage eager souls too much nowadays? After all, the light which streams forth from the centre of the soul, where God dwells, is not simply an elevating and consoling light; it is above all a light that gives gentleness and humility to the soul. Is there a subtle pride involved in the consciousness that we are advancing in humility? Surely not. At

least not necessarily. We can be very pleased to see that we are
better able to accept correction, less careful to excuse ourselves,
more at home in the last place, more kind to others, etc.; more
keenly aware of the fact that of ourselves we are nothing, and can
do nothing. As long as we are in this life there is always imperfection
and even illusion mixed with our perfection, but this need not
discourage us, nor should we discourage others because we see clearly
that they have certain imperfections. So with prayer; we can surely
find ourselves progressing in prayer without running the risk of
pride or self-complacency, knowing that there is the element of
the *Miserere* in all true prayer, and that this element has to grow
as our prayer becomes more perfect. It is not impossible, too, that
the modern distrust of degrees and measurable progress may have
its roots in a kind of fear, a fear of criticism and ridicule, a fear of
being thought a pious hypocrite, in other words a fear of losing
the esteem of others. Of course the truth is that today, as always,
the person who tries to advance along this way of union with God
will, soon or later, alienate many or most or all of his friends.

Prayer and the Virtues

In the first sentence of the Introduction, St Teresa tells us that
the book that is to follow deals with 'matters concerning prayer'.
The Interior Castle is not formally a treatise on perfection, but a
treatise on the ways of prayer. The life of prayer and the spiritual
life advance together, and at the same rate; yet they are not exactly
the same thing any more than the heart and the body are the same
thing. Prayer is the heart, or the life-blood, of the spiritual life,
but it is by no means the whole of it: it presupposes and accompanies
the practice of the moral virtues and the theological virtues. The
Ascent of Mount Carmel of St John of the Cross completes *The
Interior Castle* in so far as the theological virtues are concerned.
Certain of the moral virtues, such as humility, fortitude, obedience,
receive incidental treatment here and there throughout the works
of the two great Spanish Carmelites, but neither of them gives us

a complete treatment of these virtues. For that we have to go to
the great scholastic treatises, for example to St Thomas' *Summa*.
In reading books such as *The Interior Castle* we have to recall from
time to time the fact that these other moral virtues are also
important, for instance, that the virtue of magnanimity has its
importance in the growth of a genuine contemplative. So also
justice and the virtues associated with it have their own special
place and importance as a basis of genuine contemplation.

But of course each of the ordinary moral virtues has its own
place and its own importance in the life of contemplation, for, as
St Thomas points out, the virtues are so connected that he who
fails seriously in one fails in all. This is plain common sense, and
St Teresa knew it well. She takes it for granted that the virtues
will grow as the life of prayer grows.[3]

The main point to bear in mind is that where the life of prayer
seems to be developing while the virtues are lagging behind there
is in fact no true development, no true growth in union with God.
This is not to say that a genuinely mystical soul has no faults at
all: this was the mistake made by some of St Teresa's advisers, who
told her she was deluded. Some faults take a long time to root out;
some faults are never overcome as long as life lasts – they are left
to us that we might know our own weaknesses. These are beneficial
and indeliberate, and are quite distinct from those deliberate
attachments, those grains of hypocrisy, self-seeking, self-complacency

---

3. The higher ways of prayer with which St Teresa is concerned in *The
   Interior Castle* involve a kind of 'supermorality' where virtues such as
   self-sacrifice, love of solitude, the acceptance of humiliations and
   vulnerability of heart take over from the moral virtues. There is even
   a sense in which the mystic is 'broken', totally dejected like Elijah, or
   full of fear like St Paul. But it would be a disastrous mistake to think
   that ordinary goodness of life and the moral virtues of justice, temperance
   and the rest are left behind. They are the grid on which the whole
   superstructure rests, and the heavier the superstructure the more
   'strain', so to speak, this grid has to take, and the more strongly must
   it be reinforced.

which serve as a barrier to God's grace. The true life of prayer breaks down all these barriers gradually.

The 'Dangers' of Prayer

'As far as I can understand it, the door of entry into this castle is prayer and meditation' (I, i, par. 7). There is question of mental prayer, the prayer that is meditative, *con consideración*, but the saint tells us that she speaks of 'prayer' and not of 'mental prayer', for all true prayer has the quality of meditation, of 'taking thought'. Otherwise vocal prayer is simply the mechanical repetition of words, and is valueless. The only exception to this is the case where we repeat words which we have already thought about – the meditation 'carries over' so to speak.

The saint is here expressing in summary form what she had said at some length in the twenty-second chapter of the *Way of Perfection*. Her doctrine in both places seems to have as background a certain opposition to mental prayer and an emphasis on vocal prayer on the part of certain people. Mental prayer and the world of mental prayer (which is the Interior Castle) was one of the saint's great discoveries, and one of her principal motives in founding her monasteries and initiating a new kind of religious life. It would seem, however, that there were many who regarded the way of mental prayer to be full of dangers. In Chapter 21 of the *Way of Perfection* the saint gives a list of the kind of remarks that were made about people who embarked on the way of mental prayer: 'It is dangerous,' 'That's how so-and-so was lost,' 'This other was deluded,' 'It is not for women: it is quite enough for them to say the *Paternoster* and *Ave Maria*.'

It must not be thought that this kind of criticism is frivolous or malicious. It arises from a genuine problem and brings us close to one of the great whirlpools of controversy of the Christian conscience. It is the whole matter of the *mystical* that is here in question. Those who advance along the ways of union with God are brought into a world that is very wonderful yet also strange and terrible. God has chosen his Church as the mediator between himself and mankind, yet this mediation does not lessen his desire to form a bond of love directly with the individual soul. How is the soul that is receiving graces directly from God in prayer to come to accommodate itself to receiving all from Mother Church? In *theory* the answer is quite simple. Such a soul must choose a spiritual director who is capable of guiding it in the Church's name along the ways of prayer. In practice, however, the soul comes up against the difficulty that it is not being understood, for nobody can lead another along these ways unless he has already travelled them for himself, and they are few, very few, who go far along this road. Those who do advance will almost certainly come under suspicion among their more down-to-earth brethren for whom mysticism is synonymous with illusion and morbidity, or, at best, extreme oddness. St Teresa had to wait for help until she met St Peter of Alcántara, and it is significant that she was directed to him not by a priest but by a woman friend of hers.

St Teresa's solution of this problem is in effect this: the ways of prayer may be dangerous, but the truth is that God calls us all to these ways, for he asks us all to pray. All admit that we must say vocal prayers such as the *Pater Noster* and the *Ave Maria*. But in fact if we examine what we are saying in these prayers we find that we have already embarked on the ways of prayer and union with God. And surely nobody can argue that we must *not* attend to what we are saying — 'I do not call that prayer at all,' she says (I, i). And so, in the *Way of Perfection* the saint takes the *Pater Noster* and shows that it is full of meaning, a meditation book all by itself, and that it leads the soul onward and upward to full union with God.

We do not know how far St Teresa's solution to the problem is original, but it is certainly brilliant and convincing. Not only is it clear that the proper saying of the *Pater Noster* involves 'praying' in the sense of mental prayer, but the very petitions of this prayer itself are a vindication of mysticism, which is simply the kingdom of God in the soul. As for the dangers that await us, is there not a special petition at the very end framed specially to meet the case – 'Lead us not into temptation, but deliver us from evil'?

The problem just mentioned was very much in the saint's mind when she was writing the *Way of Perfection*. Here in the Mansions it is in the background. It is a problem that arises in the initial stages of the journey, that part with which the *Way of Perfection* deals. Here in the Mansions she is writing for those who have conquered these fears and are boldly set on the path to the heights.

Entering the Castle

Prayer, then, is the doorway to the Castle. In the context, this is a kind of truism, for the Castle has already been described as a castle of prayer.

And yet the saint does in fact give some valuable indications, even at this point, as to the *kind* of prayer that is the necessary minimum for entry into the Castle. In the second to last paragraph of the first chapter she presents a portrait of ordinary worldly Christians who are 'very much immersed in worldly affairs' yet have 'good desires' and sometimes 'commend themselves to God, and think about the state of their soul, though not very carefully.' Somehow these souls enter the lowest Mansions of the Castle, but 'many reptiles get in with them', and so they are prevented from dwelling peacefully in the Castle and appreciating its beauty.

At this point St Teresa becomes conscious that the treatment of the first or outer Mansions is of little profit to the contemplative nuns for whom she is writing. She is too sensible to insist heavily, as do some directors and guides, that we are all beginners all the time. Rather she begs their indulgence on the grounds that 'there is no other way' in which she can set out her ideas on prayer.

The Soul in Mortal Sin

The second chapter of Book I treats successively three main themes: firstly, the soul in mortal sin; secondly, self-knowledge; and thirdly, the activity of the devil. There are, besides, certain important incidental observations – that on the basis of the

Carmelite Rule in the penultimate paragraph is particularly important. The treatment of the various themes serves to shed some light on the main theme of the discussion: the state of the soul of the beginner in the ways of prayer. But the reader who expects a clear and formal discussion of the nature of the First Mansions will be a little disconcerted. Here, as elsewhere in *The Interior Castle,* the saint allows herself to discuss the whole range of the spiritual life. This is an important feature of the book, and should be borne in mind throughout. The chapter is almost complete in itself, and might be taken as a small treatise on the life of prayer.

The difference of climate between the sixteenth century and our own is brought home to us very powerfully by discussions such as in this passage. It is almost inconceivable to us that contemplative nuns should derive benefit from horrific descriptions of the soul in mortal sin and from the resultant fear of offending God (par. 5). In our pessimistic and fear-ridden century the ordinary contemplative finds these descriptions simply depressing and frightening, and rarely finds any help in them. Indeed, not a few contemplatives are so sensitive to the atmosphere of our times that they have to make a great struggle to overcome morbid feelings of guilt and absolute unworthiness. For such people the 'Little Way' of St Thérèse is full of appeal, whereas passages such as this one in *The Interior Castle* serve to turn them away from the spiritual treasure-house of the Mother of Carmel.

This problem is a general one. There are passages in St Augustine, St Bernard and St Thomas, which are so much out of tune with our way of feeling and thinking that they serve only to depress and disconcert the soul. There is in the Church not only development of dogma but also development of feeling and attitude, so that what is in the most perfect harmony with the mind of one age strikes a false note in relation to the mind of a later age. The fundamental beliefs have not changed, but their true meaning has come to be more fully understood.

So it is that it is better not to make too much of this and similar passages in St Teresa's writings. She is describing the soul that lives in deliberate and conscious opposition to God, the source of all goodness, and we can have the strongest confidence that we have been preserved from this. But there are, it seems, souls, not a few either, in the state described by the saint, and we can help them by our prayers and sufferings. If we have already 'the greatest fear of offending God' then instead of forcing this fear any further we can resolve to pray more often and more fervently for sinners.

The second result mentioned by the saint as following from the vision of the soul in mortal sin is very helpful and profound: We see that what is truly good in us has its source outside ourselves: it comes from God. Yet this same God it is who dwells within us, so that the more we are true to what is deepest in ourselves the more we draw from this source.

Self-Knowledge

It is not easy at first reading to discover what place St Teresa accords to self-knowledge in her Castle. The First Mansions are, it seems, the mansions of self-knowledge ('the first rooms – that is the rooms of self-knowledge', I, ii, par. 8); yet self-knowledge belongs it seems to all the Mansions ('however high a state the soul may have attained, self-knowledge is incumbent upon it' – ibid, see also VI, ix). It would seem that what is meant is that self-knowledge is the beginning of progress in prayer, but that it is not something which we leave behind after a while; rather does it grow as we advance and, indeed, if it is not growing we are not advancing.

Self-knowledge for St Teresa is almost synonymous with humility, and, for her, humility is the staple solid food, the bread of the spiritual life. But one can have too much bread, and she seems to be more conscious in this chapter of the dangers attending self-knowledge than of the need for it. She sees clearly that self-knowledge is not complete in itself, that it is worse than useless unless it is combined with knowledge of God. By itself it simply depresses us, dries up the springs of action. Here, as in many other places in her writings, the saint castigates pusillanimity. It is worth remarking that although she stresses greatly the importance of humility, St Teresa places far more emphasis on magnanimity, and gives the impression that she regarded pusillanimity as the greatest of all enemies to spiritual progress. We need only look around us to see how right she was in this: for the one person who is held back from progressing in the spiritual life through pride, ten are held back by the fact that 'they will not disengage themselves from the slough of cowardice, pusillanimity and fear' (I, ii, par. 10).

It is sometimes said that Christian ascetic writers place too much emphasis on self-examination and self-accusation. The practice of the daily examination of conscience (it is said) leads to morbid introspection and to meagreness of soul. St Teresa's way of self-knowledge obviates this danger completely. What she says in effect is: let your examination of conscience be a contemplation of the divine attributes, a recalling of Christ's passion and death, Christ's meekness and humility; a contemplation in which our faults and lapses appear, yes, but appear only to be swallowed up in this marvellous light of God's presence. This is diametrically opposed to all systems of counting faults; and yet it is large enough to allow us to see our faults and to make very specific resolutions. But the atmosphere and light in which we move is that of God's presence not that of our own poor nature. We are, as it were, looking through a window at a beautiful landscape; the window is always misting over, and we are cleaning it, but we are concerned far more with the view than with the window. To concentrate on the window without ever looking through it would be foolish and stultifying.

The Devil

Perhaps the most disconcerting thing in St Teresa's writing is her attitude to the devil. He is as much part of the spiritual scene as the Blessed Virgin, or the spiritual director. She sees him as at once spiritual and material: he can enter into our thoughts but he can also hide in the pages of a book.

For St Teresa, the devil is present all the time on the stage of the spiritual life, engaged always in undoing God's work or trying to prevent it. He has power to simulate apparitions of Christ and the saints; he has the power to perplex and confuse; especially he has the power to throw the soul into deep depression. In everything that is done for God's glory the devil must get his innings, so to speak. And yet the devil is always subject to God, and is never given more power than God permits; we need not, therefore, be really afraid of him.

In its essentials the saint's doctrine in this matter is the same as that of sacred Scripture, and the fathers, and all the great spiritual writers. Perfection would be a simple matter if it was a question only of God and the soul, but the third protagonist is always on the stage – the Adversary, the accuser who must be heard and given a certain scope, for the reason that the human will has somehow given him a footing. God does not force the will but draws it on sweetly, strongly, very delicately, respecting its freedom, its spontaneity. Those who cannot understand why Satan should have so much power, why there is so much sin and suffering in the world, do not take account of the infinite gentleness of God, that gentleness and delicacy that is as much a divine attribute as omniscience and omnipotence. The material creation is a most beautiful and delicate dialogue between creature and creator by which a whole world is gradually drawn out of chaos; so also the spiritual world in which the soul is born again and brought to maturity is full of that same dialogue and delicate co-operation. And in all this the Adversary is present, watching to distort and destroy, for Satan has freely chosen to oppose God in all his works, and God has chosen to overcome Satan not by force but by that infinite love and gentleness that always draws good out of evil. When the Body of Christ is fully built up Satan will have no more power to harm it.

Satan is always present as long as our present state lasts, yet it would seem that the kind of power and presence that is given to him differs from one age to the next according as mankind develops towards the fullness of Christ. He worked and showed himself somewhat differently to St Teresa and her contemporaries than he does today. So it is that some of the things she experienced and some of the things she says do not find immediate application with us.

What she has to say about the devil's activities in the present chapter, however, is just as relevant now as when it was written. Those who set out on the way of perfection very easily fall into the habit of criticizing those about them, finding them lacking in that spirit of earnestness and mortification which they themselves genuinely possess at the moment. If this critical spirit can be made to grow, then there is dissension, dislike, all kinds of bitterness and strife. The devil tries to achieve this, and very often succeeds. The great weapon against him is fraternal charity, more and more of it. We might add that this is always the best of all weapons against Satan. It is like a strong acid that cleans away all impurities in the soul, and so gets rid of all the devil's works and pomps. With her admirable sense of the essential, St Teresa sees this clearly, and is careful to emphasize it here at the beginnings of the journey into the Interior Castle.

The Call to Perfection

The First Mansions are occupied by those who have begun to practise prayer, that is, to take thought about the things of God, but are still worldly in outlook, distracted and prone to sin. This general state admits of many varieties and degrees, and St Teresa is careful to explain that there are very many rooms in these outer Mansions. But common to all of them is a certain immersion in worldly affairs, and a consequent deafness and dumbness as regards divine converse.

Now the soul enters the Second Mansions by making a definite break with the world. It hears the call of God (par. 3) and answers it, and so it gets away from the occasions of sin, the 'reptiles' that insinuate themselves everywhere in the outer Mansions. It would seem that the transition from the First to the Second Mansions has a certain correspondence with the transition from the world to the cloister when one decides to embrace the religious life. It is, of course, possible that a person may have advanced very far in prayer before entering the cloister, and, on the other hand, it is possible that a religious may become deeply immersed in worldly preoccupations; but there is, nevertheless, a certain correspondence, so that we may say that the religious novice is normally within the Second Mansions and that the saint's directives concerning this state as given in this chapter and in Chapters 11 and 13 of the *Life* have special relevance for direction of beginners in the religious life.[4]

The process of disengagement from the world is usually very painful – the saint likens it to the 'clash of arms' and 'the noise of canon'. She may have been thinking of her own experience in leaving her father's house for the Convent of the Incarnation when, she tells us, it seemed to her as if every bone in her body were being wrenched asunder.

We find evidence of this struggle in the lives of many of the saints, and it may seem that, because of the heights they reached later on, even at this early stage they were somehow different from ordinary mortals. This is not true. This elementary decision to give all to God involves the same kind of struggle for everybody, and there is hardly any soul that has entered the religious state or the priesthood who has not felt it. As a rule, it is not a question of great possessions in the form of material goods, but rather of the affections that chain down the heart, and only reveal their strength when we try to break them. It is indeed a deep and terrible drama, and there are many who are defeated in the face of it, and turn away sad, like the rich young man. But it is better that it should be deeply felt once and for all, for if the victory is gained then, a great leap forward has been made.

In the fourth paragraph of the chapter under discussion, the Saint enumerates some of the ways in which the call to perfection

---

4. It is, of course, also possible to make this decision without entering a monastery or convent; and St Teresa would admit this. Many of her 'soul friends' were very much *in* the world, if not *of* the world. Yet she did see her convents as strongholds of prayer, to which the ardent lover of God was normally led. The Carmelite commits herself to the front line of the spiritual battle; others may well fight beside her, carrying, so to speak, a 'free lance'.

comes: good conversations, sermons, books etc. Remembering her own struggle of three months (*Life* 3) she adds that we need not lose heart if we do not respond to the call to perfection at once. Like many women saints she is very conscious of the importance of good *desires*. For many people, men or women, this is better psychology than the insistence on the 'moment of grace'. We are weak creatures, and it is not always wise for us to face great obstacles all at once; often it is necessary to wait on grace, knowing that God can build on our desires to overcome the obstacle.

Although there is an unmistakable parallel between the description given here of the passage into the Second Mansions and the saint's own decision to become a nun, it does not follow that married people are excluded from advancing in the ways of prayer. Some of the saint's most valued companions in her journey upwards were married people. But for many souls the decision to go forward into the ways of divine intimacy coincided with the decision to enter religion: the latter decision brings the former to a definite point, demanding an early solution.

For all the conflict and drama involved in it, the call to perfection is yet something very sweet and gentle: it is the voice of the Bridegroom gently calling the Bride to himself. Indeed, the way of progress in prayer is a way towards an ever deeper sweetness and gentleness, for the Lord who dwells in the innermost Mansions is infinitely gentle and sweet. Yet he is also a consuming fire that burns away all that is sentimental and self-indulgent.

Aridity

When the fire of divine love feeds on the affections of the heart there results interior sweetness and delight. This general state varies in intensity, and has many different forms. In some of its manifestations it has a certain quality of sensible or sensuous feeling, which may in certain cases lead to sensual feelings and motions. These latter are not directly intended nor indulged in and are best ignored. Some modern psychologists would dismiss all sensible consolation as basically sensual; in this they follow Freud's conception of the soul, according to which the whole of the affective life is sensual and sexual in the strict sense. This conception is rejected by many psychologists, such as the followers of Jung and Adler, and so it must be remembered that even within the domain of psychology this is merely an 'opinion'. Some of the Quietists in medieval times seem to have regarded all sensible consolation as unholy. The Church *condemned* this position as expressed in the following proposition: 'In the spiritual life all sensible feeling is abominable, impure and unclean.'[5]

As a rule consolations become more calm, profound and deeply joyful as the soul advances. Gradually the fire of God's love begins to take hold of the deeper levels of the soul and this process involves a certain darkening or 'drying up' of the lower levels. The process is analogous to that of education in taste: in order to come to appreciate good music we have to put aside bad music; this may mean a period when our musical sense is in aridity since it does not get what it wants, and it does not yet want what it is getting.

It is easy to become attached to sensible consolations, and if we do, our progress is much impeded. St John of the Cross was very conscious of this, and his Mount of Perfection is largely aimed at counteracting this attachment. The soul that would advance quickly and in the right direction must enter by the narrow gate of the *Nada* (nothing). It simply seeks God, leaving aside both earthly goods and heavenly goods (consolations). St Teresa is making the same point when she says the really important thing at this stage

5. See H. Denzinger and C. Rahner, *Enchiridion Symbolorum* (Rome: 1946) n.1250, where this proposition is ascribed to Molinos. In general the spiritual tradition has tended to purify and transcend the sensual by means of ascetical practices, and to recover something of its energy at the mystical level. On the other hand the official Church has tended to defend the way of the common man and to distrust the 'exalted' emotions of the mystic. This tension is one of the constants of Christian history largely overlooked by historians. It seems likely that some of the insults that were levelled at St Teresa in her lifetime, as also the effort to discredit her writings after her death, came from this kind of tension.

is 'to labour and be resolute and prepare ourselves with all possible diligence to bring our will into conformity with the will of God' (II, i, par. 9). The soul must not seek consolations but simply God's will, leaving everything to God. Thus the foundation is properly laid and there is no danger of a collapse. This kind of attitude will carry us through right to the end.

It is easy to get the impression from all this that the soul in the Second Mansions is usually in a state of aridity. This is not so, however. Rather, this is the time of consolations of a sensible kind such as the saint herself experienced when she had entered the Convent of the Incarnation. But it is also a time when the danger of becoming attached to consolations is especially large, and so a word of warning is necessary.

The state of aridity may be felt at all stages of the spiritual life, but as the fire of God's love begins to burn more and more deeply the presence or absence of sensible warmth matters less and less. The will that is deeply united to God possesses its own warmth, which is profound, secure and stable. This warmth may flow back into the domain of the senses and even cause a sensible bodily warmth. What the soul has to learn at the early stage is to bear patiently with aridity, and to try to strengthen the will to proceed onwards, applying itself to the basic virtues without which prayer is of little value.

The Carefully Ordered Life

To the Third Mansions belong those people who lead a carefully ordered spiritual life 'They avoid even venial sin [i.e. deliberate venial sin]; they are fond of penance; they have their times for recollection;[6] they use their time well; they engage in works of

---

6. *suo horas de recogimiento*. Peers translates 'they spend hours in recollection' (p. 221) which gives the wrong impression. It is only later, after the mystical frontier has been passed, that people quite spontaneously spend hours in prayer. On the other hand, we must be careful not to underestimate the scope and depth of the types of Christian experience covered by the Second and Third Mansions.

charity; they are careful in dress and speech and in the management of their house if they have one' (III, i, par. 5).

Such people have advanced very far, and have put sin resolutely behind them. This has been possible only with the help of divine grace; and this fact alone is sufficient to show that the Lord wishes to bring them farther, into the innermost Mansions. This is in fact their great desire, for their taste has been purified: they desire heavenly things rather than earthly things. Those in the Second Mansions are still in or near the field of battle, in which the world and the spirit fight for mastery. It is a battle in which there are many engagements, and in which victory comes only by dint of perseverance. Those who have gained the victory enter the relative security of the Third Mansions. In the Second Mansions all mortal sin has been put away; there are no longer these occasional falls that come to those in the First Mansions, but there are still some deliberate venial sins, for the battle with the world is going on, and the soul tries to make terms with the world from time to time. Such deliberate faults are absent in the Third Mansions, though there are still many indeliberate faults; indeed these are present even in the Seventh Mansions.

It is not these faults that are holding the soul back from further advance. Rather it is a kind of unconscious selfishness. The soul easily becomes smug, especially as it shows great perfection in externals and wins good reports from others. St Teresa remarks, not without irony, that the soul at this stage has a certain excess of order and routine. It is well-ordered even in its penances. 'There is no fear that they will kill themselves; their reason is well in control' (III, 2, par. 8). It has not yet found that love that overcomes all reason.

It would seem that there are very many people, secular and religious, who remain all their lives in these Third Mansions. They have achieved a certain routine of righteousness, and they have not the will to rise beyond it. As a rule it seems that souls quite naturally rest at this point, so that there is great danger that they will never go any further. The way by which God shakes them out of the rut is suffering: he sends them various trials to chasten and refine the spirit, and prepare the way for the delicate unctions of the Fourth Mansions.

At this point everything depends on the soul's reaction to the Cross. The saint gives us a lively description of the reactions these people of 'carefully ordered life' have to the crosses sent them by God. These people *seemed* so well established in virtue, and did so well as long as the sun shone on them, as long as they were able to pursue their own way, their own routine of prayer and works of piety. But then the cross comes, and they simply cannot accept it. They lose their goods, or people despise them, or they are put aside in some way: and they cannot understand how such things can happen to *them*. 'It is no use offering them advice, for they have been practising virtue for so long that they think they are capable of teaching others' (III, ii, par. 1).

Such people are as a rule rather careful about their health. They find plenty of good reasons, and in fact have good reasons, for taking care of themselves; but this timidity keeps them back from the higher ways of prayer. They are solidly encased in their own reasonableness.

There are some, however, who allow the cross to do its work, whose will to attain to union with God is strong enough to hold on while the storm rages. It is souls such as these that advance into the Fourth Mansions, and come to experience infused contemplation. Unfortunately, however, there are many who fail to accept the Cross and who run away from it. They lack generosity of soul, and are not taken into the ways of contemplative prayer. This is a great pity, for the Lord's graces are there for all.[7]

---

7. The cross at this stage may take any one of a variety of forms: physical illness, failure in business or vocation, an emotional entanglement, a nervous ailment. The main point is that the soul is shaken out of its routine; the apple-cart is upset. This can lead to some kind of breakdown, or to a hardening of the personality, or, finally, to that opening and flowing which allows God's love to come in and take over.

Mystical Prayer

The most important advance in the spiritual journey is that which
takes us from the Third to the Fourth Mansions. The soul in the
first three sets of Mansions is in the ways of ordinary prayer, and
the means by which it establishes contact with God is meditation
– that is, the interior contact of mental prayer; for, of course, there
is always vocal and liturgical prayer and the contact with God they
involve. The Fourth Mansions are entered when the soul begins
to enjoy mystical prayer – what St Teresa here calls supernatural
prayer.

What is mystical prayer? It is the experienced presence of the
divine in the soul, a certain spiritual warmth and light which the
soul does not have to labour to attain: it is *given*; the soul is passive
– hence the name passive contemplation. The soul seems to be
drinking the living water of God's love; God's presence pours in –
hence the name 'infused' contemplation (Latin *infundere*, to pour).
This infusion admits of very many degrees and varieties, and seems
to be accommodated in its structure and accompanying phenomena
to the spiritual physiognomy of the person involved.

Infused contemplation is partly transient and partly stable. The
glow and fervour of the experience does not last very long as a
rule, a few days or weeks usually. But the deepest part of the
experience, that which unites the will to the will of God, does not
disappear, and remains on as a deeper adhesion to God and a fuller
detachment from creatures.

There is much controversy as to whether infused contemplation,
or mystical prayer, lies in the normal way by which the soul journeys
to God. Can a soul arrive at the heights simply by the practice of
the virtues and a kind of active prayer – 'active contemplation' –
or is it essential that mystical prayer be reached in order that the
soul advance to the heights? St Teresa seems to teach that there
are some souls of an active nature for whom the mystical order is
closed; these must not be forced to adopt the mystical way. On
the other hand, she is quite certain that God calls all to the mystical
order, that the graces are there if the soul only disposes itself.

Commentators are hard put to it to reconcile her various statements on the subject. One thing is clear, however: for St Teresa the mystical way is the sure way to the heights, to the fullness of God's love, to the divine espousals and marriage. She does not align herself with those who fear mysticism; she would have us all go forward boldly along this road. Nevertheless, it must be said that she judges spiritual progress not by mystical experience, however deep and genuine, but by growth in that charity described by St Paul in 1 Corinthians 13.

Consolations: A Distinction

As soon as St Teresa begins to describe what she means by 'supernatural' or mystical prayer she finds herself struggling with an important distinction that is very difficult to express accurately. It is clear that the infusion of knowledge and love of God that is the essence of mystical prayer brings greater delight to the soul. The soul is filled with a kind of fragrance 'as if in these interior depths there were a brazier on which were cast sweet perfumes' and this sweetness even extends at times to the body: mystical experience in this its joyful aspect involves therefore a marvellous sense of well-being compared with which the highest mundane pleasures are shallow and unsteady.

Now the beginner in the ways of prayer, who, in Teresian terminology, inhabits the Second or Third Mansions, usually receives moments or times of deep sweetness, a sense of peace, of union with Jesus in the Blessed Sacrament, of the fatherly providence of God, etc. In emotional natures the thought of one's sins may cause tears which are sweet rather than sorrowful, or tears may flow from a simple consideration of God's goodness, or from the vivid realization of some scene in the Passion. Thinking of the humanity of Christ, his Sacred Heart, his divine countenance, a great fervour of love may arise in the heart through a kind of commotion of the blood and this may lead to vehement motions and cries of longing. Some of these phenomena may be experienced by souls in the later

Mansions, especially those that have to do with sorrow for sin, but as a rule they decrease as the soul becomes more deeply united to God.

These phenomena are frequently bound up with discursive meditation. By means of deep and sympathetic reflection the soul is able to call up these emotions. In a certain sense it is in control of these phenomena. Not entirely, however: there are times of aridity when no consideration will arouse any pious feeling, when the only feelings present are disgust and weariness. But at other times the soul is able to arouse its own feelings by means of reading and meditation, though there is a certain strain and laboriousness about it that can at times leave the soul depressed.

The consolations that come in the early stages of the life of prayer are not all of this kind, however. Most of them are peaceful and deeply satisfying. In this they resemble mystical prayer or infused contemplation and the two may easily be confused. They are nevertheless quite different, and it is very important to distinguish clearly between them. St Teresa is very anxious to do this, though she is not at all satisfied that she has done so. Here as elsewhere she attributes her failure (or seeming failure) to her lack of learning. She must have known that the learned men were also puzzled by these phenomena, but she was right in feeling that learning would have provided her with various terms and concepts that she might have used to express her meaning.

Although the saint begins to try to express this distinction early in the first chapter of the Fourth Mansions she goes off at a tangent, so that when later on she takes up her manuscript again she feels somewhat lost and in fact has to begin again. So it is only in the second chapter that the distinction comes to be drawn.

The distinction is first expressed in terms of mediacy versus immediacy, by means of the figure of the fountain and aqueduct. The bowl that is near the fountain is filled immediately without labour, and it is filled to overflowing; the bowl that is far away from the fountain cannot be filled until an aqueduct is built and all kinds of intervening chutes and pipes. The point is that the one process is quite laborious and uncertain, whereas the other is certain and without labour. The sweetness that we bring about through considerations are somewhat laborious and a little disappointing; the sweetness of infused contemplation is abundant and is simply received into the soul: except for its activity of receiving, the soul is passive.

This basis of distinction is, however, rather unsatisfactory, and the saint puts it aside in favour of another, which goes far more deeply into the matter. (This in fact was the ground of distinction which was first brought up early in the first chapter.) This centres around the phrase from Psalm 118 *dilatasti cor meum*: thou hast enlarged my heart. Infused contemplation enlarges the heart, causes an interior dilation as if the whole experience was the unfolding of something that was within – here we have the beautiful figure of the brazier and the perfume which spreads its fragrance throughout the whole soul. Some authors speak of an interior sense of smell as they speak of other interior senses but St Teresa makes it clear that there is no question here of any real fragrance – fragrance is simply used as a metaphor to express that for which there is no terminology available. Neither is there question of that opening up of 'the doors of perception' which can be induced by certain drugs, or by certain techniques of meditation. What is in question is a certain profound possession of the heart by the divine presence, that gives a sense of enlargement and the breaking of bonds. Ordinary consolations have not this quality: they may possess the soul but they do not have the power to open it up and enlarge it.

The result of infused contemplation is an increase of union of the will with the divine will – this is the best of all tests of its genuineness. We might put it in another way by saying that the best test of its genuineness is the *detachment* it brings with it. Ordinary consolations do not really increase detachment in any lasting way.

Through infused prayer the soul passes from particular loves to universal love. This consequence is not mentioned by St Teresa, but it is the obvious moral counterpart of the psychological dilation of the heart to which she refers. If the enlargement of the heart is to be anything more than a transient experience it must involve a larger charity. At its highest, divine charity is truly universal, giving to all that deep and unfailing love that the human heart in the order of nature only gives to a few. This does not mean that there are no distinctions, no special friends, but it means that people are now specially loved according as their beauty of soul, their inner reality, is more deeply known, and not because of superficial qualities or natural relationships.

It must be noted, finally, that though St Teresa clearly places infused contemplation on a higher plane than ordinary consolations she does not in fact say anything to disparage ordinary consolations. Rather does she assume that they are an integral part of the whole spiritual process, having their own place and their own advantages.

The Prayer of Quiet

That infused prayer which characterizes the Fourth Mansions is discussed very fully in Chapter 31 of the *Way of Perfection* where it is named the Prayer of Quiet.

Since the psychological method of St Teresa and the Spanish mystics generally is rather disconcerting to many people, it may be well to attempt to express the nature of this prayer in other terms.

The Prayer of Quiet is simply the prayer of the soul that has found a certain repose in resting in the arms of God. St Teresa herself used the simile of a child at the breast. The soul that has reached the Prayer of Quiet is the soul that has come to experience a certain sweet repose in the love of God, a repose so deep and strong that it detaches the soul from all created things. It is in fact an awakening of the God of love in the heart, an awakening that may be connected with some divine attribute or manifestation, with the Divine Childhood, the Sacred Heart, the motherly presence of Mary, or that may be simply a flame and glow of love not connected specially with any mystery.

There is here a deep union with God of the will, the power of loving. At this stage the powers of perception and apprehension, though conscious of this marvellous love, are not as yet really caught up into the divine embrace. In other words, though the heart is full of love, the mind still wanders at times, and may indeed be full of the most fantastic distractions.[8] St Teresa tells us that in this situation it would be useless to try to get the mind to fix itself on subjects of meditation, or in general to try to achieve deeper union with God by means of intelligence. We must simply allow ourselves to rest in this love that is filling our hearts. This does not mean that we are no longer responsible for our thoughts, that we can allow bitter or proud or self-indulgent thoughts to possess our minds. On the contrary, we can only preserve this union of hearts if we keep our house well in order by the practice of all the virtues. The point is that we cannot fix the mind on God in the way that the will is fixed on him, and so we simply ignore distractions and keep our attention on the act of loving, encouraging this activity with great gentleness.

What is really essential to the Prayer of Quiet is union of the will with the Will of God, not so much the will as a faculty of decision, for this union has begun earlier, but with the will as a faculty of union, of espousals and marriage between spirit and spirit. Now this union can be present not only in a joyful way but also in a dark and painful and arid way. This arid Prayer of Quiet is generally said to be of the same kind as the Passive Dark Night

---

8. In St Teresa's terminology there is suspension of the will but not of the memory or understanding. Other authors use the term ligature from the Latin *ligare*, to bind, for the will is bound up or held by God. There may be suspension or ligature of any or all of the powers of the mind. It may be noted that St Teresa and her contemporaries made use of the terms of what is now called 'faculty psychology' not only in their writings, but in their everyday conversations. So, too, the word 'soul' was as commonly used and as acceptable as the word 'person' is to us. There is no way of reading St Teresa without tuning in to this terminology.

of Sense of St John of the Cross. In this state the soul is constantly and deeply concerned with God, but the vital springs of the heart seem dried up, and there is a feeling of utter darkness and loneliness. It demands no little courage to keep on seeking God during the times of darkness and aridity that are a feature of the spiritual life at all stages; this is especially true at this stage, for the soul is still weak, and not yet accustomed to this new world of joy and sorrow.

The Prayer of Quiet, like all mystical prayer, has two levels, a superficial intensity of joy or sorrow, which is transitory, and a deeper level of union with God and detachment from creatures, which is of its nature permanent. The soul is no longer timid and calculating in its attitude to spiritual things. It is ready to suffer great things for God, and at times may experience a certain love of suffering which is by no means a masochistic falling back on one's own emotions but the opening up of the spirit to the great world of sacrificial love. In its early stages this love for suffering may be so acute that it involves a real need for assuagement; so it is that we hear of saints and servants of God who have had a thirst for austerities. But this stage is transitory, and is usually connected with the transitory elements of joyful union. The more stable result of the Prayer of Quiet is not so much a desire for penance as a readiness to undergo hardships for the sake of love – this perhaps in spite of a sense of physical and moral weakness.

Finally, it is worth noting that the Prayer of Quiet, like all mystical prayer, may vanish or almost vanish from remembrance as regards its transitory side. But it remains on in its effects, in its deeper level, in the detachment from creatures and attachment to God it brings with it. We are not concerned here with the question as to whether these effects can be attained in some other way, through some non-mystical means. What is precious either way is the good effect itself, that deep peaceful union of the will with God, intermittently known to consciousness, by which we truly abide in these inner Mansions of the soul.

The Prayer of Recollection

By recollection St Teresa means a certain concentration or unified attention of the mind – an attention, that is, to God and divine things.

This attention is, of course, implied in all mystical prayer, so much so that St John of the Cross describes mystical prayer as a 'loving attention'. But attention to divine things is essentially something which the soul can develop for itself after the fashion in which we can learn to control our attention and develop concentration in the domain of study. The more we become interested in something the more easily we can concentrate on it, until the time comes when we become absorbed almost in spite of ourselves. According as we develop a love for divine things, so do we develop a power of attention to these things; and this attention is the prayer of recollection.

How is the prayer of recollection related to the Prayer of Quiet? In the *Way of Perfection* the main difference seems to lie in the fact that the Prayer of Quiet is 'supernatural' (i.e. mystical, passive) while the Prayer of Recollection is not. In the *Mansions*, however, the Prayer of Recollection is regarded as supernatural. It is 'a recollection that also seems to me supernatural' (IV, iii, par. 1). It 'cannot be had for the seeking but comes to us only when God gives it to us.' (ibid, par. 3) How then does it differ from the Prayer of Quiet for which it prepares the way? By the fact that it works through meditation. The mind is concentrated on God but not in such a way that it is simply drinking in the glory of the divine presence. Rather is it engaged in examining some part of divine truth and drawing affections from it.

But is not this kind of prayer within one's own power, allowing for the ordinary operations of grace? It may be said to be within our power physically, but not morally. Most people who are trying to lead a life of prayer very soon meet with a great problem of distractions. At first prayer is easy, for they are receiving consolations and perhaps some touches of the Prayer of Quiet. But then there comes a kind of flatness and weariness, as if the soul were travelling across an interminable plateau. Perhaps a better figure would be that of marking time: the soul seems to be simply marking time. The period of meditation is full of distractions, and it seems, in spite of all assurances to the contrary, to be time wasted. This state may last many years, and the soul feels quite unable to advance beyond it. Then, perhaps subsequent to some renewal of fervour, or after the acceptance of heavy crosses, the soul begins to find prayer somehow fruitful and easy. It is as if a door had swung open within the mind and revealed a divine treasury of thoughts. This door does not open whenever the soul wills it. Indeed it may remain closed again for some time, even for years. As a rule, however, the door is thrown open when the soul gives itself to prayer; and it is clear that a new stage has been reached. Meditation may still be rather 'scrappy' and laborious at times but there is, in general, a new sense of contact with divine things and of the fruit-fulness of a life of prayer.

The Prayer of Recollection, then, is largely acquired by our own efforts aided by 'ordinary' grace. Yet there is need of a special grace to establish the soul in this way of prayer. For this prayer involves a strong adhesion to God, and a great degree of detachment from creatures, and this normally demands a special grace. This grace does not involve any deeply felt experience of the presence of God, any special inflowing of peace and joy, and so it is not strictly speaking a mystical grace. Yet what is lasting and most precious in mystical graces is found also in this special grace – detachment from creatures and attachment to God. It is not surprising then that St Teresa is willing to speak of the Prayer of Recollection as 'supernatural' (i.e. mystical), even though she has already stated that the Prayer of Quiet is the *initial* mystical prayer.

Recollection is a great spiritual gift, and the soul that has attained to it even in small measure should thank God for it. Although it involves meditation, the movement of the mind from one point to another, it easily passes over into the Prayer of Quiet, in which the soul rests in God and uses meditation only as a bridge to attain this rest.

The Prayer of Union

The Prayer of Union is the prayer of the Fifth Mansions and of the Third Degree of Prayer described in the *Life*. It belongs to the order of mystical prayer, being a deepening and intensification of the Prayer of Quiet. Indeed, all the kinds of prayer dealt with in the Fourth and subsequent Mansions belong together and are simply modes of the infusion of the Presence of God into the soul, that experienced presence which is accompanied either by great warmth and sweetness or by deep darkness and distress. In all these states we can distinguish the vivid experience of joy or sorrow, which is transient, from the deeper level of attachment to God and detachment from creatures. It must be remembered that a soul may have come to live in any of these Mansions, even the Seventh, and yet find, with St Thérèse of Lisieux, that its habitual state is one of aridity and monotony; but it will be always deeply and exclusively concerned with divine things, and will not really give itself to any human interest or pleasure.

But we must return to the Prayer of Union. This is not yet Spiritual Betrothal, much less Spiritual Marriage; that is to say, the union of the soul with God is not yet constant or complete. There is nevertheless, a true and marvellous union of spirit and spirit that is far more striking than that of the Prayer of Quiet.

The Prayer of Union is a kind of inebriation. The soul discovers that it is somehow deeply in love with God. If the Prayer of Quiet may be described under the figure of the child asleep in its father's arms, the figure that seems best to suit the present state is that of the man who has fallen deeply in love, who wants to do nothing but sing the praises of his beloved. 'O God what must that soul be like when it is in this state. It would fain be all tongue, so that it might praise the Lord. It utters a thousand holy follies, striving ever to please him who thus possesses it' (*Life*, 16, par. 4). The soul in such a state may break out in exclamations of love, and if it does not succeed in hiding its state (as it will normally strive to do) those around it will think that it has become unbalanced and will perhaps speak of 'strain', 'emotionalism', 'religious mania', etc.[9]

It is obvious that a state of this kind will have variations of intensity, and that it will be to some extent subject to the psychological law of action and reaction. Not that it is subject to this law in the same way as is the state of first fervour, which involves the more superficial emotions, and is more the soul's work than God's work. In the Prayer of Union the soul's vicissitudes seem to be arranged by God: it is *given* joy and fervour, and again it is *given* distress and darkness. The times of darkness bring very great suffering, for the grain of wheat must die, the silkworm must be changed into the butterfly. The time of fervour may last for days or weeks, but the time of darkness will inevitably come; if it does not come there is something wrong. 'If anyone tells me that having arrived at this stage he finds that all is peace and joy I should say to him that he has not arrived at this stage at all' (V, ii, par. 10).

The Prayer of Union itself, in its most fervent manifestations has within it a certain distress. Essentially it is the distress of unfulfilment. The soul is deeply in love with God and cannot rest until it possesses him fully. In a sense it is at peace, yet in another

---

9. Obviously this state may have some features in common with obsessional states, just as poetic inspiration and manic behaviour have features in common. But to argue from this to identity is to commit a fallacy or *non sequitur* analysed long ago by Aristotle. The fallacy consists in assuming that because X and Y have characteristics a, b, c, d in common they must, therefore, be the same or at least have some further important point in common. Most detective stories are based on this fallacy: the reader and everybody else is taken in, but the great detective has a flash of insight sparked off by some small detail, and he sees that some assumption collapses and reveals the culprit. It is quite incredible how widespread is this 'sin of the mind' today; for instance in accusations of Gnosticism levelled at certain thinkers or in the attachment of labels such as 'liberal' or 'conservative' to certain positions. The mystic is especially open to being misrepresented in this way, for mysticism resembles so many attitudes and states that are, in fact, essentially different.

sense it is restless and full of grief, exclaiming with St John of the Cross: 'O give me all of Thee: For Thou alone canst heal my sorrow.' There is peace in so far as the Beloved is present, but this presence is only partial, and so it serves to emphasize the absence of the Beloved.

At this stage it is common to experience a need for expression, especially for poetic or artistic expression, and this need may recur from time to time throughout the remainder of the spiritual journey. The results may be of artistic value or may be quite worthless artistically; either way such compositions should be treated with great respect for they are sincere expressions of the soul's love. It is significant that all the canonized saints of the Teresian Reform have left us poems telling of their love of God.

Love of the Neighbour

After having written most enthusiastically about the Prayer of Union, St Teresa turns aside in Chapter 3 of the Fifth Mansions to underline the importance of fraternal charity.

She begins by pointing out that the Prayer of Union is of little use unless it has within it a union of our will with the divine will. She tells us: 'This is the union which I have desired all my life; it is for this that I constantly pray to our Lord, and which is most clear and secure.' (V, iii, par. 6)

This union of will is not to be confused with that delectable union of will which belongs to the Prayer of Quiet. The will is at once a faculty of enjoyment and a faculty of choice; it is the will as a faculty of enjoyment that is in question when we speak of union of will in the Prayer of Quiet – this union of course is deeper still in the Prayer of Union, where there is union of the understanding as well. But the will is also a faculty of choice, and it is in this sense that we speak of our will conforming to the will of God. This union of will may be quite without delectation, but it is most durable and precious, and is indeed the basis of all spiritual progress. It has been present in some measure from the beginning of the life of prayer; but it will increase as the soul goes onward from one Mansion to the next. Otherwise the soul is not in fact progressing.

St Teresa repeatedly warns us against seeking or even praying for mystical graces. It is otherwise with this grace of conformity with the will of God. This is something to be sought after and prayed for constantly. Moreover it is a gift which does not easily lend itself to delusion.

This conformity with God's will shows itself in the practice of the virtues, and above all in the practice of the virtue of charity according to the dual commandment of the love of God and the love of the neighbour. 'The Lord asks only two things of us – to love himself and to love the neighbour. It is in this direction we must strive' (V, iii, par. 8).

The saint goes on to point out – she is following St John the Evangelist though she does not refer to him – that the practical test and sign of our success in keeping the commandment of loving God is our success in loving our neighbour. This, then, is the 'acid test' of all spiritual progress. By this we can determine whether we are really advancing from one Mansion to the next, or whether we are simply being led by our emotions, or deceived by Satan. If a person is selfish, unhelpful, unwilling to suffer for others, to make a real effort to put up with difficult people, then he can be sure that he is not really advancing in prayer. Similarly the censorious person, the backbiter, the man of jealous mind can never advance along the ways of prayer until he tries to change his fundamental attitude. For it is the attitude that is most important. There will always be many faults and failures, things done or said 'on the spur of the moment', and these will serve to remind us of our frailty, but it is the basic attitude that counts, our deliberate policies; it is at this deeper level that prayer and conduct are interwoven, so that our prayer is purifying our attitudes, and our attitudes of love and reverence and forgiveness are enlarging the heart to greater infusions of graces of union.

Any mystical doctrine that ignores this matter of charity, or puts it in parenthesis, is incomplete and unsound where it is not positively false and dangerous.

It is in the love of the neighbour that prayer and apostolate are bound together in the hidden life. We do not enter into the ways of union in order to leave behind us the hurts and afflictions of life among our fellows. Rather do we lay ourselves more open to these hurts and afflictions – nobody is more exposed to the barbs and arrows of life in the group than the enclosed religious. This is an essential part of prayer; it might be called the raw material of prayer. There are, besides, a thousand afflictions and anxieties arising from our family or our friends or the general situation in which we find ourselves. All this enters into our prayer and opens our hearts to our kind, to sinners, to the miserable, to the whole world. Nobody is more attuned to 'the human condition' in which he finds himself than is the true contemplative. It is through this attunement and openness that the mystic becomes a warrior in the great battle described by St Paul in Ephesians, chapter 6.

Dangers of Complacency

The soul that has attained to the Prayer of Union is so deeply attached to God that it would seem impossible for it to fall away and forsake him. Nevertheless, it is the soul at this stage that is in question in the following somewhat frightening passage:

> The devil attacks the soul in the most subtle ways, undermining it in small ways by giving evil the colour of good, leading it on to matters which he makes it understand not to be wrong. And so, little by little the understanding is darkened, the will is weakened, self-love grows, so that, in one way or another, the soul comes to cease to do God's will and to indulge its own wishes. (V, iv, par. 7)

The saint has described with some finesse a gradual process by which self-love comes to be substituted for God's love. It must be remembered that the Prayer of Union gives a certain power to the soul that is very flattering and exhilarating – virtue has become easy, for the soul no longer desires any thing but God alone. Very subtly and gradually self-love takes advantage of this situation, so that there is a danger that the soul may lose all that it has gained, and may return to a selfish worldly life.

Here, too, may arise the danger of some form of mystical aberration such as Quietism or Illuminism. Mystical writers usually condemn these aberrations in a very austere and absolute manner and sometimes with scant reverence. This is wrong, for such people are really striving to serve God and are perhaps engaged in a specially terrible and subtle struggle with the spirits of wickedness, a struggle in which they are cruelly sifted and purified. It is the duty of ecclesiastical authority to protect the ordinary faithful against the misunderstandings which may arise in grosser minds through the statements of the mystic, but this should not lead us to lose our reverence for those who have been brought some distance along this marvellous road.

At the beginning of the Second Book of the *Dark Night of the Soul* St John speaks of the dangers that beset the proficient in the ways of prayer, and he uses language very similar to that of St Teresa. 'The devil is accustomed to fill them with presumption and pride, and strives to make them think that God and saints are speaking with them, and they often trust their own fancy. . . . Thus they become bold with God, and lose holy fear, which is the key and custodian of all the virtues.' It is in order to remedy this state and bring the soul to a more perfect humility that the Divine Lover brings it into the depths of the terrible Dark Night of the Spirit. Even when the presumptuousness and self-complacency of the soul is not very obvious, or very grave, it is necessary that it should be brought to feel the fullness of the truth of its own nothingness, and the times of deep darkness accomplish this best of all.

St Teresa does not treat of this darkness here, but she makes it clear that the soul must learn a deeper humility, and that its further progress depends on this. The nearer the soul comes to God the more it recognizes its own wretchedness and insufficiency. But this must not be confused with the state of self-rejection in which a person brings to bear on him or her a cold, unloving, critical light. Here all is love and humble, trustful self-acceptance.

Trials

The first chapter of the Sixth Book of the Mansions is devoted to a description of some of the trials which the soul has to face as it advances towards the fullness of union with God.

This chapter provides the nearest parallel that we find in St Teresa's writings to something that occupied a central place in the writings of St John of the Cross – the Dark Night of the Soul. They are both speaking of the cross, and it is clear that their experiences meet in the depths, as it were; nevertheless, the difference between the two accounts is also striking. In St Teresa's account, external factors, such as ill-health, the opposition of good people and the incomprehension of confessors, play a very large part; in St John's account these are not ruled out, yet what is described is deeply interior and personal and is spoken of almost entirely in terms of divine causality. God has placed the soul in this Dark Night. Reflection of these and other points of difference gives us a more clear and balanced view of the common kernel, the universal element in these trials. The common element is not so much darkness as the Cross, but it is the cross in its most terrible and purifying aspects, the cross of the Agony in the Garden and the *Lamma Sabacthani.*

If we examine the lives of the great saints we shall discover that many of them were brought to the point where 'prophecies were made void' (1 Cor. 13). The lights and assurances which sustained them were called into question by others, and – far more terrible – by themselves. So it was with St Joan at the end; so it was with St Gemma Galgani and St Margaret Mary. So it was with St Bernard, with St Francis (when his whole concept of poverty seemed to be rejected even by his own), with St John of the Cross in those last terrible days at La Peñuela and Úbeda (when he told his friend Ana de Peñalosa that his soul was in 'a very poor state'). This is the final great purification, the turning-point beyond which charity alone remains, a charity fire-tried and indestructible, humble, calm, sweet and mightily strong. This is the preparation for the death of love; those who have passed through this fire are on the way to dying of love in the way that Jesus Christ died of love. They know the Dark Night; they know the truth of Gethsemane and Calvary.

This first chapter of the Sixth Mansions is most useful to contemplative souls at all stages of the ascent to union. It is a pity that some are prevented from making use of it by the fact that it is found under the heading of the *Sixth* Mansions. We are again reminded of the disadvantages of the saint's method of making such a strong distinction between the various stages of the spiritual life. This chapter (like so much else in the book) cuts across all these divisions, and is simply a little treatise on the trials of contemplative souls.

Yearnings

As it comes nearer to God the soul experiences very strong desires and yearnings. They may become so strong as to cause sighs and tears, and in the case of certain temperaments they may have physical repercussions.

Every religious soul feels the desire for God more or less keenly. It is the fundamental desire to love and be loved, to know and be known, that is in every human heart. Usually, this desire seeks its object first in human persons, each of whom has something of the divine beauty and charm, for they are made to his image. It is a remarkable fact that so many of the great saints underwent very deep experiences of human love. As a rule they describe their experiences in terms of self-rebuke, as if everything connected with these experiences were entirely regrettable, and this obscures the fact that these friendships played an important part in the growth of the heart and the whole personality, and prepared the way for the only love and the only lover that fully satisfies the heart.[10]

---

10. It can happen, and it does happen, that some fantasy image of God or Christ is used as a substitute for human relationships. It can be a way of avoiding the wounds and challenges of real human encounters. The soul that genuinely seeks the living God soon finds that this

The soul finds her fullness in the beloved. Love has opened up
for her a new world, a new atmosphere; above all, love has revealed
to her that splendid and most exquisitely beautiful Other whose
presence is joy and all good things, whose absence is sorrow and
loneliness. . . So it is too with the soul that has come to know and
love God even a little. The whole domain of feeling is deeply stirred
and troubled being 'enkindled in love with yearnings'.

The yearning for God lasts all life long in the soul that has come
to know him. At a certain stage, however – that of St Teresa's Sixth
Mansions – these yearnings may become very deep and violent.
This arises from a special mystical or 'supernatural' activity by which
God awakens the soul to a deeper knowledge of his beauty and
sweetness. Both St Teresa and St John of the Cross speak of a wounding
of the soul which is at once delectable and painful.

In this state the lover of God may be led to strange and
extravagant behaviour. He may wish to cast off all encumbrances,
to rise beyond the ordinary necessities of food and clothing, and
to run through the world telling of God's love and glory. Even when
the lover's behaviour is not as extreme as this, there may be a certain
exaltation and 'inebriation' about his way of acting that will lead
those around him to think he has gone mad, or is at least slightly
deranged. This is but a particular manifestation, of course, of
something which attaches to the spiritual life all through – the
cross of misunderstanding. Those who are not prepared to bear
this cross will not advance very far.

---

fantasy world is shattered, that she is forced to open to others,
perhaps to contend with the masculine which she has been flying
from in the name of a spurious virginity. So too, the 'monkish' man,
if his search for God is genuine, will be forced to contend with the
world of the feminine, with that part of himself which is vulnerable
and full of tears. In this connection the ikons of the Sacred Heart of
Jesus and the Immaculate Heart of Mary can place before man and
woman the challenge of human completeness, though this kind of
devotion can also be used as an escape into a fantasy world.

In some souls these yearnings remain deep and hidden, so that there is little or no external manifestation of them. This was the case with St Thérèse of Lisieux. She had illimitable desires, and admitted that at times these were a real martyrdom, but she never lost her calm and poise, and she kept her real state of soul so much hidden that even her sister Marie was greatly surprised by what Thérèse revealed to her.

In the case of St Teresa of Avila, however, these wounds of love are palpable and overwhelming – the soul 'begins to tremble and complain', is 'conscious of having been delectably wounded', 'cries aloud', (VI, ii, par. 2) is 'penetrated to its very centre'. (ibid, par. 4) In fact, the passages in which she describes these yearnings are among the most glowing and ardent that have ever been written on the love of God. Nevertheless this state, though it may last for years, is but a passing one. Later, when the soul is at rest in the Seventh Mansions, the desire for God is deep and calm and entirely serene. At least this is the soul's habitual state: the Lord may give it from time to time a taste of its former joys and pains, though this is not usual. Its yearnings are now deeply based in the will; the whole order of feeling has been purified and fortified so that it is able to respond quietly and deeply to the presence of the Beloved.

All yearning for God is itself an exercise of love and adoration, and it is therefore pleasing to God who is Love Itself.

Locutions

The soul that has come to love God has come to speak to God interiorly. And sometimes within the silence of contemplation the Divine Lover speaks words of love and comfort to the soul.

In order to understand these 'locutions', as they are called, we must begin by putting aside two kinds of phenomena that might be confused with them.

There is a state of mental aberration in which a person hears 'voices', and sometimes what is 'said' is of a religious nature. As a rule there are in these cases other clear signs of illness. There are cases, however, when the person who hears the voices is quite normal in every other way, and when these voices have a spiritual import we are faced with a very delicate problem that only a fool will pronounce on dogmatically. When the problem is handed over to a psychiatrist he will naturally treat it within the limits of his science, and will talk of schizophrenia and such like. There may be nothing more to it than this, but it is wiser, nevertheless, to reserve judgement, for the spiritual and the pathological may present many features that are common, and may in some cases be interwoven. Most psychiatrists presented with the case of St Joan, a peasant girl who hears voices and insists on wearing men's clothes, will decide that she was mentally ill. Treatises have been written by 'the psychologically minded' to prove mental aberration in St Thérèse of Lisieux, St Teresa of Avila, St Gemma Galgani, the founder of the Trappists, Cardinal Newman and many others of the cleverest and sanest men and women of all ages. The truth is that there is more in human character than the psychiatrist or psychologist sees.

Nevertheless, there are many cases where it is clear enough that the hearing of voices is 'pathological' in the sense that there is some abnormality of character. St Teresa recognizes this – it is one of these cases which she puts under the general heading of 'melancholy' – and she gives some excellent practical advice for dealing with it in convents. There is no use, she tells us, in trying to persuade the person herself that her voices are illusory – she cannot accept this. The thing to do is to listen to her and make no comment except that sanctity does not consist in such things (which she will, as a rule, admit), and to give her manual work to do and healthy recreation. (Obviously this approach demands much tact and much humility on the part of the superior if it is to be effective.)

Of another kind altogether is the voice of Fancy within us, that doppelgönger that comes to have quite a large place in the lives of some delicate and imaginative people. Sometimes there is an interior dialogue, sometimes it is a monologue or just a sentence or two. This chattering within can be impish. It sometimes presumes to foretell the future, and even serves as a vehicle for the truth. Mostly, however, the voice of Fancy is senseless and pointless, and involves no danger of illusion for the ordinary person.

All divine locutions are given to the soul for the purpose of strengthening and enlightening it. They belong especially to the stage of the Sixth Mansions, for it is at this stage that the spiritual journey is most difficult and disconcerting. In one way they are a sign that the soul is advancing; this is especially true of the substantial locutions which demand a certain sensitivity to the divine action. But in another way they are a sign of weakness, for their main purpose is to enlighten and strengthen the soul in an external way as if by a prop or support: they help the soul forward but they do not transform it as does the Dark Night and the carrying of the cross. Hence it is a definite sign of progress when these favours begin to disappear. Moreover, there are some strong and humble souls who are given little or nothing in the way of external helps, and yet advance very rapidly.

There are other external helps besides locutions. Sometimes we open the Scriptures or a spiritual book at some statement that may solve a pressing problem, or break up a dark mood. Again the soul that is really strong is not much helped in this way, nor is it right to be anxious about receiving signs of this kind, if only because the appetite for them is never satisfied. Or again we receive an interior peace and assurance on some matter about which we have been very worried. Or somebody says the word for which we have been waiting, and we feel strengthened and reassured. (It is noteworthy that God often uses the humblest instruments to serve his purposes in this matter, some very prosaic person, some insignificant event.) In every way the good God is helping the soul to arrive at that 'place' where he himself dwells far beyond all words and symbols. His presence is most truly revealed to us, not through miraculous intervention, but through charity in the heart.

Intellectual Visions

In treating of the Sixth Mansions St Teresa has much to say about ecstasy and rapture, and it is certain that these played a large role in her own spiritual development. We find accounts of these and similar phenomena in the lives of many saints and servants of God. On the other hand, there are very many souls who have clearly reached the Seventh Mansions without ever having experienced that kind of ecstasy or rapture which St Teresa describes – St Augustine, St Thérèse, St Bernadette are perhaps examples. In parts the *Mansions* is more a spiritual autobiography than a treatise on the common elements of contemplative prayer.

Far more common than ecstasies or raptures are intellectual visions, as they are called. The terminology here is somewhat disconcerting for what is described is not a vision in the ordinary sense, nor is it intellectual in the strictly philosophical sense. There is a question of a certain interior presence partly pictured and partly felt. For example Christ seems present to the soul as he was at the Crowning with Thorns: there is a picture of a thorn-crowned head before the mind interiorly, a picture that has a certain stability and impressiveness about it that does not belong to the creation of imagination. This picture is, however, suggested rather than defined; and if we try to focus it clearly we shall fail to do so and will feel a kind of distress. The content of the experience may vary. It may concern our Lord, or our Lady, or a saint, or the angels. It may last for hours, or days, or longer. Usually it has the effect of consoling and strengthening the soul. This strengthening, of course, is external, as in the case of locutions. It would seem to be given to the soul because of the great crosses it has to bear in these later stages of the spiritual ascent.

It would seem that there are very many ways in which souls may be given this kind of extraordinary help, and it would be quite wrong to see one person's experiences in terms of another's. The words 'see', 'hear', and so on, are used by each person according to the type of experience given to him. We must not think, for instance, that somebody like Sister Josefa Menendez, who claimed to see our Lord and speak with him, saw him as we see a person across the table from us, or as St Teresa saw the Trinity. The Lord has innumerable ways of showing himself to his own. And all agree that the best vision of all here below is that in which we find God in love, in deep 'darkness', and so enter more deeply into his mysteries.

Jubilation

The way of prayer and close union with God is a way of much suffering, of many crosses. It never ceases to be this, and very often death itself involves for such souls a real Calvary. We have seen that St Teresa regarded as suspect any way of prayer in which the cross was absent. What Edith Stein calls 'The Science of the Cross' is the great secret of holiness: those who refuse to apply themselves to this science will never become holy. Neither will they learn true wisdom, the wisdom of St Thomas Aquinas, who was able to assert that he learned everything at the foot of the cross.

Nevertheless, the life of prayer is full of joy, and the life of union with God is immeasurably happier than any other kind of life. In the early stages of prayer there is the simple joy of serving God, the testimony of a good conscience. Later the soul is given moments of deep sweetness, of intense consolation, and may be given a profound felt peace that spreads through the soul like a healing balsam. As its operations become more spiritual the joys it receives become more delicate, more interior. St Teresa describes one variety of this kind of joy in a lovely passage towards the end of the sixth chapter of the Sixth Mansions: 'Sometimes the Lord bestows on the soul moments of jubilation and a strange kind of prayer. . . . The joy of the soul is so very great that it cannot keep it to itself but wants to express it to everybody that all may praise the Lord' I, vi, par. 10) These moments of surpassing joy are perhaps rare in the case of most people, the joy that comes from entering ever more deeply into the heart of Christ, and living his mysteries, is more continuous, though this too can be inserted, as it were, within times of darkness. In the case of the Sorrowful Mysteries, and union with the agonizing heart of Christ, the joy is a joy within darkness, a joy compatible with a great load of sorrow. There are many other joys that the prayerful soul experiences. Especially delicate and beautiful is the joy that comes from these exquisite touches of God's guiding providence which can hardly be called miracles, and yet are more than coincidence, for example the finding of a book that we needed just then, an unexpected visit or encounter some day that is a special private day of jubilee with us. . . Such favours occur at all stages of the spiritual journey.

Besides these joys, which are more or less passing, there is a deep 'substantial' joy that is the very atmosphere of the truly prayerful soul. This joy is of itself above the order of sensible feeling, dwelling in that purest region of the spirit that is independent of all moods and vicissitudes. Great pain or great grief may obscure this region for a while, but not even these can really destroy it, or diminish it in the least – rather does the peace and joy of this region become all the stronger and deeper through pain and grief. This is not to say that the pain or grief is lessened, for the spirit does not communicate any of its well-being to the sensibility, as it does in normal times, any more than the sun gives light in total eclipse, though it is shining just as strongly as ever. Yet the personal response to the situation, the way in which the pain and grief is accepted, depends largely on this hidden peace and joy in the superior part of the soul, which truly rejoices in suffering for the sake of the Beloved. When the eclipse or separation is total, there is a terrible sense of dereliction and desolation – the atmosphere of the *Lamma Sabacthani*. The poor sufferer may cry out for mercy, for relief, saying 'I can bear no more'. Yet that hidden peace and joy will show itself to the beholders in a strange dignity and sweetness of countenance, and the sense of acceptance will be constantly breaking through the cries of anguish. This does not mean that such a soul is strong all the time. A martyr may break down under torture of mind and body, as St Joan of Arc broke down, and yet be completely orientated to God in the will. And the Lord gives strength after weakness.

Apart from times of deep suffering, the peace and joy that is in the spirit gives serenity to the whole personality. Thus the soul attains a certain measure of beatitude even here below, for it has found the Beloved in the darkness.

Meditation: The Humanity of Christ

There are few things that cause more confusion than the statements of spiritual writers on the subject of meditation. In the first place the term is variously understood and defined, and even when it is defined clearly we may find that the definition does not in fact cover the uses of the term in the subsequent discussion. At one moment meditation seems the simplest exercise imaginable: at other times it seems a most difficult mental operation. Then we are told that a time comes (and that early in the life of prayer) when meditation is to be put aside: this is extremely disconcerting for the person who has never succeeded in 'making' a meditation.

Sometimes what is described as 'simple meditation' involves for most people a psychological impossibility, for example that one can take some topic (such as the goodness of God) and explore it systematically for a whole half-hour, taking three aspects of it in turn, this without the aid of reading matter or writing materials. Spiritual writers and preachers give us sample meditations which are in fact little treatises carefully put together by their authors.

Now there is a passage in Chapter 7 of the Sixth Book of *The Interior Castle* which is of the greatest value in the clearing up of this confusion. The passage has not received the attention it deserves, perhaps because it is at first sight rather obscure. The saint makes a distinction between two kinds of meditation, that in which there is 'the discursive use of the understanding' and that in which 'the memory brings truth before the understanding' (VI, vii, par. 11). The first kind is the meditation of beginners and is soon left behind by the soul that advances in the way of prayer; the second kind is necessary at all stages of the spiritual ascent and especially in the Sixth Mansions. Let us examine this distinction more closely.

In the first kind of meditation the mind goes along step by step, *discurrendo*, 'running along', not remaining for more than a moment or two at any one point. 'We begin with the Agony in the Garden and the mind follows right up to the Crucifixion. Or we take one episode, such as the arrest of Jesus, and we consider all the details of the scene one by one – the betrayal, the flight of the apostles, and so on' (ibid.). Obviously this kind of meditation is much helped by reading and pictorial representation. Indeed it is doubtful whether, apart from times of special consolation, this kind of operation is possible without external aids. What is to keep the mind from going off at a tangent according to the laws of association of ideas and images? It is true that the soul that is completely given to God and entirely detached from earthly things will not easily turn aside from the spiritual, even for a moment, but the beginner in prayer has not yet arrived at this stage – and yet meditation is supposed to be the way of prayer special to beginners. It would seem in fact that this kind of prayer is hardly possible without some external 'sensible' aids. This alternative would seem to be distractions or vacancy of mind, and this in fact is frequently the lot of people who spend a fixed period of time in meditation, and who have not yet reached the stage where the heart can seek only the things of God. Some writers say that God is working in the depths of the soul through all this; but there is no evidence for this, nor is it explained why this divine operation has to wait for such times of distracted 'meditation', why it cannot take place all the time in the person who truly desires it. What is true, of course, is that time given to God in this way is always pleasing to him, as long as the intention is to be with him and to know and love him better.

Now it is a well-known fact that this discursive meditation becomes burdensome to the soul that is advancing towards the higher kinds of prayer and union with God. The soul has come to attach itself to God in a more simple and intuitive way. The mind does not want to 'run around' but to stay still and ponder on the divine mysteries. It is here that the second, higher kind of meditation has its place. 'The memory brings truth before the understanding' – some words of Scripture, some particular mystery or some aspect of some mystery is recalled to mind, and this acts as a bridge by which the soul crosses over into the world of divine things, the world of God's love. The memory may not initiate the process: the words may be read or heard. For such a person one meditation

book is as good as another, for all the soul looks for is a topic or
heading, some kind of bridge on which to cross over into the world
of prayer and union. Sometimes the mind remains concerned with
the same truth for several days, and this will be the best bridge
for it to use during this time – in fact the soul may find it next to
impossible to use any other bridge during this time. As a rule the
inspiration of the soul at this stage will follow the liturgical cycle,
at least in its main lines, and there arises a wonderful harmony
between liturgy and contemplation, each helping the other. The
soul loves above all a certain serenity and reverence in the recitation
of the Divine Office and is greatly chafed by extremes of terse
correctness on the one hand, or slovenliness or frivolity on the
other. The externals of the liturgy are no longer an adventitious
help, but rather the reverent expression of the sacred mysteries.

This way of meditation must be practised by the soul at all stages
of the life of prayer. It is true that at the highest stage in the Seventh
Mansions it becomes second nature, for the soul at this stage
'never ceases to walk with Christ our Lord but has him as a constant
companion in a most wonderful way, which is at once divine and
human.' (VI, vii, par. 10) There is a sense then in which the soul
at this final stage does not as a rule have to concern itself with
meditation, does not have to exercise that diligence which was
necessary in previous Mansions.[11] Since it has Christ for its constant
companion it will be turned to him constantly and habitually.
Nevertheless, this companionship is full of variety and discovery,
and here the Scriptures, the liturgy and all that concerns Christ
and his Church finds its place within this companionship. It is
from out of this companionship that we can best of all contemplate
nature and man: the beauty of landscape and of God's creatures,
of bird, flower and tree, the friendly animals that serve us, the
marvellous variety and exquisite pathos of a world that awaits the
coming of Christ in glory: the greatness and littleness of man, the

---

11. 'In the Seventh Mansions it is very seldom that the soul has to exercise
    this diligence.' Peers translates *esta diligencia* as 'this activity', which
    gives a false impression.

admirable works of his genius, 'the still sad music of humanity', all the tears and laughter of human life, man's strange and wonderful history. Since all things have been made through Christ, the man who walks with Christ will have an interest in them all. Perhaps this is one of the main differences between the Sixth and Seventh Mansions, that the soul in the Sixth Mansions is still engaged in the endeavour of establishing this companionship with Christ and must be diligent lest the creature come between the soul and God the Creator: in the Seventh Mansions, however, this companionship has been achieved, and it is possible to act from within it, opening the heart and mind to the whole of reality. It is a pity that some genuinely holy people maintain a certain guarded attitude towards secular values even when this is no longer necessary. How their friends who admire their virtue would love to see them more expansively human! Somewhere along the way that negative attitude towards creatures that is essential if the soul is to give itself completely to the Creator – somewhere this negativity has been over-emphasized, or presented as if it were an end in itself, and it is very difficult to break through this attitude later on.

We seem to have gone aside from the topic of meditation, but this is not so in reality. For this higher meditation whose centre is Christ is not something confined to our times of prayer. It is something deep and constant and involves a whole attitude to life. As it becomes more profound it enters more and more deeply into the human condition, into its sorrows especially, its immeasurable pathos. It enters into the mystery of human iniquity, suffering it in the injustices and cruelties, the coarseness and selfishness that it encounters: thus the heart bleeds with the heart of Christ. It enters into the mystery of the Cross, understanding that this is the way for every companion of Christ, coming gradually to accept the chalice that has to be drunk. It enters into the mystery of joy and glory, the joy and glory that is to be, and also the joy and glory that is given to us abundantly even here below.

Meditation on the Christian mysteries is meditation on the person of Christ at once human and divine. St Teresa will have nothing to do with the theory that the soul in the higher activities of prayer goes beyond the humanity of Christ to the pure Godhead. If the highest contemplation is without images, having contact with the divine through faith, hope and charity in deep obscurity, then it would seem that all images of the humanity of Christ are left behind at this stage. This would seem to be the burden of the tradition of the 'Hid Divinity' that goes back to Pseudo-Denis, is clearly discernible in works such as *The Cloud of Unknowing*, and is not absent from the writings of St John of the Cross. Prayer at its highest is a naked intent, a 'loving attention' which looks to the divinity itself beyond all particular images or concepts. Attention to Christ's humanity and the circumstances of his life could destroy the sublime generality and indeterminateness of this prayer.

As we have seen, St Teresa set herself against this conception in the celebrated twenty-second chapter of the *Life*, and here, again, in the *Mansions*, she takes the same stand with even more firmness. 'I assure you, daughters, that I consider this to be a dangerous road and that the devil could end by making us lose our devotion to the Most Holy Sacrament' (VI, vii, par. 15). She is clearly conscious of the fact that those who go beyond the humanity of Christ, if they are superficial people, will enter into a state of sentimental unreal absorption (which in fact would be the antithesis of the exalted state described in *The Cloud of Unknowing*). But she is most of all conscious of the marvellous love that is in the heart of Christ and of the wrong done to his heart by going away from him in this way. The truth is, of course, that the more deeply we enter into the heart of Christ the closer we bind ourselves to his humanity, and yet the more we go beyond all particular conceptions, we are in a world where all is love and no word is spoken, where heart speaks to heart, where the 'general loving attention' spoken of by St John of the Cross is realized in its most perfect way.

This meditation on the Christian mystery is at the heart of the life of Christian prayer. It is the fruit of ascetical and mystical experience and it is never cast aside or transcended. Its great model is our Lady 'pondering all these things in her heart'. It is a far higher activity than that usually termed meditation, that activity which hardly goes beyond the level of the senses and is concerned with images and pictures, with 'considerations' spelt out one by one, with 'points' and 'conclusions'. This method is useful only to the beginner, to those who are new to the world of divine things, and it is doubtful whether it is useful to all of these, for the person of lively and aspiring mind will want to think, to ponder, to explore the mighty world of the Scriptures and of God's dealing with men, will want, moreover, to bring within the radiance of the Christian mysteries the whole of life, all that God has made. This meditation is not simply theological enquiry, though theological enquiry in all or any of its branches may form part of it, for it involves attitudes of adoration, praise, contrition, exaltation, reparation, etc. Above all, it involves that general attitude of loving attention which is the ground of all contemplation.

The Abode of Peace

The highest stage of prayer distinguished by St Teresa is that in which the soul dwells constantly with God in God's own dwelling at the soul's centre, that is in the Seventh Mansions.

At this stage the soul is almost always at peace. Even in the Sixth Mansions the soul was subject to times of great distress; in fact it may have been plunged for certain periods in deep darkness. Now it has attained to a durable substantial peace that is very rarely disturbed, and is never broken for long. This tranquility must not be confused with inertia, or with the placidity of the soul that has stopped trying to advance, and has made its own a quiet, un-adventurous mode of existence: this kind of person has never left the Third Mansions or has returned to them after some slight experience of higher states. Strange to say, this timid unadventurous person is often full of self-complacency, and is convinced that he has really arrived at the end of the road. He who has attained to true tranquillity is very different from this. He is not smug or self-satisfied, or critical of others. He is not inert but full of zeal, and has about him even in old age the enthusiasm of youth. He has much to suffer, for he has accepted fully the cross of Christ.

Next to fraternal charity the love of the cross is the 'acid test' of progress at this level of the spiritual life. St John of the Cross was at this stage of deep and tranquil union with God when he was able to say 'Lord, let me suffer and be despised for thy sake.' Those who come to the Seventh Mansions will be able to pray this prayer with him and mean it. They may not be able to pray it always, but they will be able to attain to it at times, and their whole life will be lived in the shadow of it. Those in the Fourth, Fifth and Sixth Mansions are able to accept it and appreciate the cross, and they may feel at times a great love of suffering, but they have not come to the true deep continuous love of the cross of Christ. Sometimes in the earlier Mansions the soul is given a kind of sensible joy in suffering; at this final stage this is entirely absent: the cross is now the bare cross and the suffering that is felt at times is terribly deep. Yet there is a new calm and peace in suffering and a readiness to carry on without the least consolation or reassurance.

Here we encounter the phenomena of polarity or *doubling* which is found in every soul at this level but may also be experienced at the earlier stages of the journey. It is in fact no more than the prolongation into the life of prayer of the psychological fact according to which the same person may experience at one and the same time feelings that are quite contrary: joy and sorrow, love and hate, fear and confidence. It is as if there were two levels in the soul, as if the soul were somehow 'doubled'. In the higher states of prayer this phenomenon has a peculiar depth and poignancy: the soul is at once full of light and warmth and yet plunged in deepest darkness. It is sometimes thought that very holy people have no great sufferings because they find a deep joy in suffering in union with Christ: we might be tempted to think that the joy overcomes the sorrow, that such people do not feel such things as pain and humiliation and misunderstanding. But the truth is that they are more rather than less sensitive than others, that they feel things in a way that is particularly exquisite and deep, that they may experience quite extraordinary depths of darkness and despair. For instance St Thérèse felt that her belief in a future life had completely vanished, that she found herself eating at the table of unbelievers. St Francis experienced a poverty of soul far more terrible than any material poverty. St John of the Cross found himself low and depressed in that last terrible period when some of his brethren closed in to destroy him. And yet they will all say they are in great peace, that they are full of joy in the midst of great tribulation. They are able to support those around them, being full of a marvellous strength and courage and a strange radiant gladness. Thus it was that St Thérèse was able to write some of her most ardent poems of the love of God during that last eighteen months when her soul was in deep darkness. It is sometimes said or implied that the Dark Nights spoken of by St John of the Cross are passing phenomena and that the soul that has reached the summit of the Mount of Perfection is beyond all these trials. This is a great error, for it can easily lead to a kind of depreciation of the cross of Christ and a mistaking of mediocrity for sanctity. It is *in* the Night, in the midst of darkness that the Beloved is found. That is why the soul is represented in the fifth stanza of the poem, of which *Dark Night of the Soul* is a commentary, as addressing the night in words of joy and gratitude: '*Oh Night that joined Beloved with Lover, Lover transformed in the Beloved.*' The darkness remains, but the heart is illuminated interiorly by the light and fire of love that burns within.

But however one interprets St John of the Cross there is absolutely no doubt at all about the fact that the cross is at the centre of the spiritual life as long as we live in this world. That is the teaching of the gospel; that is the example of Christ: that is the story of every saint. In fact the cross becomes heavier as the soul advances in virtue and is able to bear a heavier load.

And yet it can be said that once the soul has reached the Seventh Mansions it possesses marvellous joy and peace. It has entered the abode of peace. It has discovered within itself the springs of substantial joy.

It is the light and warmth of love that brings forth this joy; indeed the love and the joy are one. This love cannot be lost, and the soul knows it cannot be lost, for it is Love Itself that is loved. There is a union of lover and beloved that is indissoluble.

This union is often called Spiritual Marriage and the achievement of it is sometimes marked by an interior vision of the Trinity or the humanity of Christ, and there may be even some inner experience such as the experience of receiving a ring from the Divine Lover. In this terminology the Spiritual Marriage takes place in the Seventh Mansions and Spiritual Betrothal in the Sixth Mansions.

Although St Teresa uses this figure and although it is very beautiful and very fitting, nevertheless it gives the impression of something very definite and very extraordinary and has the effect of making people think: 'This cannot be for me.' Besides, it lends itself rather easily to the type of shallow pretentiousness that likes to make use of mystical terminology.

The term 'transforming union' is also used and this is more satisfactory. But here also the impression given is of something strange and mysterious; and the genuine spiritual person is rather put off by it.

It seems to me that the state described by St Teresa as that of the Seventh Mansions is best understood in terms of peace and love. It may be called 'peace of soul' or 'essential peace', or, best of all, 'perfect charity', (i.e. perfect according to the imperfect human mode). This perfect charity in which the soul is fully at peace is the goal of all spiritual progress and the highest state of prayer to which a man may attain in this life. And the test of it will always be our readiness to accept the cross of Christ. In the ordinary ways of life the practical expression of this readiness is the exercise of fraternal charity: 'In this shall all men know that you are my disciples, that you have love one for another' (John 13.35).

The charity of the soul in this state is no ordinary charity. It is the charity of Calvary, the charity through which a man will lay down his life for his brethren, for the coming of God's kingdom into every heart. It is a charity that goes out to the whole world, that would bear on its shoulders the woes of all who suffer. And it is made to experience this victimhood to the full, so much so that it is in no danger of being puffed up because of the great graces it has received. The cross is present in a particularly terrible and piercing way; sometimes the mystic is cast off by all, and seems to be cast off even by God's representatives, as happened in the case of St Joan of Arc. One way or another the cross lies deep and heavy across the life of the man or woman who has been exalted so greatly by God.

It may be asked: does the soul that has reached this exalted state realize its own position? Here the phenomenon of doubling is again evident. On the one hand the soul knows with great, deep, calm certainty that it has in truth been brought to the heights, and it rejoices in this. On the other hand it feels that it is indeed living in the depths and that it is a castaway: the *De Profundis* and the *Miserere* seem to express most perfectly its knowledge of its own situation. A stanza of St John of the Cross's poem 'Upon love's chase I went my way' expresses the matter perfectly:

> The further upward did I go
> In this great chase of love so high,
> The baser, humbler soul was I,
> The more exhausted did I grow.
> 'No hope of conquest!' did I say,
> But as I sank so low, so low,
> So high, so high did upward go,
> That in the end I reached my prey.

Here then the soul rests in the centre of its own nothingness where God himself dwells. It has entered even here below into a world of surpassing joy. It is invulnerable, independent, completely at peace. It has found Love, and in finding Love it has found itself and found the source of all joy.

PART TWO

ST JOHN OF THE CROSS:
MAN OF FIRE

CHAPTER 4

THE WAY OF MYSTICAL LONGING

John Sings his Song of Songs

On 2 December 1577, when he was 35 years of age and unofficial chaplain to the Carmelite sisters of the Convent of the Incarnation outside the walls of Avila, John of the Cross was attacked in his little hermitage and roughly taken prisoner by order of the Calced Carmelites. His captors took him to their monastery in Toledo and put him in a narrow cell or enclosure ten feet by six, a dark foetid place where he was kept for nine months until he managed to escape.[1]

It was in the course of this imprisonment that he wrote the *Spiritual Canticle* (*Cántico espiritual*), his longest and most dramatic poem in 39(40) five-line stanzas. In its imagery and theme it is based fairly closely on the Old Testament Song of Songs or Song of Solomon, yet it is by no means merely a translation or a commentary on the Hebrew poem in its Latin version which, of course, John knew very well. The Song of Songs sings of human love between man and woman, that yet may be applied anagogically or ascendingly to the love of the human soul for God in the Holy Spirit. John's poem is all about the love between the human soul as Bride and God in Christ as Bridegroom; it uses human love and the beauties of nature as metaphors or analogies to express the joy and glory of divine love in the human soul given and received.

Here we are in the region or ambience of the spiritual or

---

1. On the quarrel between the Calced or Ancient Carmelites and the Discalced or Teresian Carmelites, see E. Allison Peers, *Spirit of Flame* (London: SCM Press, 1943), ch. 3.

spiritualized senses[2] which open to a 'heavenly' world that must not be held or possessed. John piles up metaphors taken from the senses and the joys of sense, yet these joys are pure joys never weighed down by that possessive desiring that dies in its own fulfilment, as in the satisfaction of bodily hunger and in sexual ecstasies. John would have had no difficulty in accepting the physical explicitness of Milton's *Paradise Lost* or even of D. H. Lawrence's *Lady Chatterley's Lover*, but would have wanted the man–woman relationship made permanent and self-transcending, opening indeed to the glory of the love at the heart of the Trinity in the fullness of 'the living flame of love', which is the Holy Spirit.

Before making contact with the *Spiritual Canticle* it is well to look carefully at the drawing of Christ on the Cross which John made when he was chaplain to the nuns of the Convent of the Incarnation in Avila (1574–77). John had very little to say about visions and tended not to make much of them but it seems that this image of the crucified Christ came before his inner eye vividly and suddenly while he was at prayer, and he made a sketch of it immediately. The American Carmelite translation describes it as follows:

> The sketch is of Christ crucified, hanging in space, turned towards his people, and seen from a new perspective. The cross is erect. The body, lifeless and contorted, with the head bent over, hangs forward so that the arms are held only by the nails. Christ is seen from above, from the view of the Father. He is more worm than man, weighed down by the sins of human beings, leaning toward the world for which he died.[3]

---

2. See N. D. O'Donoghue, 'St John of the Cross and the Spiritual Senses', in *Leeds Papers on Saint John of the Cross*, ed. M. A. Rees, (Dublin: Trinity and All Saints College, Dublin: 1991) pp. 49–62.
3. From *The Collected Works of St John of the Cross*, tr. Kieran Kavanaugh and Otilio Rodriguez (Washington, DC: Institute of Carmelite Studies, 1964, 1979, 1991, p. 37).

A short time afterwards, in his narrow prison in Toledo, John was to live something of the dereliction and loneliness and engulfing pain of this vision, and it was out of this that the *Spiritual Canticle* came to be written. John had eyes and heart for that beauty and purity and goodness that would 'undo the twist in the cosmos' (John 1.29, thus interpreting the Greek), by sustaining that twist and thus overcoming it. John's bridal soul went forth like an arrow towards this marvellous beauty foreseen long ago by Isaiah and glimpsed so miraculously by Plato, in the second book of the *Republic*. But John did not leave physical beauty behind as merely dangerous and imperfect, rather he made his poem come marvellously alive by way of the colours and shapes and sounds and fragrances of nature and the physical creation. The whole poem is a triumph of that analogical poetry in which the physical becomes spiritualized without losing anything of its own special charm, pathos and identity. Only the original Songs of Songs understood in its spiritual, anagogical dimension can compare with it in the Judaeo-Christian tradition.

Several points are worth recalling before we look closely at the first part (st. 1–12) of the *Spiritual Canticle*. Firstly, we are dealing, as in all the poems of St John of the Cross, with a poem on prayer, and not ordinary or active prayer but mystical or, as John called it, and Teresa also, supernatural prayer. This had an exact meaning for both John and Teresa. It meant a kind of speaking with, or opening to, the Divine Source in which the Divine Other took in some way the initiative, and the human agent was more receptive than active; not passive but actively receptive, not by way of the intellect primarily and essentially, but by way of the will. Thus the first part of the *Spiritual Canticle*, though it is full of considerations or thoughts, is moved all the way by a deep, even painful (yet joyful) longing in the outgoing, feeling, emotional side of the personality. In a sense this is full of striving to the point of stress and turmoil, but the whole dynamic or movement of the soul or inner self is ruled by that which is drawing it so strongly and constantly. This pull and the longing that is at the centre of it comes from a tremendous experience of the presence of the Beloved who has come and gone. This is clearly and poignantly expressed in the first stanza in which we can, as it were, hear the longing of all who have been left alone and grieving.

Secondly, John claims rather astonishingly that every single thing he says is to be found in the Bible. Just as Martin Luther and John Calvin found the Bible constantly and uniquely a source of illumination, so John found the Bible not only illuminative but also unitive, essentially the story of the union of the soul with God and God with the soul. But whereas the Reform tradition has on the whole avoided the Song of Songs, or understood it as a song of human love and human lovers, John is at one with those classical Jewish commentators who saw it as a kind of Holy of Holies, the centre and compendium of the whole of revelation. A certain Rabbi Aquiba said in the second century BC: 'All the world is not worth the day the Song of Songs was given to Israel. All the writings are holy, but the Song of Songs is the Holy of Holies.'

Not the least of the achievements of John – perhaps indeed his greatest achievement – is to have renewed with marvellous poetical imagination and theological depth this ancient text and to have, by his unique understanding of Scripture in its mystical sense, shown that the Song secretly permeates the Old Testament and is fulfilled in the New Testament.

Thirdly, it must be noted that the poem and the prose commentary were written at different times and at different stages of John's development. The poem is not only the longest of John's poetic works but also the first of his 'great' poems, in which his own special mystical pathway is, so to speak, 'discovered' and its elements assembled: dark night, rejection of attachment to the 'goods of heaven', ecstatic bridal mysticism leading to mystical marriage, union of sense and spirit. The poem emerges clear and radiant, with 'the glory and the freshness of a dream', from the squalor, dereliction and loneliness of his prison cell in which his legitimate (it must be said) superiors felt themselves totally justified in breaking down what they saw as his stubborn, disobedient wilfulness: they would have released him at once into a position of honour if he had capitulated and given up 'all this nonsense' about reforming the Carmelite order.

It must be borne in mind that John was as much a stubborn reformer as Martin Luther and might have repeated 'Here I stand; I can no other.' And, like Luther, John pinned all his faith on the cross of Christ, in a *theologia crucis* as against a *theologia gloriae*. John, like Teresa, managed to stay within the ancient Catholic unity centred on Rome, but he must have had times of deep doubting and 'soul-searching' in the loneliness of his prison in Toledo. His own Reform brethren seemed to have forgotten him, as Teresa was to complain, and indeed he was surely led to pray the *Lamma Sabacthani* prayer of Jesus on the Cross; indeed it is clear that his poem takes off from that.

The commentary runs to sizeable book-length and it was written in the serenity of a time when he had escaped from his Toledan prison and was held in honour by his Reform brethren. It sets out to explain the poem to his women disciples who had begged him to do so. While the poem may be said to be written out of John's feminine self, seeking fulfilment from the all-fathering, all-mothering anointed Emmanuel, the commentary is written out of John's masculine self and masculine presence of Father-confessor to the nuns at Beas, strong and radiant women demanding beyond any denial the masculine other that John mediated. The sense of being a spiritual father to many daughters was precious and central to John and indeed he had profound things to say about spiritual fatherhood. When somebody asked him about Teresa he said that she was very much his daughter (*muy hija mia*) and was indeed criticized for daring to say this. John did have many men disciples, especially among his Carmelite brethren, yet it seems clear that it was among women especially that he found that receptivity of response that he asked for and perhaps deeply needed. In the relativity of masculine and feminine John is a profoundly masculine man as Teresa is a profoundly feminine woman. Because of a negative under-standing of celibacy John's relationship with the many women in his life (as, reciprocally, Teresa's relationship with the men in her life) is deeply misunderstood if it is seen as merely incidental or as coldly ministerial. Rather was it an essential part of his development and personality as a man of mystical prayer and as a teacher.

One can ask how far John was true to his original poetic inspiration in responding to the requests of his spiritual daughters and transforming his poems into commentaries on the ways of mystical prayer. Certainly the commentaries themselves are beyond price each in its own right, yet they tend to obscure and, as it were, flatten down the original surge of inspiration in the poetry. It is therefore necessary to allow the poems and the commentaries each their space and vibrational field, for the poem does not disappear or dissolve into the explanation of it, but rather continues to have its own impact as a poem. In other words, a work that lives under the sign of Beauty strikes in on the heart and the instinctual-emotional level of our being as much as, and indeed rather than, or more than, the level of analysis and understanding.

Spiritual Canticle (stanzas 1–12)

The method which John follows in his commentary on the *Spiritual Canticle* is to take the poem stanza by stanza and begin in each case with a general introduction (*Anotación*) to the whole stanza which is then set down in its entirety and explained (*Declaración*) line by line or phrase by phrase.

Stanza One

The first stanza reads:

> Whither hast thou hidden thyself, And hast left me, O Beloved, to my sighing?
> Thou didst flee like the hart, having wounded me: I went out after thee, calling, and thou wert gone.[4]

---

4. I am following the translation in E. Allison Peers, *The Complete Works of St John of the Cross*, Vol. II (London: Burns & Oates, 1957), Redaction B.

The first stanza says everything and the next eleven stanzas are but a development of the one theme of loss and longing. In his commentary John tells us that these first stanzas refer to the state of beginners – that is the Purgative or purificatory way. However, these stanzas are the exclamations of one who is not only a poet of genius but who is very far advanced in the ways of mystical prayer, at the level of the Seventh Mansions of St Teresa's *Interior Castle*. These stanzas can be assimilated to the traditional Purgative way of beginners only inasmuch as mystical prayer involves a kind of purification in the mode of receptivity by which the soul is happy to receive only what is given to it.

The reference to the hart in this first stanza links John's *Canticle* firmly with the Song of Songs, where the Bridegroom is likened to a hart of the mountains in the suddenness of his comings and goings, by which he deals wounds of longing to the Bride who is all on fire with love for him. These spiritual woundings, John tells us, are 'delectable and desirable' (par. 19). He also refers here (par. 17) to the phoenix that is said to rise from its own ashes, and to Psalm 72(73) in the old Vulgate translation (vv. 21,22): John interprets this in terms of the spiritualization of the senses, especially of sexuality (par. 18).

Stanza Two

> Shepherds, ye that go Yonder, through the sheepcotes, to the hill,
> If perchance ye see him that I most love, Tell ye him that I languish,
> suffer and die.

The shepherds of stanza 2 are identified by John in his commentary with the soul's 'desires, affections and sighs' (par. 2) which she, as it were, sends towards the Bridegroom. Elsewhere John uses Romans 8.26 in this context. The sheepcotes are, John tells us, 'the hierarchies and choirs of the angels' (par. 3) who offer our prayers to God as in the ancient Christian liturgies such as the old Latin Mass. The 'angels' as they appear in the New Testament hold an important place in the Carmelite understanding of prayer, and, characteristically, John makes large use of the Old Testament texts about the angels.

Stanza Three

Seeking my loves, I will go o'er yonder mountains and banks; I will neither pluck the flowers nor fear the wild beasts; I will pass by the mighty and cross the frontiers.

The third stanza shows the Bride in a resolute mood, facing dangers from above and below, resisting all blandishments and allurements (the flowers) (par. 5) and the devil (the mighty) (par. 9). The thought here is traditional and unremarkable in its content. It could be dull and heavy but John, fine poet that he was, brings it to life with strong clear images and forceful ringing diction ending with 'y pasaré los fuertes y fronteras', words triumphantly on the march.

Stanza Four

O woods and thickets Planted by the hand of the Beloved!
O meadow of verdure, enamelled with flowers, Say if he has passed by you.

In stanzas 4 and 5 John looks at the world of nature and represents the soul already wounded by divine love (stanza 1) as seeking some vestige or reflection of the creator in the physical things that have been created.

In the commentary John explains that the 'woods' refer to the traditional four elements of earth, water, air and fire and the 'thickets' to the multitude of beings to be found in earth and water and air, 'while the element of fire concurs with all in animating and preserving them' (par. 2). All these things are, for John, directly created by the Beloved, so the question of the dark side of 'nature red in tooth and claw' is shelved or ignored. The green meadows are the physical heavens above us and the bright flowers are the angels and the faithful departed.

It must be remembered that the Bridal Soul that speaks is already on fire with love, so the question of the existence of God does not arise as it arose later on at the end of the nineteenth century for Thérèse of Lisieux. So we need not expect that John will involve himself in questions of the existence of God. He would have had to look at such questions in his theology studies at Salamanca and here he shows himself conscious of them by quoting St Paul's dismissal of atheism in Romans 1.20 and also St Augustine's search for God by way of creation in *Confessions* 10.6. God is somehow immediately present to John as a source of light, of longing, even of darkness. John is not far from Illuminism here, and his followers were hard put to defend him against the charge of following his own inner light and ignoring the Church and the Sacramental order. We are here at the heart of an ongoing adventure in prayer where John of the Cross and George Fox face a common inquisition.

Stanza Five

The fifth stanza, which is one of my favourites, tells the answer of the creatures, of that creation which includes, let us recall, the starry regions and the depths of the great oceans.

> Scattering a thousand graces, He passed through these groves in haste, And looking upon them as he went, Left them, by his glance alone, clothed with beauty.

Here we have John's uniquely beautiful celebration of Cosmic Christology, a theme that goes back to St Paul and Origen, surfacing on and off throughout the Christian centuries and shining forth briefly and yet powerfully in the grandiose prayerful vision of Pierre Teilhard de Chardin in our own day. In its prayerfulness, especially as it is expressed for instance in *Le Milieu Divin*, Teilhard's vision might seem to be an extended meditation on this fifth stanza of the *Cántico espiritual* with its unmistakable echoes of Hindu *Shakti*, of the Jewish *Hasidim* and of the Mohammedan *Sufis*.

The commentary on stanza five explains that Christ, who is the Logos by which all things are made, may be said to pass through the world of nature 'in haste' because he was passing on from the 'lesser works' to the 'greater works' (par. 3), which are the mysteries of the Incarnation. This is very helpful and clarifying in relation to Cosmic Christology and the other Christian mysteries, but to stop here intellectualizes what is a deep human feeling in face of the marvellous, hidden beauty of nature and that 'dearest freshness deep-down things' of which G. M. Hopkins speaks[5] – the feeling that someone has been here and has departed in haste. This feeling may be quite legitimately explained in rational terms, but *as poetry* it opens up to eternal Beauty rather than eternal Truth and should retain its own special glory as such. The Bride (i.e. the human soul) at this stage is stricken and wounded by eternal Beauty.

Stanza Six

Ah, who will be able to heal me! Surrender thou thyself now completely.
From today do thou send me now no other messenger, For they cannot tell me what I wish.

The wound dealt by eternal Beauty incarnate in Christ can only be healed by a full vision of this Beauty, a full possession of the Beloved that finally surrenders to the longing of the Bridal Soul. But in order that this mutual surrender should fully come about, the human soul would have to be released from the corruptible body, and so, in this life, the Bridal Soul must live in a kind of longing unto death.

In his commentary on stanza 7, John uses the metaphor of 'wounding' quite elaborately, speaking of the festering of the wound and the coming of death; strangely he died himself in this way at the age of 49. He was in his own measure living and dying in accordance with his vision and sketch of the crucifed Christ.

---

5. Gerard Manley Hopkins, 'God's Grandeur (written 1887).

John did not, could not, accept any other messenger than the crucified Christ. It is by way of the cross and his death on the cross that Christ was able to draw all things upward in accordance with chapter 12, v. 32 of the Fourth Gospel. And John writes, in par. 4 of the commentary on stanza 5: 'And thus, in this lifting up of the Incarnation of His Son, and in the glory of His resurrection according to the flesh, not alone did the Father beautify the creatures in part, but we can say that He left them all clothed with beauty and dignity.' There is a note of tenderness here which is essential to the understanding of John's Christocentric Bridal mysticism. It is perhaps most clearly expressed in John's poem: 'A Shepherd Boy', which we will return to later.

Stanza Seven

In the seventh stanza the poet is still talking of those messengers which tell the Bridal Soul of the wonders and beauties of the Divine Bridegroom.

> And all those that serve Relate to me a thousand graces of thee,
> And all wound me the more And something that they are stammering
> leaves me dying.

'Those who are free' or 'those who serve' (the word *vagan* can bear either meaning) are the rational creatures who surround the Bride and seem to be full of 'news' about the Bridegroom who came and vanished. These rational creatures are both human and angelic, speaking outwardly or inwardly to the Bride. The world of the angels shows itself by inner *intimations* and *inspirations*, audible and visible to the spiritual senses as they are awakened by mystical prayer. The 'stammering' is the witness of those who have had some glimpse of the ineffable glory and goodness and beauty of the Divine Bridegroom.

Stanzas Eight to Eleven

The theme of 'wounding' and 'dying' comes up again in stanzas 8 to 11 which are an intensification of the theme of longing.

> But how, O life, dost thou persevere, Since thou livest not where thou livest,
> And since the arrows make thee to die which thou receivest From the conceptions of the Beloved which thou formest within thee?
> Since thou hast wounded this heart, Wherefore didst thou not heal it?
> And wherefore, having robbed me of it, hast thou left it thus And takest not the prey that thou hast spoiled?
> Quench thou my griefs, since none suffices to remove them, And let mine eyes behold thee, Since thou art their light and for thee alone I wish to have them.
> Reveal thy presence And let the vision of thee and thy beauty slay me; Behold, the affliction of love is not cured Save by thy presence and thy form.

'The death for longing' and 'longing for death' is poignantly and powerfully expressed in the poem whose refrain is 'dying because I cannot die', a sentiment echoed by St Teresa in a poem of similar refrain and content.[6] The second stanza of John's poem reads (in the Peers translation):[7]

> This life that has been giv'n to me
> Is but true life's negation – nay,
> 'Tis death that comes with each new day,
> Until I live, my God, with Thee.
> Hearken, O Lord, to this my plea,
> No longing for this life have I
> Who die because I do not die.

---

6. E. Allison Peers, *The Complete Works of St Teresa,* Vol. III (London: Sheed & Ward, 1957), p. 277.

7. Peers, *Complete Works of St John*, Vol. II, p. 427.

The Bridal Soul so deeply longs for the Divine Bridegroom that it could die for very longing. But added to this is the recognition that the joy of the presence of the Bridegroom would be too great to bear in our present state.

Stanza Twelve

> O crystalline fount, If on that thy silvered surface Thou wouldst of a suffen form the eyes desired Which I bear outlined in my inmost parts!

This stanza is best interpreted by one of John's simplest and most profound poems whose refrain is: 'Although 'tis night'. Like the *Spiritual Canticle* this was also written during his time of imprisonment at Toledo and is not to be confused with his most famous poem: *The Dark Night* (*noche oscura*). The figure of the fount or fountain (*la fonte*) is at the centre of this poem as it is of our present stanza of the *Spiritual Canticle*; in both cases it is closely connected with the theological virtue (i.e. God-centred orientation of the soul) of faith.

In the Peers translation the first stanza of 'Although 'tis night' runs:

> The eternal fount its source has never show'd,
> But well I know wherein is its abode,
> Although 'tis night.

And the fifth stanza reads:

> Never was fount so clear, undimm'd and bright:
> From it alone, I know, proceeds all light,
> Although 'tis night.

We have in this poem, as in the twelfth stanza of the *Spiritual Canticle*, the same image of a bright silvery stream flowing from a Source hidden and far-off yet very present and intimate. My own God, my own Source, deep in my ownmost self, in deepest darkness.

There within this darkness, a many-layered darkness, God dwells. The soul that has been visited by the Holy Spirit of God lives in deepest longing that this visit may be repeated and not any longer as visiting merely, but as a total constancy. Yes, of course there is faith flowing forth like a stream of silver surface within which the gold of the Divine Presence is hidden; in this sense this Presence is already possessed, securely held in the darkness of faith. We are here at a dramatic moment of the Reformation, where John remains within the ancient Church and Luther feels he must break away from it; both were led on by the inner vision of the crucified Christ, Luther towards a theology of salvation by way of substitution (Christ has done it all; all I can do is accept this free gracious gift as it is unconditionally given), John towards a theology of union in which the Bridal Soul and the Bridegroom God live into each other in accordance with Galatians 2.20. Luther could keep his eyes closed and only the eye of faith open to the darkness of God; John wants vision in the meeting of lovers; he longs to look into the eyes of the Beloved looking into his eyes, into the most intimate depths of his soul. The silvered surface of the stream issuing from the Source is not enough; his prayer of longing becomes a kind of loving boldness, yet withal delicately expressed. Vision will come by way of the silvered surface of faith, not going away from faith, nor indeed from justification by faith, but arising within its silvery gleam and passing into the gold of vision.

    In his commentary on the phrase 'crystalline fount' John makes use of a literary device hardly used at all in his day nor indeed used with any real skill until we come to James Joyce four centuries later. It is the device by which words echo and mirror one another in sound and shape to call up unexpected gleams and glimmers of meaning. So the word *cristalina* brings up the sense of the brightness of crystal and the glory of Christ: in Spanish both are spelt *crist*. John writes: 'She [i.e. the Bride] calls faith crystalline for two reasons: the first, because it is from Christ her Spouse, and the second, because it has the properties of crystal in being pure in its truths, and strong, and clear and free from errors and natural forms' (SC 12, par. 3).

'The eyes desired' are the eyes of the Bridal Soul that have a sudden clear vision of Jesus Christ, the Divine Bridegroom. Here we are close to St Augustine's 'faith seeking understanding' (*fides quaerens intellectum*) and some distance from the justifying faith of Luther, which is self-sufficient and happy in its darkness. Yet the clarity John is seeking is not by way of intellectual rational effort, but rather received as a gift from above, not unlike St Teresa's visions of Christ that came as a sudden gift to her through prayer.

It must be noted that both for John and Teresa, this kind of mystical vision lies under the judgement of theology, in practice that union of revelation and reason as it flowered in medieval scholasticism and was given a kind of definitive statement by St Thomas Aquinas and the celebrated Salamanca theologians (the Salmanticenses) who influenced John directly through his own studies and Teresa indirectly through her beloved 'learned men'. For both, mystical enthusiasm was tempered by a strong intellectual tradition. Yet the presence of the Inquisition tended to place all mystical enthusiasm under the suspicion of Illuminism, that is to say the acceptance of a personal inner illumination which placed the mystic outside or at least outwith the sacraments and discipline of the universal Church. There was real danger for John in translating his poetry, hidden by its own symbols, into clear unambigous prose and we can understand why he was led to make a second redaction of the *Spiritual Canticle*, since it was and is always possible to find different levels of meaning within this kind of highly symbolic poem.

The 'eyes desired' bring not only a clear *vision* of the Beloved, which essentially belongs to the Bridal Soul after passing through death, but also a total blissful *union of love* with the Beloved in that Spiritual Marriage in which 'each lives in the other, and the one is the other, and both are one through the transformation of love'. (SC 12, par. 7) This is not quite the fullness and perfection of union and marriage but it is all that can be accomplished in this life. John is convinced that it was to this degree accomplished in St Paul and that he is interpreting rightly not only the Song of Songs 8.6 but also St Paul's claim of living union with Christ in Galatians 2.20: 'I live, yet not I, but Christ lives in me.' Indeed John feels strongly

that all his poems and commentaries are simply interpretations of
Scripture. It must be borne in mind that, for medieval hermeneutics,
the anagogical or ascending (mystical) sense had an honoured place
and was by no means seen as fanciful or merely rhetorical. In certain
passages such as the present it would seem that, for John, the literal
and anagogical senses coincided; in other words, St Paul is expressing
an experience that he has lived through and is living through. Here
a very serious question arises for the Christian theologian: how
far is the mystical or anagogical exegesis of Scripture true in the
sense that it is the basic literal meaning of the text as John claims
for his interpretation, not only of the Song of Songs 8.6 but also
of Galatians 2.20. A positive answer to this question would herald
a revolution in the Christian theology of biblical interpretation.

CHAPTER 5

THE DARK NIGHT

The Mysterious Adventure of the Cross

As he enters into the longing for divine union expressed in the *Spiritual Canticle* John, as we have seen, claims that he is simply expressing in his own way the same experience of union with Christ, the Bridegroom of the Bridal Soul, expressed by St Paul in 2.20 of the Epistle to the Galatians: 'I live, yet not I, but Christ lives in me'. There is an outline within the depths or entrails of the soul both in the order of knowing or faith, and in the order of loving by which 'the Beloved lives in the lover and the lover in the Beloved.' (SC 12, par. 7) Both lover and Beloved are one 'through the transformation of love', *transformación de amor* (ibid.).

Now if we look carefully at the Epistle to the Galatians we find that the more complete text at 2.20 reads, 'I have been crucified with Christ; it is no longer I who live, but Christ who lives in me; and the life I now live in the flesh I live by faith in the Son of God, who loved me and gave himself for me' (RSV). At the very centre of the mystical prayer of John is an imitational sharing of the Cross and crucifixion of Jesus Christ. The sketch or outline of Christ crucified is a sketch of the life of John himself freely and fully accepted, in the response to the call to total discipleship. For John, as for Teresa, the full acceptance of the way of the cross was and is the highest and most deeply paradoxical of the adventures in prayer, and this is true of all those who follow the way of Christian mystical prayer.

The sign of the cross was deeply indented in John's life from the beginning. His father, Gonzalo de Yepes was rejected by his own family and died when John was only two years old, leaving his widow Catalina Álvarez in dire poverty, and all this meant, in those pre-welfare days, of suffering amd humiliation. She was repulsed by a wealthy priest, her late husband's uncle who turned her away with her youngest son, a two-year old toddler, in her arms, tiny and sickly: the child that was to become John of the Cross, thus already following closely in the footsteps of the incarnate Son of God. As a boy John was given a small job in a local hospital and thus had an early initiation into the ways of human suffering. He had to depend on patronage for his education to the priesthood and very early chose a life of great and constant austerity. After his 'vision' of the cross came his nine-month imprisonment and all its privations and humiliations. Later he was rejected by his own brethren of the Reformed Carmel and died of a painful ulcer which reduced him to something like the state of pain and dereliction depicted in his drawing of Christ crucified. More deep and terrible were the states of inner desolation which he has so vividly described in his *Ascent of Mount Carmel* and *Dark Night of the Soul*, those deserts of the sensibility and darknesses of the whole spiritual landscape.

It might be thought that John would have found some comfort in his Carmelite brethren and sisters. It is true that as long as Teresa lived (i.e. until 1582) he was protected by her powerful patronage, and it is true that he was much loved by the sisters. Yet it was this very love and veneration in which he was held by the sisters that brought about that storm of opposition and controversy among his Carmelite brethren in which, with Jerome Gracián, Teresa's great friend, he became engulfed after the death of Teresa. It was within this cloud that he died; indeed it could be argued that it was the pressure of this barrage of accusations that brought about his death; he was the kind of man who would never bend but could, like all men and women, be broken or indeed worn down by constant pressure. His very tender, and indeed paradisal, relations with women were distorted and totally misunderstood by men of coarse mind and speech. A certain Diego Evangelista had put together a dossier 'two fingers thick' to quote the vivid description of a certain nun who had a glimpse of it. The same Diego said when he heard of John's death: 'six months more and he would have been expelled from the order'. Later, he went around giving talks on John's holy life and writings.

Much more could be said about the depth and constancy of the presence of the cross in John's life and how truly and realistically he lived up to his chosen appellation John *of the Cross*. But the task at this point is to explain why John could equally be called John of the Resurrection. One can talk of that doubling (*dedoblamiento*) of the soul according to which the soul is at once in deep darkness and sorrow and marvellous joy and light. This is common to all those who experience mystical prayer in its fullness, and true even of Jesus Christ himself as shown, for example, at the Last Discourse. And one can try to explain how totally opposite this is to the doubling of the schizoid personality which leads to disintegration. The doubling of the soul of which the mystics speak rests on a strong and well-integrated sense of identity, and the doubling comes at the level of feeling as expressing a strongly coherent self-understanding and Source-understanding. It is not a question of moods following each other but rather of a constancy of feeling that involves a deep sense of suffering, more or less intense as the 'darkness of God' comes upon the soul, yet always accompanied by a substantial and vitalizing joy *that communicates itself to others* as a kind of serenity and well-tempered optimism. No calamity can disturb this serenity for long. Like the needle of a compass it returns to its centre no matter how it has been shaken and seemingly disturbed. In the mystical 'doubling' the two sides complete each other. They are both aspects of that great love and union that bind the Divine Bridegroom to the Bridal human soul. Not only are they aspects of the one mystery of love but they are aspects that cannot be separated as is set forth by St Paul in his second letter to the Corinthians, which is from beginning to end a defence of the paradox of strength and weakness that radiates from the cross.

Almost all the pictures we have of John emphasize a kind of bleak and relentless asceticism which give an almost totally false impression of one of the world's greatest poets of ecstatic love. This iconography looks exclusively at the ascetic side of John and seems totally unconscious of two things: his poet's love of beauty and the sheer tenderness of his love of God.

For John of the Cross beauty, *pulchritudo*, *hermosura*, was seen as one of the lights above the mind and one of the attributes of God. Either way it reflected everything and was reflected in everything. In a sense, this was pure Hellenism deriving directly and indirectly from Plato, Plotinus and Dionysius the Areopagite. In another and no less important sense this divine attribute was the very atmosphere and presence of the Holy Spirit as the bond uniting the Father and the Son. The Holy Spirit was also, experientially for John, the living flame of love or flame of living love, the fire within the heart that became the light in the mind in the journey through the darkness. Moreover this Holy Spirit of eternal beauty was the signature and footprint of the incarnate Son of God in nature and in man.

From the point of view of the mirroring of beauty in the experience of the deep union of the Soul and God, it will help to look carefully at stanza 35 (36) of the *Spiritual Canticle* and at the explanation of this stanza in the commentary. We have already looked carefully at the first twelve stanzas of this, John's longest and most complete poem; and we saw how this first part expresses deep mystical longing, that is to say, the longing that is also a calling and drawing in the mystical or receptive mode. The second part (st. 13–21) speaks of the preparations for perfect union and the third part (st. 22–40) deals with that fullness of union which is called the Mystical Marriage of the human lover and the Divine Beloved. It is in stanza 35 (36) that John expresses the fullness of this union.

> Let us rejoice, Beloved,
> And let us go to see ourselves in thy beauty,
> To the mountain or the hill where flows the pure water;
> Let us enter farther into the thicket.[1]

The whole commentary on this stanza should be read to catch the

---

1. E. Allison Peers, *The Complete Works of Saint John of the Cross*, Vol. II (London: Burns & Oates, 1957), Redaction A, p. 156.

exultant quality of John's mystical writing, but here I want to look especially at the final line: *Let us enter farther into the thicket*. The thicket (*espesura*) is not only 'the marvellous works and profound judgements' of God, but also 'trials and afflictions, insomuch as they are a means of entrance (*son medio para entrar*) into the thicket of the delectable wisdom of God; for the purest suffering causes and entails the purest knowledge' (SC 35, par. 8).[2]

We must be careful here. John does not want suffering or ask for it. What he longs for and asks for is the presence of the Beloved in joy and glory, but the way to this is through the purifying mysterious thicket of suffering,[3] what Teilhard de Chardin calls 'the passivities of diminishment', what Shakespeare calls 'the heartache and the thousand natural shocks that flesh is heir to'. Only John of the Cross, or rather his way, can really answer Hamlet's question here; it is in T. S. Eliot's words 'the only hope or else despair'.

Those who still find John's 'wisdom of the cross' rather cold and bleak and heartless should read carefully John's tender little poem 'A Shepherd Boy' (*un pastorcico*), which was based on a popular love poem. Nowhere is John's magical touch as a poet so clearly evident. It concludes:

> Then climbs he slowly, when much time is o'er,
> Into a tree, with fair arms wide outspread,
> And, clinging to that tree, forthwith is dead.
> For Lo! his breast was stricken very sore.

The boy is the boy Jesus who is called in the Gaelic pietistic tradition *Isogan* or Jesukin, as in the poem traditionally associated with St Ita. The beauty and freshness of boyhood and young manhood is a theme that links Hellenism and Christianity. Plato expresses it frankly in the portrait of Socrates in the *Symposium* and *Phaedrus*. Socrates is, we are told, incredibly fond of boys, yet

---

2. Ibid., p. 159.
3. See *Living Flame of Love* II 23–30.

when one of them, Alcibiades, persuades him towards bed companionship the night passes in total chastity, a chastity echoed in the picture of John the disciple whom Jesus loved lying on his breast at the Last Supper and sharing the Mother of Jesus on the death of the master himself.

We are in a world of deep upward-moving tenderness which flowered in the medieval devotion to the pierced heart of Jesus crucified. This devotion becomes cosmic both in John's celebrated sketch of the crucifixion and in recent times in some of the writings of Teilhard de Chardin. It has become a central theme in nineteenth and twentieth century iconography and devotional verse, but it is a theme demanding not only deep spirituality but a very special tact and delicacy. It is no small part of John's poetic genius that 'A Shepherd Boy' has a place among his great, if not his very greatest poems.

We are told on good authority that John had a strong devotion to the Child Jesus, and this became traditional in Carmelite spirituality. It is related to the theme of the eternal childhood of God which takes a feminine form in the ancient celebration of the presentation of Mary as a young girl in the temple, about which certain mystics, such as Mary of Agreda, have written copiously. A delicate and tender love of children is a natural and beautiful thing in men and women, and has a certain connectedness with the religious sense that needs careful maturing. The fact that this maturing is sometimes tragically lacking in some priests and ministers of religion points to the need for that strong asceticism which John of the Cross lived and preached.

The Journey in the Dark

It is well to recall and to keep in mind this pulse of tenderness and warmth as we accompany John in his greatest and most terrible adventure in prayer, that of the journey in the dark, a theme which he has made specially his own, though it is central to the Dionysian tradition, as for example in the fourteenth-century *Cloud of*

Unknowing. We do not know whether or how far John knew of the *Cloud* but certainly he accepted the general mystical principle of 'unknowing', that union with God may be reached by love and not by thought. It is a work of will and not of intellect or understanding or imagination. The author of *The Cloud of Unknowing* speaks constantly of the work of prayer as a 'naked intent of the will'. In it the intellect is in darkness but so also is the will, which is not supported by any glow of feeling as it tries to pierce the darkness and enter into union with the Divine Source beyond the darkness. There is question of a journey through the darkness in which the darkness or dark night grows deeper and deeper, so much so that it seems that all is lost. Later, in nineteenth–century followers of John, the night becomes the total night of total atheism, but John himself belongs to the age of faith where God is always present, though in a hidden or even rejecting way, and here John explores the mystical sense of the complaints of Job and of the psalmist in the *De Profundis* mode.

The terror and drama of this journey in the dark is vividly expressed in John's poem, 'Upon love's chase I went my way'. In this poem the soul becomes a huntsman of the skies and the Divine Bridegroom becomes the prey (*caza*) that is being sought in the far heights and is finally captured after a desperate chase that seems hopeless at a certain stage. 'The dreadful force of dazzling light,' brings a kind of blindness in daytime and it is only at night that success is possible. This means that the way of intellectual knowledge becomes impossible and the powers of knowing must be put on hold at all levels of knowing. But there must also be a darkness of the will attained through humility and self-relinquishment, 'my own self I could not see'. The Bridal Soul has to sink lower and lower into total humility, that 'meekness' lauded in *The Cloud of Unknowing*. Freed from the weight of its own pride and selfishness the human spirit ascends freely into an ever-darkening sky. It would seem that the word *oscura* must be given its full weight here as in the second stanza of *The Dark Night*. This is John's best-known poem, one of the half-dozen or so poems which rise like Mount Everest beyond all that man or woman has written or sung concerning the mystical receptive union of the human spirit with God, as the unique and uniquely fulfilling lover of the human person in all its infinite dimensions as *capax dei*, as the Bridal glory by which the infinite eternal glory of God is reflected and fulfilled.

In this great poem in praise of night, the darkness becomes a living medium or presence that unites the lover-poet with the divine beloved, and is thus, in John's theology, a presence of the Holy Spirit appearing within the darkness. John's eulogy of the darkness is more accurately a eulogy of the dark *night*, which is an ambience of total darkness, where all seeing by way of light is excluded, where the spirit must find new eyes and a new seeing. There is need of a profound transformation of the spirit at several levels, and this is the great task of the spiritual journey by night to the summit of the Mount of Perfection, a journey that for John can be made only by night, a night of ever-deepening darkness in which alone it is possible for the eternal divine lover to appear.

Thus, the darkness of the poem (and of some other poems on the same theme) is a positive entity or ambience in which another and deeper perception than that of light arises within the psyche. As perception, by way of light, produces a whole world of experience, varied and colourful, so too, under a different sign, perception by way of darkness reveals a whole world of deep and lasting experience that can add up to a radical transformation and divinization of the whole person. Part of the doctrine of John of the Cross and the tradition to which he belongs is that the dimension of darkness opens up the best, perhaps the only, way of union between the soul and its Divine Source. This is not to ignore or deny the dimension of light, but rather to purify the soul so that it can open to the light in a deeper and more transforming way.

The poem was written after John's escape from his Toledo prison around 1580 when John was chaplain to the Carmelite sisters in Beas in the sunny land of Andalusia in Southern Spain, and this atmosphere pervades the whole poem. It was shortly afterwards that the twin treatises the *Ascent of Mount Carmel* and the *Dark Night of the Soul* were written as an explanation and elucidation of the poem. The poem, like all John's poems, issued directly from the love of God; the treatises may be said to issue from the love between John and his Carmelite sisters. Both poem and commentary are radiant with the glow of this love, yet the sign of the cross lay deeply indented in all this; his love of God was misinterpreted as Illuminism, his love of women was misinterpreted as self-indulgence. He had to go forward in darkness and dereliction in a deep dark night. It is of this the poem speaks; and it is this that is explored by the two treatises based on the poem.

The poem runs to eight stanzas. Of these the first three have to do with darkness and longing, opening out in the prose commentary into a detailed description of the four nights, the fourth and fifth stanzas are transitional, telling of the Journey by night which unites the lover-poet with his divine beloved, and the last three are full of the joy and fulfilment of this union as accomplished. The first three stanzas find their traditional source and imagery most importantly in the Book of Job, while the last three find their source in the Song of Songs.

The commentary for all that it is John's longest and most comprehensive treatise, never got beyond a full treatment of the first two stanzas and a brief introductory explanation of the third, just at the point where the dawn is breaking, and it remains unfinished both as *Ascent* and *Dark Night*. It may be said to lay the foundation of what is called 'Sanjuanist' spirituality but it does not really go beyond the foundations towards that fullness of union described so ecstatically in the rest of the poem. For this we have to pass on to the other commentaries, the *Spiritual Canticle* and the *Living Flame of Love*. They take over at the point where the dawn is breaking, so that it all adds up to a complete exposition of the spirtual ascent in darkness and in light. But it's all there, folded up, as it were, in that one great poem *The Dark Night*. Whoever reads this and enters into it may share to some real extent the Sanjuanist spiritual journey.

It soon becomes clear that for John, as commentator on his own poem, there are four separate but interrelated zones or levels of darkness which the soul or spirit encounters in its journey towards that union with God as the Beloved which is the task of all spiritual endeavour. In the poem there is only one dark night, only one ambience of darkness, yet it is not difficult for John as commentator to show that the darkness deepens as the image is developed in the first two stanzas. And as the darkness deepens it seems that the spiritual wayfarer passes from the level of sense or sense perception to the level of spirit or spiritual perception. This, on the one hand; and, on the other there is a passage from an active journeying in the ambience or atmosphere of night and darkness to a passive or receptive encounter with a deeper presence of that same darkness. So we have the rather intimidating schema or pattern of four dark nights through which the soul must pass on the way to union with God: the Active Night of Sense, the Active Night of Spirit, (both of these are the subject of the *Ascent of Mount Carmel* and have all to do with the prayer of human effort), the Passive Night of Sense and the Passive Night of Spirit (these are the subject of the second treatise, the *Dark Night of the Soul,* which has to do with the receptive or truly mystical side of prayer wherein God, as it were, takes over and plunges the soul more and more deeply into darkness).

The Dark Night of Sense

The active night of sense (*Ascent* Bk 1) is the traditional *via purgativa*, the purgative way of asceticism or self-denial, in which sensual desires, emotions and passions are kept within the bounds of reason and the structure of the virtues. John expresses this ascetical programme with total clarity and absoluteness in what might be called a commando fashion, more suitable for the training of heroes, spiritual heroes to be sure, than for ordinary living. There is involved a training of the will and the passions, which puts the use of reason and common sense 'on hold' for a while. We are at the level of sense perception and the desires and pleasures that lie at the roots of sense perception, the desires and pleasures of beautiful sights and sounds, of taste, odour and touch, including what the Scholastic tradition named the *delectationes tactus*, the 'delights of touch' most vividly sought and found in physical sex. The darkness here is a darkness of desire and sensual fulfilment within which ultimately a higher order of desire begins to appear, a desire for the Divine Presence and what it brings of fulfilment and peace.

It might seem that what begins to appear within the darkness is a spirtual desiring and fulfilment to replace the grosser desires of the body that have been transcended. But according to John these spiritual goods, or 'goods of heaven' as he names them, can become objects of attachment no less constraining than physical goods and the desire for these goods – spiritual favours such as inner sweetness and the 'consolations' of prayer – must also be put into darkness and transcended. This is clearly portrayed in the drawing called 'The Mount of Perfection' in which we find a rough schematic drawing of a mountain towards which three pathways seem to lead. But two of the pathways, having begun to lead towards the mountain, soon go away from it. These are the paths, on the one side, of the goods of earth and, on the other, of the 'goods of heaven'. The true path is the path of *nada*, nothing, where all desire and attachment is transcended or rather placed in total darkness, a darkness not of the eyes but of all desire and all attachment. For that to which the soul is attached, whether at the earthly or the 'heavenly' level, possesses the soul and prevents it from growing. In place of the 'goods of heaven' named by John as delights and consolations, what we find in our day is attachment to some 'spiritual' trip or to the way of some master or guru which seems a precious possession until it becomes clear that the promises of the way or the master are false promises. For John the true way is without attachment to or possession of any thing or person, however great and holy, but to the all, *Todo*, that which is without limits and can never be possessed but only served and loved. In other words, the darkness that covers the whole inner realm of desire and attachment at the level of images and perceptions is a darkness awaiting the fullness of light and life.

But this journey made in darkness and deviating neither to the false pathway of the 'goods of earth' nor to the specious but no less false pathway of the 'goods of heaven' held possessively and by attachment to particular desires and images, needs a powerful inner dynamism if it is to proceed. This dynamism is love, the fire that 'burns in the heart' and becomes the light that guides the wayfarer securely through the deepest darkness, a fire and light that ultimately unites the soul with the Source that in its deepest centre it has sought from the beginning.

In the active night of sense the wayfarer has chosen the way of the *nadas* in the darkness of all sensual desire and attachment, whether through the 'goods of earth' such as earthly possessions and the various forms of sensual pleasure that can possess the soul through the senses, or through the 'goods of heaven' which are indeed spiritual in their appearance but are received into the soul or psyche in a sensual and narrowly selfish way. The wayfarer must rise beyond all this. But it is beyond one's power to do so. One neither knows nor can one tackle the deep subtle folds of selfishness and self-absorption that stand in the way of deep and lasting purification and transformation at the level of the senses. This can only come from God, the Source Itself, *la fonte que mana y corre*: the fountain freely flowing. This flowing comes by way of the passive dark night of sense (DN. Bk 1).

I have tried to give a positive meaning to the concept of darkness and the image of the dark night which is central to the mystical philosophy and theology of St John of the Cross. It must be said, however, that John begins his commentary on his poem *The Dark Night* by saying that 'Night is nothing but the privation of light' (*Ascent* I.3 par. 1)[4]. And he adds 'to deprive oneself of the gratification of the appetites in all things is like living in darkness and in a void' (ibid.).

It is clear, however, that in this passage John is thinking almost exclusively of the *active* dark night. When we come to the treatise on the *Dark Night of the Soul*, which forms the second part of a kind of diptych of which the *Ascent of Mount Carmel* is the first, the darkness,

---

4. Kieran Kavanaugh and Otilio Rodriguez, tr., *The Collected Works of St. John of the Cross* (Washington, DC: Institute of Carmelite Studies, 1964, 1979, 1991) pp. 121–2.

which is indeed 'the darkness of God' and is received passively or receptively by man, takes on a positive if not a substantial character. It *does* things to the soul, purifying, transforming, deifying. Indeed, in John's understanding of the spiritual journey, nothing is of any importance compared with this sanctifying darkness. Without it the soul (that is to say the human person as related to the source of all Goodness, Truth and Beauty) is deeply flawed, deeply selfish and self-enclosed even though it gives its energies to the spiritual journey. In a long and devastating analysis which forms the substance of the first book of the *Dark Night of the Soul*, the deep and pervasive faults and imperfections of the soul that has made its way along the steep ascent of mortification and self-denial are described under the heading of the seven 'deadly' or 'capital' sins, which at a lower level corrupt the soul in various ways and in effect draw together the main lines of traditional Christian asceticism. The soul cannot really tackle these imperfections by itself, all the more so because they are not definite sins but rather imperfections that cloud and shadow the whole soul. Their roots are largely hidden, and the darkness of the passive night of sense acts so deeply on the soul that it can expose them and eradicate them.

In this connexion of the penetration of the soul by the dark fire of divine love (for this it is), John uses an image already common in the mystical tradition, and shows how much he stands within the tradition which links him with fourteenth-century English mysticism and the fifteenth-century Rhineland mystics. This is the image of the log of wood that is at first dark and smoking and gradually becomes clear and glowing (DN II.10). So it is that the dark flame of transformation, dark indeed to the soul in its manifold imperfections, becomes gradually bright and glowing and full of fragrance and glory. This process is described in the last six stanzas of the poem *The Dark Night*, as also in the verses and prose commentaries on the *Spiritual Canticle* and the *Living Flame of Love*.

In the passive night of sense, no active progress is possible because God has, as it were, taken over to chasten, deepen and purify the soul at the level of those sensual feelings and desires that lie at the root of sense perception and the alluring world of sight and the other senses, including the region of eros and the *delectationes tactus*. At this time, in this darkness, much that seems and indeed is, innocent in the world of human joys and human relationship is taken away or 'put on hold'; those who become fixed or fixated at this stage become inhuman and puritancial, and in fact John is sometimes accused of this by those with incomplete knowledge of his vision. This is especially the case inasmuch as the active and passive dark night of sense does not entirely disappear into higher realms of darkness and light, but must be always a part or ingredient of the world of the traveller into the ways of divine union. Otherwise, to use John's image taken from the Song of Songs, the 'little foxes' may come and destroy the vineyard. The little foxes are split-off grains of selfishness, sensuality, pride and the rest which masquerade as virtues such as holy indifference, humility, childlike innocence, etc. St Paul does not use the image of 'the little foxes', yet the theme of the danger of sensuality masquerading as freedom comes up again and again in his Epistles: 'You were called to freedom, brethren; only do not use your freedom as an opportunity for the flesh, but through love be servants of one another' (Galatians 5.13, RSV). This theme appears regularly in various forms.

Yet John is confident that through the sanctifying darkness of God the soul may reach a state of freedom from the pull of sensual and selfish desire where 'its house is now at rest', and it can move forward to union with God in the spirit. By the 'spirit', John means what is known in the tradition as the intellectual level of the soul. Here knowledge by perceptual images passes over into knowledge by ideas that is no longer tied down to particular images but finds a common core of light within the images which allows the soul as mind to open out to the world of meaning and understanding. Here we are in a region of light of a different kind than that of the world of that psychic experience of light by way of the physical organ of vision. We are dealing with the active and passive nights of the spirit.

The Dark Night of Spirit

The active night of spirit, insofar as it has to do with intellectual knowledge, is called by John the Night of Faith, and to this is devoted the whole of Book Two of the *Ascent of Mount Carmel*. Faith for John is a kind of knowledge through love, through the love that is the dynamic or force of the soul as it moves forward towards union with the source that is God. In this movement towards union God is dimly discerned as the object and fulfilment of that love that burns in the heart as all other lesser loves have been transcended. This purifying of the force of love within the psyche reveals a deep spiritual thirst and longing that opens up the vast reaches and depths of the spirit to that mysterious presence which alone can fulfil the measureless desires of the heart. Unless the reader shares some of the author's deep stirring of love there is no way in which the poem and commentary *The Dark Night* can be understood. We must first and all the way *feel* the poem as expressing a certain ardour and longing within the spirit. The dryness and distress of the dark night of sense, which may last for several years, involving deep loneliness and longing, has purified this original fire of love of all its impurities and hidden grains of selfishness and sensuality: 'my house being now at rest'. The soul goes forth from the house of desire, being hidden from all the forces of desire by the surrounding darkness, escaping the threefold attacks of the world, the flesh and the Devil.

The soul is seeking the Source, and the Source is seeking the soul. John is writing within a tradition of knowledge of the Source as holy and good and loving. But human ideas of holiness, goodness and lovingness are narrow and imperfect, and the more intellectually clear and imaginatively vivid these ideas are, the more they reduce the Source to human dimensions and falsify it. It is here, at this point, that all the strife and dark hatreds of religious dogmatism and fundamentalism come in. John, who stood in fear of the Holy Inquisition all his life, knew this well, and realized that the people with clear and certain ideas and images of God had gone disastrously astray, even when they had begun by following the fire in the heart and succeeded in walking the way of the dark night of sense. They had safely emerged from the house of desire only to allow themselves gradually to be drawn into one of the camps of narrow and acrimonious dogmatism. The only safe way to go on towards union with the all-holy, all-loving, all-beautiful and transcendent Source is to close the eyes to all the isms and factions, and to be led onward by no other light or guide than that which burns in the heart purified of all sensuality in the dark nights of sense. This is the way of the Night of Faith where faith is nothing more or less than that 'fire burning in the heart' that impelled the soul to make the journey towards union. This reminds us that the whole process of the dark night is, so to speak, 'set in motion' by a fire of love in the will: the soul goes forth into the darkness 'kindled in love with yearnings', and it is the dynamic of the love of God that gives life and movement to the whole jouney through the darkness. The will thus following its own desire for union with God goes forward in what John calls the 'darkness of faith', independently of all intellectual knowledge, developing its own 'eyes'. Normally the eye or eyes of the will is the intelligence as a power of knowing, but in this journey of love the fire in the heart takes on, for a while, the 'seeing' function of the light of the mind. This is possible only because the will is not led on by any partial desire but by a desire that fulfils the whole soul in all its height and depth. Thus, faith is *love finding its own eyes* within the deepest darkness by the very force of its longing at the centre of the personality.

John's doctrine at this point sheds a deep light on St Paul's concept of agape and is illumined by that concept especially as expressed in 1 Corinthians 13. There Paul is dealing with dogmatism and fundamentalism among the first Christians, and can only heal the divisions by bringing them all together into a night of faith that is also a night of charity in which all dogmatisms are rejected. For, says Paul, our knowledge is partial and our preaching is partial (v. 9) and all these will pass away (v. 8). Only love (what John calls the fire in the heart, purified and all-encompassing) will remain in the final union of the soul with God.

What John is asking of himself and of others seems extremely

simple and even easy of achievement, just as what St Paul is asking
of his Corinthian Christians seems simple, easy, and even pleasant.
All that is needed for the journey is the full acceptance of the love
that burns in the heart, without either dogmatism or self-indulgence.
Yet this way makes total and even terrifying demands. It searches
the heart and soul to the very depths, and demands such a degree
of purity and simplicity that the least grain of selfishness or self-
absorption will enter into the personality as a kind of poison that
can permeate all thought and action. Thus one can ask why so
many holy people have bits of selfishness and harshness of various
kinds clinging to them. For this John, ever the realist, offers a final
dark night, the passive dark night of spirit which provides a remedy
for them, if only they have the humility to receive it.

And so, at this higher level, the level of mind or spirit, the darkness
has a great work to do, a work by which all arrogance and rigidity
is thoroughly cleansed and burnt away. This is the place of the
passive dark night of spirit to which is devoted John's most powerful
piece of writing, that which occupies the 25 chapters of the
unfinished second book of the *Dark Night of the Soul*.

A certain space of time normally elapses after the conclusion
of the passive night of sense before the soul, having itself chosen
and habituated itself to the active night of faith, is gradually
plunged deeper and deeper into the total darkness of the passive
dark night of spirit. The night of sense has left the soul strong and
independent, a strong and unshakable witness to the presence and
glory of God. This is what might be called the world of the strong
guru, and not a few souls never get beyond this and are never truly
softened and broken in their spirit, so that the fire of love penetrates
their whole being in humility and simplicity and by a full return
to childhood and humility in the holy state of the weak guru, who
is no longer powerful and assertive, but grows ever stronger in infirmity
so that, in St Paul's words, 'Power is made perfect in weakness'
(2 Corinthians 12.9).

In the first eight chapters of Book Two of the *Dark Night of the
Soul*, John gives striking and memorable descriptions of the afflictions
of the soul in this state of spiritual darkness. In this state a person

resembles one who is imprisoned in a dark dungeon, bound hands
and feet, and able neither to move nor see nor feel any favour from
heaven or earth. He remains in this condition until his spirit is humbled,
softened, and purified, until it becomes so delicate, simple, and refined
that it can be one with the Spirit of God . . . If this (dark night) is
to be truly efficacious, it will last for some years. (DN II.7.3)[5]

According to John it is this experience that is described in many
texts of the Old and New Testaments, in Job and Jeremiah especially,
in the image of the belly of the whale in the book of Jonah, and
in many of the Psalms, as fulfilled in the passion and death of Jesus
Christ. John, as he sees his own work, is not providing any new
doctrine but rather setting forth biblical doctrine in a new way.
He is writing primarily for people fully devoted to prayer and the
journey towards divine union, yet all who seek the Source and the
face of God will in a measure encounter darkness and night in the
way he describes. This darkness may seem oppressive and depressive,
but behind it the fire of divine love is always present like the 'kindling'
of a Highland hearth that never goes out.

The experience of the passive dark night of spirit is for the few,
indeed for the very few, and it involves a degree of purity and
transcendence of human desires and terrors that seems almost
impossible to achieve or receive as a constancy. The deepest
darkness of the passive night of spirit is like a chemical solution
or lye (*lejía*) in which the soul can be dipped like a photographic
negative but in which it cannot live and breathe for long, for in
John's own words, the soul feels as if it 'were hanging in midair,
unable to breathe' (DN II.6.5) and in another image 'feels that it
is melting away and being undone by a cruel spiritual death' (DN
II.6.1).[6] This is the Jonah experience of being, as it were, buried
alive as in the belly of a great fish in the depths of the sea in which
it is only possible for the soul to pray the Jonah prayer of deep
and seemingly total dereliction.[7]

---

5. Ibid., pp. 407–8.
6. Ibid., pp. 404–5.
7. See Jonah 2, Psalm 130 v. 1–2, Lamentations 3.54.

All this takes us to the far limits of spiritual experience, to the place of the narrow gate of Gethsemane and the *Lamma Sabacthani*, where the soul can only cry out to be lifted by the heavenly Bridegroom across the final threshold.[8] But it is this threshold and this final prayer that gives meaning to the whole spiritual journey and releases the soul into the glory of heaven. This state of glory is amply described by John in his writings concerning the light, as we shall see.

For most people who are set on the spritual journey to union with God, John's teaching on the active and passive nights of sense is relevant and helpful, perhaps uniquely so. So, too, the active night of spirit as the Night of Faith makes sense, as we feel the light of reason and reasoning cannot take us the whole way into the mysterious world of the transcendent and divine. But the passive dark night of spirit, being admittedly for the few, the specially graced and exceptional ones, can be easily dismissed as of no real relevance for those many people of goodwill who are earnestly seeking union with God in truth and charity. In this respect it is well to look carefully at Chapters 1 and 2 of the second book of the *Dark Night of the Soul*. There, introduced casually and just as casually dismissed, we find the notion of 'morsels' *bocados* of dark contemplation, that is to say, touches or brief experiences of the passive dark night of spirit. These morsels are, John tells us, 'omens and messengers (*presagios y mensajeros*) of the night to come, that is the passive night of spirit. 'Thus God purges some individuals who are not destined to ascend to so lofty a degree of love as are others' (DN II.1.1).[9] It seems a pity that John speaks so dismissively of this high and holy state, for it is the state of many people who are well advanced in mystical experience and who have perhaps an important place in God's purposes and in the world of spritual guidance and spritual service. John leaves himself open in this matter to St Teresa's shrewd comment when she prays to be delivered from

8. See N. D. O'Donoghue, *Mystics for Our Time: Carmelite Meditations for a New Age* (Edinburgh, T & T Clark, 1989), chs 7 and 9.
9. Kavanaugh and Rodriguez, *Collected Works*, p. 395.

those people (i.e. her friend John, who is nevertheless a 'divine man') who must turn everything into perfect comtemplation, come what will.

John is a being of essences, clear and in a sense uncompromising; Teresa, Mother of Carmel, takes human nature as she finds it and has a mother's skill in finding words of encouragement to comfort human weakness along the straight and narrow pathways of the ascent of Mount Carmel.

But for both of them, these dark pathways are lighted by a light within the heart which is the fire of a great flame, kindled by a deeply-felt presence of a great love that is a call heard in silence as all the voices of desire cease to trouble the soul. It is by a 'happy chance' or 'grace' that this silence is encountered and this call is heard and followed.

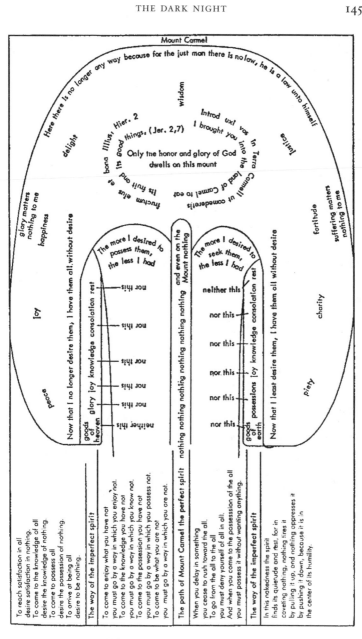

The Mount of Perfection

CHAPTER 6

THE MOUNT OF PERFECTION

The Sketch of the Mount

Let us look again at the sketch of The Mount of Perfection, which shows the whole journey as it lies backward from this vantage point of the entry into the passive dark night of spirit that indeed lies far beyond the dark night of sense and all its purifications. In this sketch, typically, John gives an impression at once of movement and rest. It is an urgent invitation to make a journey, an inner journey towards dizzying heights and depths that are all within the spirit and involve not the least change or disarray of our ordinary life.

John made many copies of this sketch involving small variations, and it was variously 'improved' by subsequent writers in ways sometimes detrimental to its unity and force.[1] The American Carmelite translation presents a well-authenticated copy of one of John's own sketches, which we will follow here. John wished this drawing to stand at the head of his great unfinished work called by some Spanish editors the Subida–Noche, that is, the Ascent–Night, or dual treatise of the *Ascent of Mount Carmel* and the *Dark Night of the Soul*.

The central area of the sketch of the Mount shows us three pathways: the middle or central pathway is that of 'Mount Carmel and the perfect spirit', the pathways to the right and to the left are both named 'the way of the imperfect spirit'. Note that these pathways are not named 'ways of the erring (or straying) spirit' as some of

---

1. See N. D. O'Donoghue, 'The Primitive Drawings of the Mount of Perfection', (*Mount Carmel*, Vol. 7. No. 3, 1959), pp. 118–25.

John's followers and editors named them. This 'improvement' may well be in accord with what John said or suggested elsewhere, but it is not in accord with his primary inspiration. He is *not* saying that those who do not follow the central path (which is in no sense a *via media* or middle way) are going astray, but that they are not following the perfect path or the path of perfection as leading to union with God.

We are told that the imperfect pathway on the right (of the observer) is that of 'the goods of earth' (*suelo*: a very 'earthy' word) while that on the left is that of the 'goods of heaven'. Five separate goods are named in each case of which four share a common name, though John is clearly speaking at two separate, though analogical levels. These four are joy, knowledge, consolation and rest (*descanso*). The fifth good is, in the case of the 'goods of earth' named as possessions, and in the case of the 'goods of heaven' as glory. None of these goods is condemned as harmful or destructive and it is necessary to remind ourselves that we are not dealing with the moral level of right and wrong, virtue and vice, but rather with that mystical level which assumes a grid of moral virtue (honesty, justice, temperance, etc.) on which it is built. We, John's readers, are in the position of the rich young man who has kept all the commandments from his youth and is firmly based in virtuous habits. If I lack this basis because I have some addiction or bitterness in me or am dishonest in my dealings with others then John will very gently take away his sketch and tell me it is of no use to me. But if I have truly decided to follow the way of union with God then the sketch is a map for me to follow.

It is worth noting that the ways of the imperfect spirit are called simply 'ways' giving the impression of a certain spaciousness (*camino*) whereas the true way is called *senda*, a track, with a hint of the steepness and straightness of the true upward path.

To repeat: neither the 'goods of earth' nor the 'goods of heaven' are seen as evil or destructive in themselves at the level of ordinary morality. What is destructive is *attachment* to these goods and this not at the moral level but only at the mystical level, that is to say the level of the journey towards union with God in active and receptive prayer. If we hold on desperately to things that can never fulfil our deep-down desire for the infinite beauty and glory of the eternal all-giving Source that has given us life, then we are closed against the divine gift of the Holy Spirit of God. We are closed against the seven gifts of the Holy Spirit, all of which are receptivities by which we can open more and more deeply to the Source of all giving and transformation.

The word desire comes in at this point, and we must be careful here. Desire is good; we are created creatures of desire. But small and narrow desires stand in the way of those ever larger desires and desiring that are the deepest dynamic of the prayer adventure of union with the infinite Source of our Being. Where the Buddha teaches his followers to go beyond all desires, John – and here he is simply plumbing the depths of the Christian tradition – tells us to go beyond all limited desires in order to open ourselves to the desire for the Source, for God is seeking the soul as the love that 'will not let me go'. At this point one should read what Teresa of Avila has to say in the first book of *The Interior Castle* concerning the beauty and grandeur of the human soul. John is assuming all this, assuming too that the desire of the Bridal Soul for the Bridegroom God is fully and more than fully met by the desire of the Bridegroom God for the Bridal Soul. Images such as that of Rachel bewailing her children and the father waiting day after day for the prodigal son do but express an aspect of the deep things of God that is central to the Old and New Testaments.

Before we leave this central section of the sketch of the Mount we must look at the third pathway, that of the perfect spirit. The original here might be more accurately rendered as 'the spirit on the road to perfection' for there must be no least hint of the presence of what is called 'the performance principle' along the mystical journey. The right way is the way of 'nothing' or *nada* seven times repeated as both earthly goods and heavenly goods (or rather the attachment to them) are firmly rejected and *nada* chosen at every level. One time a medical doctor, a good man in his way, was heard muttering as he left the room or 'cell' of a student with some small ailment, with a picture of the famous Mount above his bed – 'and on the mountain, nothing, and on the mountain nothing'. But, of course, John might equally have written: on the mountain everything. This will be clearer when we examine the famous aphorisms at the foot of the sketch.

The upper part of the sketch of the Mount, although it is drawn on the same vertical plane as the lower part nevertheless should be seen horizontally, for here we are *on* the Mount which is named Mount Carmel. A text from the second chapter of Jeremiah marks the centre of the summit. Our English translation keeps to the original latin of Jeremiah 2.7 with its reference to the 'land of Carmel', where the original Hebrew has 'land of plenty', so that the RSV translates the whole text as: 'I brought you into a plentiful land to enjoy its fruits and its good things.' These good things are identified by John as the virtues of soul and states of mind that are ranged around the summit and have at their centre wisdom or *sabiduría*: the Spanish word has a somewhat more contemplative and ruminative quality about it as of a cow happily chewing the cud; John would not have rejected this image any more than he would have rejected the hen and her chicks as an image of divine charity.

On the left hand side of this upper section of the drawing we see four shinings or irradiations of heavenly glory freely given by the Holy Spirit and freely received by the human soul in its spiritual depths. It must be carefully noted that this glory is received in peace and joy and happiness and delight but is not possessed like the glory that has to be transcended at the lower level of the pathways to the summit. This point is of the highest importance and might be explained in modern parlance by saying: 'If you are looking for a spiritual trip and exalted 'highs' don't go near John of the Cross or you'll be slaughtered without mercy. Lots of goods; but only if you don't waste time looking for goodies.'

On our right-hand side as we look at the summit, with its text from Jeremiah, and its central virtue of wisdom – *sabiduría,* we find four virtues or attitudes of soul which balance at the level of action the four virtues or receptive attitudes by which the soul-spirit opens up to mystical contemplation. These four virtues must be carefully understood. Clearly they have to do with the active life of the second great command of love of the neighbour. We are here in the world of the 'goods of earth', of people's needs and demands, of social and political involvements. Piety has to do with individual and family claims (John never tried to 'escape' these in choosing monastic life); charity with wider social claims, the claims of the neighbour however it arises (not idiot compassion but a wise and lucid concern for others); fortitude with all the difficulties that a life of active compassion entails (not excluding the adventures of prayer); justice which may involve political action even within the narrow limits of a religious order or institution (John was imprisoned, tortured and finally done to death by the factions and cliques around him). When one looks at all John suffered at this level of action and engagement it is almost impossible to take seriously the words he attaches to all this: *suffering matters nothing to me.*

But John is not saying that the spirit at this level does not *feel* suffering, but rather that such a spirit is not as it were 'blown off course' by suffering, however deep and deeply felt. Even if such a one should cry out, as did the holy Job or indeed Jesus himself, yet there is peace in the depths or heights, on the summit of the Mount, where only the honour and glory of God is of any importance. And John finally adds to the sketch-map of the journey of mystical or receptive prayer: 'Here there is no longer any way (*camino*) because for the just man there is no law; he is a law unto himself.' In all this it is important to bear in mind that John is not, he would claim, speaking for himself but simply presenting the challenge that is there for every Christian at the centre of the gospel, as in Galatians 2.19, 20.

Let us now focus on the counsels or maxims at the foot of the sketch. These maxims are divided into four sets according to the central division of the three paths: 4, 4, 3 and 1, moving from the reader's left to the right. The division into four sets seems natural enough, yet if we look at Chapter 13 of Book One of the *Ascent*, we find that these maxims run on and that the single maxim in the fourth set sums up the other eleven and, moreover, is accompanied or completed by a further and final maxim, which reads: 'When it [i.e. the soul] covets something/in this desire it is wearied.' It is central to John's understanding of spiritual psychology that all desire for anything less than God causes weariness (*fatiga*) and that, alternatively, weariness is a sure sign of attachment to something or somebody less than God. John would approve of G. K. Chesterton's celebrated quip that Satan fell by the force of gravity, weighed down by self-importance.

The first four aphorisms all have to do with desire and desiring. The original Spanish term is perhaps better translated as 'seeking' rather than desiring; it gives the impression of unquiet busyness which may indeed, Martha-wise, have God or Christ for its object but does not really meet God (or Christ) or really *listen*, in receptive prayer. We must remember that for John there is always a question of prayer as seeking and finding the creative Source of the suppliant's being. Four objects of seeking are named in this first set of maxims: satisfaction (*gusto,* i.e. feelings of satisfaction in one's prayer), knowledge (*sabor,* i.e. the illuminations that may come through prayer), possession (*poseer,* i.e. something tightly held as a possession) and being (*ser*).

Let us look carefully at this last. The verbs *ser* and *estar* are notoriously tricky in Spanish, and here *serlo todo* over against *ser algo* seems to affirm (with St Teresa) that all true value or self-identity is to be found only in God and never in the way of common wordly valuation. So it is that the more one seeks *ser algo,* to *be* somebody in a worldly sense, the farther away one is from *serlo todo,* which is the true valuation of oneself as open to God (*capax dei*) and is also the way of true peace as we come safely to rest 'in the centre of our humility'.

The second set of maxims has all to do with the very difficult and delicate matter of that development of taste which is a large part of education of every kind. On the assumption that, say, Shakespeare's *Hamlet* is better than a diet of schoolboy comics, how is a boy to be led from the one to the other? Clearly there must be a period of non-enjoyment and deprivation, very gradual perhaps, by which the taste for the better literature is gradually formed until the mature man really enjoys *Hamlet* rather than the schoolboy comics. John's maxims are an application of these principles of ordinary teaching to the spiritual journey from the love of material corruptible things to the love of God and truly heavenly things. The pupil has to go forward in the dark until a new appreciation begins to dawn within it. In this process it is clear that it is essential to have a master and to have trust in this master as the Carmelite sisters, and brothers, had in John.

In the third set of aphorisms John gets rather carried away by his Senequita side and the reader sometimes needs disentanglement. The word all, *todo*, is taken in two different senses, as indeed it is also sometimes in English. It can mean 'each' as when we say all the eggs in this basket are fresh, or it can mean 'all together' as when we say 'all the eggs are too heavy to carry'. John's basic message is that the human soul must seek God who is all and refuse to attach itself to any other single thing. To reach or reach towards the All (which is God) we must go beyond all things, that is to say each single thing and even the totality of all things as distinct from the All which is God. So, the second of this third set of maxims reads: *To go from the all to the all/you must deny yourself of all in all*; and this means: to go from the totality of human finite things to the Being who is all (i.e. God) you must detach yourself firmly from whatever you desire to have in particular things. Note that the words 'rush toward' are better translated 'rest upon.'

The last general maxim sums it all up and is at the very centre of John's ascetical doctrine.

> In this nakedness the spirit
> finds its quietude and rest, for in
> coveting nothing, nothing tires it
> by pulling it up, and nothing oppresses it
> by pushing it down, because it is in the
> centre of its humility.

The Spiritual Marriage

John's ascetical teaching loses half its meaning if we do not keep in mind that John is primarily a writer of love poetry. As John sees them, the passive dark nights are simply the benign presence of God delicately weaning us from childish things so that we may come to a free, at first perhaps painful, receptivity to larger, more humanly fulfilling, more spiritual possessions – the hidden treasure, 'the pearl of great price'. John takes this process for granted as central to the active nights; in the passive nights God takes over, as it were, in so far as the human person is receptive. In all this a work of transformation is being achieved which culminates in the Spiritual Marriage of God and the soul. In expressing this, John was true to the tradition in making use of the Old Testament Song of Songs in an anagogical or upward-looking sense, and as he was dying, having been cast aside, as he had prophesied, 'like an old rag', he asked that the latin text of the Song of Songs be read to him.

Indeed it might be said that all the moods and metaphors of John's writing, poetry and prose, tend to polarize themselves between two great Old Testament witnesses to the human religious condition; the Book of Job and the Song of Songs. It must be added, however, that these polarities are seen as fulfilled and transcended in the figure and teaching of Jesus Christ as shown forth in the New Testament. John's claim that he says nothing in his commentaries that is not already present in Scripture is not to be taken either rhetorically or defensively, but rather expresses a deep and steady vision on his part of the hidden but entirely real meaning of the text: 'Since he who speaks therein is the Holy Spirit' (*Ascent,* Prologue, par. 2).

Both the *Spiritual Canticle,* John's longest and most imaginative poem, and the *Living Flame of Love*, at once serene and ecstatic, are in their entirety expressions of the moods and metaphors of the Song of Songs, and in both cases the commentaries, full and detailed as they are, are centrally concerned with the joys and glories of the Spiritual Marriage and its immediate antecedents. This happy state of love and union is expressed in many images and exclamations, so that, all in all, the ardours and modalities of love attain a sustained emotional power of unexampled richness and intensity. Indeed, the depths of the darkness and terrors of the nights is more than balanced by the height and perfection of the many joys of the state of Spiritual Marriage.

The darkness and the light belong together and must not be separated either way if the mystical poetry and teaching of John of the Cross is to be understood. Together they form a unique exploration of the depths and heights – the Himalayas – of the range of the experiences of the human soul at all levels.

In order to see how John manages to link his highly personal account of the divine union and Spiritual Marriage with the principle of action and exteriority, it is well to look at the commentary on stanza 29 of the *Spiritual Canticle*. Here the lover is at once lost to everyday activities, even those devoted to the service of God and the service of others, and devotes herself entirely to the work of contemplation. This is the way of Mary as against the way of Martha, and John has no doubt whatever that Mary has 'chosen the better part' (Luke 10.42).

John is very consious of the fact that in his day, as in our day, as in the days of Martha and Mary, the way of 'pure contemplation' can be seen as lazy and selfish. The Mary-soul seems to be wholly concentrated on her personal story, on her personal fulfilment, while people all around are in need of food and support and enlightenment. In the face of this, John comes out boldly with the principle that the man or woman who engages fully in the way of contemplative mystical prayer is doing far more for those in bodily and spiritual need than are those who devote themselves, however heroically, to corporeal and spiritual works of mercy, binding and healing the world's wounds.

Here is how John expresses himself at this point:

> It must be noted that as long as the soul has not arrived at the state of union of love with God it is proper that it should give expression to its love in both the active life and the contemplative. However, when it has arrived at the state of union it is not proper that it should devote itself to any activities and external observances which might serve as an impediment, even in the least way, to giving its full attention to the contemplative love of God, even though they may be of great service to God. For even a little of the pure

contemplative love of God (*un poquito de este puro amor*) is more precious before God and the soul, and of more advantage to the Church, even though the soul seems to be doing nothing, than all the external works put together (*todas esas otras obras juntas*).[2]

It is extremely important to look more deeply into the question of the communal or social power of mystical prayer and the place of the mystic in the whole 'economy' of salvation. There are several horizons to be looked at, or towards, if we are to put the mystical element in its proper context within Christianity and generally within the drama of the human soul and the Divine Source.

In the first place, we must look again at the very great mystical text, the Book of Job, seeing it this time as opening up a very mysterious horizon of light and darkness in which the darkness is not any longer the transforming darkness of the 'inaccessible light' of the Deity but the fearful engulfing darkness of Satan, the Accuser, the Adversary, that is present all the way throughout the story of the Christ-mystery in the New Testament. We are not in the world of God and man but rather of God, man and Satan, one of whose names is Fear. Because of some deep mysterious connivance within, mankind has become subject to Satan, and it is only by the Incarnation that this subjection can be broken. But it cannot be broken by power or force but only by way of sacrificial love. Every evil thought, every least connivance, gives power to the Adversary. Every act of the love of God on the part of men and women diminishes this power and lets in the power and presence of Christ to the human heart. The divine power and presence cannot come into the human heart by force but only by way of love. In this 'inflowing' of the Holy Spirit of God, the mystic acts as a receptacle or aqueduct into which the Divine Source flows freely and constantly, casting out fear and the works of darkness.

The mystic is deeply involved in this opposition of light and darkness, and the battle being fought in the souls of men and women, and not simply in this or that individual but on a universal scale

---

2. Stanza 29, Introduction, par. 2 (my own translation).

involving human unity and solidarity. The more deeply the mystic is illuminated and enflamed by divine love in its purity and power, the more the living flame of love issues forth into the darkness and coldness of the human condition. This is not something open to observation, but it is deeply felt and experienced by those who give themselves to prayer at any level. Here we are in view of the horizon of human unity and solidarity, and the mystic dwells naturally and constantly within this horizon. We live in a world ruled by Satan, the Lord of Cruelty, Hypocrisy and Pride, and this because men and women have connived with this master. The woman or man at prayer, especially at the highest mystic level, is giving a human response to God's love so that this love can enter the world ever more deeply and illuminate the dark cruel hearts and lost places of the world. All who fight or oppose evil are warriors in this battle, but only the mystic, totally God-centred, totally spirit-filled, can form a human mediation for the entry of the purity and power of God. Only thus can the battle for the soul of man be won. Only thus can there come to be a new heaven and a new earth. Only thus can the physical incorruptible world of resurrection and transformation emerge from the darkness of corruption and the terrible hold of the Adversary.

PART THREE

ST THÉRÈSE OF LISIEUX: CHILD OF THE LITTLE WAY

CHAPTER 7

THE LITTLE WAY OF SPIRITUAL CHILDHOOD

The Adventure of Growing Up Very Suddenly

It came suddenly at Christmas 1886 when Thérèse was on the eve of her fourteenth birthday: she had been born on 2 January 1873, the youngest of five sisters, much cossetted and loved by parents and older sisters. She was a happy child, affectionate but strong-willed and stubborn. She could have become a spoiled child; she could have grown into a little monster seeking her own way in everything, imposing her own will on all around. But there was much firmness as well as affection in her early training by a very ascetic and Christ-centred mother. She, however, soon died a painful death of cancer leaving the little Thérèse an orphan at the age of four and a half. Her elder sisters, one of them especially, tried to take the place of the departed mother, but this could be only partially successful and the young Thérèse became tearful and timorous and sensitive to an extent that in her own words made her 'almost unbearable'.

Thérèse was at the doorway of womanhood and, it seemed, quite incapable of passing through that doorway. What came suddenly at Christmas 1886 changed all this: for Thérèse herself, for those around her in her family and in school, for the whole world, Christian and non-Christian, for all the years to come. Precisely after Mass and Holy Communion on Christmas night, she found herself quite mysteriously taken across the threshold into a maturity which never left her. In the course of the few steps upstairs to change her bonnet as she returned from Midnight Mass, the over-sensitive, babyish, fourteen-year-old girl became a woman who would from that moment on react as a woman, think as a woman, shed her tears when they were appropriate as a woman.

The incident itself that announced or revealed this sudden transformation from childish girlhood to mature womanhood was a very simple one and is best told in Thérèse's own words.

It was December 25, 1886, that I received the grace of leaving my childhood, in a word, the grace of my complete conversion. We had come back from Midnight Mass where I had the happiness of receiving the *strong* and *powerful* God. Upon arriving at Les Buissonnets, I used to love to take my shoes from the chimmney-corner and examine the presents in them; this old custom had given us so much joy in our youth that Céline wanted to continue treating me as a baby since I was the youngest in the family. Papa had always loved to see my happiness and listen to my cries of delight as I drew each surprise from the *magic shoes,* and my dear King's gaiety increased my own happiness very much. However, Jesus desired to show me that I was to give up the defects of my childhood and so He withdrew its innocent pleasures. He permitted Papa, tired out after the Midnight Mass, to experience annoyance when seeing my shoes at the fireplace, and that he speak those words which pierced my heart: 'Well, fortunately, this will be the last year!' I was going upstairs, at the time, to remove my hat, and Céline, knowing how sensitive I was and seeing the tears already glistening in my eyes, wanted to cry too, for she loved me very much and understood my grief. She said 'Oh, Thérèse, don't go downstairs; it would cause you too much grief to look at your slippers right now!' But Thérèse was no longer the same; Jesus had changed her heart! Forcing back my tears, I descended the stairs rapidly; controlling the poundings of my heart, I took the slippers and placed them in front of Papa, and withdrew all the objects joyfully. I had the happy appearance of a Queen. Having regained his own cheerfulness, Papa was laughing; Céline believed it was all a *dream*! Fortunately, it was a sweet reality; Thérèse had discovered once again the strength of soul which she had lost at the age of four and a half, and she was to preserve it forever![1]

---

1. *Story of a Soul: The Autobiography of St Thérèse of Lisieux,* J. Clarke, tr., OCD. (Washington, DC: Institute of Carmelite Studies, 1975), p. 98.

In one moment, as the 14 year-old girl went lightly upstairs in her father's house, the human child emerged from the shadows, and all the demands and dependence of human childhood, into the heavenly light of Divine Childhood, into the vestibule of that state into which Jesus of Nazareth, the Christos, the anointed one calls all those who would follow him to Gethsemane, to Calvary and to the glory of the Resurrection. Thérèse could now hold her childhood in such serene possession that she could take her childhood along with her in total spiritual maturity. She could at once in full self control share with her father and sister the gaiety and gladness now possessed in maturity. But we must look more closely at what Thérèse later called her 'complete conversion'. We need to look at what came before and what came after.

It has been noted that the year 1886, leading on to her fourteenth birthday on 2 January 1887, was a very important one for Thérèse. It was in the course of this year that her two-year attack of scruples came to a head after her sister Marie had entered the Lisieux Carmelite convent. Scruples or scrupulosity is a form of neurotic anxiety that can attack people of sensitive conscience at any age but is most often encountered at adolescence. It made life a misery for Thérèse after her elder sister Marie's departure for the convent, and all she could do was pray and pray. This prayer however took a peculiar turn inasmuch as it looked towards her two sisters and her two brothers who had died before Thérèse was born. This has never been a common Christian or Catholic practice, and it is an early indication of Thérèse's power of carrying commonplace pieties to cosmic conclusions.

In this case the commonplace piety told her that dead baptized children were with God; it was the intensity of her need that brought these beings into the living present, so much so that her scruples disappeared in a deep inner peace. She felt that there was something miraculous about this, but more profoundly she felt she had made a link with heavenly companions who were never far away. What is most important, however, is that Thérèse is opening a secret door to the other side of prayer, a door on the other side of which prayer passes over from the region of asking to the region of receiving, a region in which great things may happen in a single moment; may happen, not miraculously but naturally, for that is the nature of things on the other side of prayer. *There* all is gift, for the suppliant wills nothing but what God wills, so that God is totally without constraint in giving what he is asked to give.

In becoming a mature woman this 14 year-old girl became a mother, became in her own pious parlance, 'a mother of souls'. This was of course a metaphor but it was a heroic metaphor, the metaphor in which, in a heroic spirit, a truth is not weakened but strengthened and indeed expresses a reality deeper than its original. As Thérèse thought and spoke it, the motherhood of souls carried more pain and care and ultimate glory than ever could ordinary motherhood of human children destined to die in the fullness of time, no matter how well cared for. As Thérèse and her Carmelite forebears, Teresa and John, understood it, soul-motherhood and soul-fatherhood opened up beyond time and mortality to eternity and immortality, giving every least decision, every least action another dimension, endless day or endless night. So it is that when Thérèse tells us of an experience whereby she suddenly finds within herself 'an insatiable thirst for souls' she is not indulging in a flight of pious rhetoric but telling of a deep, totally transformative, all-consuming desire and thirst that arose within her with the piercing urgency of a sword in the heart, which culminated in what was to be an Act of Consecration to Merciful Love.

We shall speak of this later. Just now it is well to ponder a little on Thérèse's first soul-child, a callous and unrepentant murderer named Pranzini. Again I shall tell the story in Thérèse's own words.

> I felt in the depths of my heart *certain* that our desires would be granted, but to obtain courage to pray for sinners I told God I was sure He would pardon the poor, unfortunate Pranzini; that I'd believe this even if he went to his death without *any signs of repentance* or without *having gone to confession*. I was absolutely confident in the mercy of Jesus. But I was begging Him for a '*sign*' of repentance only for my own simple consolation.
>
> My prayer was answered to the letter! In spite of Papa's prohibition that we read no papers, I didn't think I was disobeying when reading

the passages pertaining to Pranzini. The day after his execution I found the newspaper '*La Croix.*' I opened it quickly and what did I see? Ah! my tears betrayed my emotion and I was obliged to hide. Pranzini had not gone to confession. He had mounted the scaffold and was preparing to place his head in the formidable opening, when suddenly, seized by an inspiration, he turned, took hold of the *crucifix* the priest was holding out to him and *kissed* the *sacred wounds three times!* Then his soul went to receive the *merciful* senctence of Him who declares that in heaven there will be more joy over one sinner who does penance than over ninety-nine just who have no need of repentance!

I had obtained the 'sign' I requested, and this sign was a perfect replica of the grace Jesus had given me when He attracted me to pray for sinners. Wasn't it before the *wounds of Jesus,* when seeing His divine *blood* flowing, that thirst for souls had entered my heart? I wished to give them this *immaculate blood* to drink, this blood which was to purify them from their stains, and the lips of my '*first child*' were pressed to the sacred wounds![2]

It seems clear that Pranzini needed to change his attitude, that he had been closed to the world of love and compassion until the end, and that the young Thérèse had a clear conception of his moral state. The case of another soul-child of hers was somewhat different. Fr. Hyacinthe Loyson was a famous Carmelite preacher who could not accept the dogmatic definition of Papal Infallibility in 1870 and joined those Catholic theologians who formed the Old Catholic Church. As it happened, Thérèse's final communion before her death was on the feast of St Hyacinthe and she 'offered up' this communion for Fr. Loyson, who nevertheless continued on what Thérèse could only see as his erroneous course: he died in 1912. It would seem that Thérèse's prayers remained unanswered, yet, as far as we know, Fr. Loyson made a good Christian death while still a member of the Old Catholic Church. Moreover, Fr. Loyson was by no means alone among devoted Catholics in finding the 1870 definition of Papal Infallibility hard, if not impossible, to accept.

---

2. Ibid., p. 100.

Was Fr. Loyson blinded by pride or led onwards by the light of conscience? Perhaps he, too, had his own adventure in prayer, which led by strange paths to his last words which sound like an echo of Thérèse ('My sweet Jesus'), and may well have 'connected' with her in some way.

At this point we need to call in question the assumption that Thérèse Martin simply and piously accepted the theological mind-set given to her by pious parents and pious priests who were all of one word, a mindset that precluded all questioning. We know that Thérèse in the last 18 months of her life had to endure a terrible 'dark night of faith' and we shall look at this later. It is generally assumed that this was a trial sent by God out of a blue sky so to speak. It was indeed a trial and a kind of Gethsemane, but it is not the kind of trial we meet with in Thérèse's two great sixteenth-century mentors, even though one of them, John of the Cross wrote more powerfully and piercingly of the Dark Night of the Soul than has ever been done. We know that Thérèse knew John's writings very well and spent two of her most formative years studying these writings almost exclusively. Yet for all his understanding of the psychology and mysticism of darkness, intellectually John walked in the light of the age of faith whereas Thérèse in late nineteenth-century France was as much a daughter of Descartes and his lonely doubt under a closed heaven, as she was a daughter of John of the Cross and Teresa of Avila. As far as we know she never read the *Discourse* or *Meditations,* nor did her parents, but she could not in her short life have escaped the ambience of universal doubt all around her, nor could she fail to be painfully impressed by the gap between preaching and practice in the priests and ecclesiastics who were of so much importance in her short life.

But above all else Thérèse had to face doubt and pressure in her deep rejection of the spirituality of fear and judgement which she encountered in the Carmelite community which she joined at the age of 15. It was in facing this especially that she showed her genius and it was in this especially that she entered a crucible of doubt through which she revealed to us the face of the God of merciful love.

The Discovery of Merciful Love

Thérèse, or to give her all her names, Marie-Françoise-Thérèse Martin entered the Discalced Carmelite convent at Lisieux on 9 April 1888 and was hitherto known as Sister Thérèse of the Child Jesus. Most young women at that age would be far from mature enough to make a decision for life and in fact the law of the Catholic Church forbade it. Thérèse knew in her own heart that she had arrived at full maturity through her Christmas grace at the age of 14 and so sure was she of what she saw as her vocation that, once she had received her father's consent, she felt strong and courageous enough to take her request to enter at 15 as far as Rome and Pope Leo XIII, then an old man. He could not intervene, but Thérèse kept on seeking entry and finally had her way, against it must be said all the laws of good sense and ecclesiastical prudence. However, we must not overlook the fact that not only Thérèse's father, but also her older sisters as well as her relatives, were by then supporting her request. Who could tell that as in the case of a certain Francis from Assisi, a certain Martin Luther from Germany or an Ignatius from Spain, Rome was being pushed very hard to open to something new that would change its whole history? A poem by John Bate entitled 'Whose Frailty' gives an imaginative colouring to the whole situation.

> Whose presence in that convent at all
> was one of those quiet scandals the Church
> is so good at living with; but what no one
> had reckoned was how much she could suffer,
> nor the sheer size of her capacity
> to look back cheerfully at torturers.
> In that poor house something began to fizz,
> its energy spread everywhere;
> with astonishing speed, we all heard of her,
> radiant among the nuances of that troop
> of women, whose frailty
> never deserted them, who grappled
> hopefully with holiness, a greasy pole
> they climbed and slid down every day; seeking

light, it was their wax fed a single flame,
illuminating all of them for ever.

Something did indeed begin to 'fizz', a new fermentation, a new
understanding of Christ and Christianity, of God and creation. The
face of God became changed because this being who was at once
total child and total woman saw that face differently. The face of
the God of wrath and righteousness changed into the radiant
countenance of the God of love and mercy. So it was that Thérèse
very solemnly dedicated her whole life and her sacrificial death to
merciful love; and her whole way of prayer became what she came
to call the Little Way of Spiritual Childhood. These descriptions
easily become clichés and even sentimentalized into flowery pictures
and statues all smiles and roses, and so it is essential, if we are to
understand Thérèse's adventures in prayer, to reach towards the
glorious and terrifying reality behind these pictures.

Let us first look at another picture of God in Jesus Christ, that
of Michelangelo in the celebrated picture recently restored of the
Last Judgement. The whole picture is dominated by the face and
figure of a man expressing judgement and condemnation. One is
lost in admiration at the superhuman genius that could express so
powerfully this superhuman figure in all its terrifying justice and
righteousness. One cannot say that in thus depicting the God of
wrath and justice the artist is in any way misrepresenting the God
of the Old Testament nor the God-man of the New Testament
who comes to judge the living and the dead, for this is a strand in
the New Testament revelation which cannot be ignored. This God
of condemnation, of terror and righteousness, was part of the
doctrine of God and Christ that Thérèse received from her teachers
in late nineteenth-century France and its deep Jansenism, which
tended to put this dark and terrifying strand of Christian doctrine
at the centre of its teaching. Yet it would seem that this darker
side of Christian teaching was almost totally ignored in the ambience
of the Martin family.

But Thérèse was to meet it in the Carmelite convent in the terrible
mixture of Carmelite and Ignatian spirituality which she was

expected to make her own, and it was to trouble her deeply as she set her feet ever more firmly on the straight and narrow path of Christian perfection. She was given certain books to read, including those of Teresa of Avila and John of the Cross who were the holy founders of the Carmelite sisterhood to which she belonged. But for all their light and fire these books, nevertheless, belonged to the same medieval world as that of the Christ of Judgement of Michelangelo. Thérèse never uttered one word of direct criticism of these holy founders of her Order yet when she read of Teresa's God as 'His Majesty' (*su majestad*), or of the many maxims and cautions of St John of the Cross writing in more robust and self-confident times, she must have been cast down and deeply troubled. This was not the God of love and mercy that she had come to know. She said nothing, but deep down and in her own way she was in revolt as if the blood of her military ancestors was planning another kind of assault of the Mount of Perfection.

Thérèse went through a kind of 'dark night' as she struggled in vain to follow the traditional Carmelite 'way' such as she found set forth in the *Life* and *The Interior Castle* of St Teresa of Avila, which we must remember was mediated in the French Carmels by the interpretations of a certain Cardinal Bérulle who, it would seem, rather lacked the lightness of touch and graceful gaiety of Teresa. So Thérèse, although endowed by nature with a sharp and enquiring mind, decided to 'shut the great tomes and open the Scriptures'. It was there that she found the kind of food her soul yearned for and in a moment of genial insight found what she came to call a 'Little Way' to travel to the Source of all goodness and all grace – the Little Way of Spiritual Childhood.

The domestic lift was coming into use in Thérèse's day and she saw in it the perfect metaphor for her 'little way' to God. She was too weak to climb the stairs or ladder of perfection as the books seemed to be demanding. If she remained a little child surely she would be taken up in his arms by the infinitely good all-fathering God: here Thérèse's own saintly father was the perfect transitional mediation. And surely, surely that's what the Saviour was saying in the gospel; surely that was already promised in the Old Testament!

What Thérèse found in the Scriptures was not only the exhortation by Jesus himself to become as a little child, but certain very physical personal images which she could take deeply into her affectivity, into that emotional-instinctual realm in which the great glowing beauty of human *castitas* (chastity) flowers. Among such scriptural invitations one especially captured the attention of Thérèse, and indeed her whole spirituality is in it. It is from Isaiah 66. 12–13: 'As one whom a mother caresses, so will I comfort you; you shall be carried at the breasts, and upon the knees they shall caress you.'[3]

These words and others of the same sense and genre did not simply reassure Thérèse and comfort her as indeed many have found them comforting and helpful, no; these words pierced the very depths of her young womanhood coming into flower, or rather gave her womanhood that seed from above by which her dedicated virginity became fruitful, unbelievably fruitful. She had discovered what she came to call her 'little way' along which she wished to lead thousands, millions of 'little souls'. We are at the heart of the paradox of greatness and littleness expressed with great force and beauty in the poetry of John of the Cross, which Thérèse knew well. But she did not receive her 'little way' from John. It came directly as a great shaft of light and fire straight from Isaiah, transforming her for ever. Of course she could only let this happen to her because she saw that it was at the centre of all that she drew into her meditative heart from the Scriptures.

The Little Way, 'a way that is very straight, very short, and totally new',[4] is utterly simple and easy to grasp. A child grasps it easily out of the depths of its own constant state of dependence. But how many children really accept the state of dependence with total trust in the adult world around them? And how many adults can fully *appropriate,* in adulthood, the dependence of childhood?

In fact if one looks carefully at the elevator metaphor again it is clear that, simple as it is, it yet hides a condition that in truth demands a truly heroic humility. For if one trusts oneself to the

---

3. Ibid., p. 208.
4. Ibid., p. 207.

elevator one must firmly turn one's back on the stairs. Not only that but the active decision to do this must be strong enough and dynamic enough to endure for the whole upward journey; otherwise, as Thérèse herself saw clearly, one tumbles into that Quietism in which receptivity becomes passivity.[5]

The 'little way' involved a total rejection of the God of terror and judgement in favour of the God of love and mercy, approached with the confidence and complete trust of a child assured of being loved. This childlike confidence could only be maintained against the dark terrors of life and death by a total maturity strong enough to hold firm against the whole world. So, paradoxically, the little way of total confidence in the merciful love of God demanded a strength of soul that could only come from a total purity of love that sought nothing for itself. The story of Thérèse is the story of a being who maintained this purity in the midst of all the terrors and shadows of the earth. Some of her companions in the Lisieux Carmel were inhibited and even paralysed with fear of a righteous and implacable God; in dealing with them Thérèse was forced to face the face of the God of wrath. She knew deep down that the final and most impregnable hiding place of Satan, the destroyer, was in God's sanctuary and in the very face of God. And we must ask how this young woman – bound to obey superiors and priests who felt they had to balance the God of love and mercy with the God of justice and wrath and severity – succeeded in escaping from them all.

All Christian theological systems try in various ways to balance the images of the God of justice and wrath against the images of the God of love and mercy, since both sets of images are to be found in the Holy Book which is the guide of all Christians everywhere. When the youthful, miraculously mature, Thérèse Martin entered Carmel, she handed herself over, at one and the same time, to a group of mentors, women and men, all of whom lived according to a personal balance of the traditional imagery of the God of love and mercy and the God of justice and wrath. They

---

5. See John Beevers, *Storm of Glory* (London: Sheed & Ward, 1952), p. 172.

all looked back to the great Carmelite founders of the sixteenth-century and to another sixteenth-century Spaniard, Ignatius of Loyola, and his Spiritual Exercises. Almost all the priests who came to the convent to preach the annual retreat were Jesuits trained in the Spiritual Exercises, according to what has been perhaps one of the most thorough and efficient systems of spiritual training the world has ever seen. Already two of Thérèse's sisters had absorbed this training, and subsequently kept their poise and balance through-out a long life. There seemed no reason why their young sister should not follow in their footsteps keeping in step with the great godly army of Ignatius, especially as this young postulant, all sweetness and smiles (hiding, it must be admitted, a delicious sense of humour and a very hidden talent for mimicry), seemed so malleable and obedient and was so clearly anxious to keep in step in every little detail. Indeed, she seemed absurdly anxious to do what she was told by her prioress and mistress of novices.

Yet Thérèse all the time was deeply in revolt and had just one weapon, one martial art to express her revolt. It was one of the most powerful of all weapons: the quiet deep constant grief of the pure of heart. She could not be happy as long as the face of the God of merciful love was in any way shadowed by any image of the God of justice and wrath, the God of fear. But none of her mentors either within the convent or from outside could give her this assurance. They could not understand what this discovery of the 'little way' meant to her.

Then a strange thing happened. The Jesuit priest who was to preach the annual retreat in October 1891 suddenly fell ill and could not come. Rather desperately, a local Franciscan named Fr. Alexis Prou was called in. He was reported to be a rather inferior type, or as the Carmelite Sisters delicately put it 'he was supposed to do good to great sinners but not to religious souls'. In the event Thérèse tells us 'he was appreciated only by me in the community'. Let us listen to the story as Thérèse tells it:

> At the time I was having great interior trials of all kinds, even to the point of asking myself whether heaven really existed. I felt disposed

to say nothing of my interior dispositions since I didn't know how to express them, but I had hardly entered the confessional when I felt my soul expand. After speaking only a few words, I *was understood* in a marvellous way and my soul was like a book in which this priest read better than I did myself. He launched me full sail upon the waves of *confidence and love* which so strongly attracted me, but upon which I dared not advance.[6]

Thérèse spoke with Fr. Alexis once and only once. But once was enough, for Fr. Alexis not only approved her 'little way' but urged her to launch forth fully and confidently along that pathway. She accepted this and never looked back.

There is something moving as well as significant about the image of Francis of Assisi reaching his hand across the centuries to this young woman whose ambition was to be a burning radiant love in the heart of the Church, something moving too about that mysterious writer whom we can only name as Second Isaiah reaching the heart of this same young woman and her purity and greatness of soul from farther away still in the human story, as if time stood still in face of the love of God in the heart of a woman.

These words that pierced the heart of Thérèse and illuminated her pathway were couched in the delicate and tender images of childhood and motherhood. They might have become senti-mentalized into childishness in another kind of affectivity. In Thérèse they pierced the heart and became creative in an affectivity that was totally open to the Source and never fell back into that well of selfishness, sensuality and self-satisfaction by which pietism sometimes closes in on itself, and spiritual childhood can become spritual childishness. In Thérèse the discovery of the 'little way' did not turn her away from any of the demands of sacrificial greatness of soul and she was to change the whole way of feeling of a Church grown cold and set in its ways and desperately in need of the new Pentecost that was to come upon it 70 years on. Then she would influence the shift towards a more gentle and heart-

6. Clarke, *Story of a Soul,* pp. 173–4.

centred sprituality in the Catholic Church of Vatican II, and a more ecumenical Christianity that looked to the world of the heart in all the great religions.

The Little Way and the Test of the Everyday

Part of the difficulty of understanding the 'little way' of Thérèse is that it is all too easy to grasp it, especially if it is seen as an opting for the God of love rather than the God of justice and wrath. First it must be realized that the option for the God of love is a simplification and that we must find a place for justice as well and the ancient virtue of *vindication* and the things that are said about sin and choice in the Spiritual Exercises of Ignatius of Loyola. But, more important, we must realize that it is one thing to accept an insight in a general way and quite another thing to live out this insight in the details and difficulties of everyday life, that *terribile quotidiano* of which a pope speaks talking in fact of Thérèse and her 'little way'. Indeed the 'little way' is no more than a more or less helpful pious thought 'here today and gone tomorrow', unless we tease it out carefully in its everyday fulfilment in practice.

Thérèse at 15 was well confirmed in that maturity which, mystically or miraculously, had come to her at the age of 14. She knew that in entering Carmel she was entering a battlefield and indeed had a self-image as a latter-day Joan of Arc. It is worth contrasting this with the common understanding or misunderstanding of a young woman 'taking the veil' as expressed in a well-known poem of Gerard Manley Hopkins entitled 'Heaven-Haven: A nun takes the veil':[7]

> I have desired to go
> Where springs not fail,
> To fields where flies no sharp and sided hail
> And a few lilies blow.

---

7. *The Poems of Gerard Manley Hopkins*, eds W. H. Gardner and N. H. Mackenzie, (Oxford University Press, 1982), p. 19.

And I have asked to be
Where no storms come,
Where the green swell is in the havens dumb,
And out of the swing of the sea.

It must be said that Hopkins wrote quite another kind of poem when he in his own way had come to understand the true dimensions of a full religious commitment. But here we are concerned with the contrast between that heaven-haven of which Hopkins spoke and the truth of convent life as Thérèse understood it and experienced it in the everyday of an enclosed contemplative convent.

Thérèse should have survived the physical rigours of a Carmelite rule of life as did her three sisters who each lived to a lively old age. She was a healthy young woman, well endowed with that common sense which is part of the maturity that came to her suddenly at the age of 14. Yet she allowed herself to freeze because she never once asked for an extra blanket, either directly or through her novice mistress. She took whatever she was given in the refectory and it quickly became known that scraps and left overs of dubious freshness were accepted by her and eaten without a murmur. Ordinary common sense, of which Thérèse had a large store, should have told her to remedy these situations in a quiet way.

But apart from and in contrast to ordinary common sense there is a heroic common sense which was at the centre of the 'little way'. This is the everyday attitude of the child who has complete confidence in its parents to receive everything from them. Not that there is a daily expectation of miracles but rather a daily, hourly, assurance that, in St Paul's words, 'all things will work together unto good for those who love God (Rom. 8.28).' The young Thérèse shivered through the cold Normandy nights, for she was constitutionally hypersensitive to cold, when ordinary common sense told her to ask for more blankets, but the common sense of that cross, which the Fathering-Mothering Source had given her, told her to continue to bear it as it came to her. We shall have to look more fully into this attitude, but now it is well to look at 'little way' as it affected Thérèse's relationships with the people she met in the convent.

Let us recall the vital distinction between insight and habitual attitude or virtue, a distinction that goes back to Aristotle and Plato and is central to Thomas Aquinas and the great medieval moralists, a distinction, moreover which featured largely in the moral teaching of the New Testament, in the parable of the Sower, for instance. The insight at the heart of the 'little way' is easy to grasp and after the publication of the *Story of a Soul* many people took it thankfully to themselves, as indeed Thérèse meant them to do. It affirmed the way of love and trust in one's relationship with the Source as against the way of fear and judgement, and this was very helpful for people of real goodwill. But for people who accepted it lightly and superficially, it simply became an aid to their spiritual superficiality.

The 'little way' as a realistic, practical, habitual attitude is altogether another matter and is quite overwhelming in its demands, as it was for Thérèse herself. The *Story of a Soul* is at once the simplest and the most difficult of all the great Christian mystical texts. A child can follow it; indeed if the child in us has died we cannot follow it. The most profound philosopher, the most far-sighted theologian will find opening up all around far horizons almost beyond our ken, challenges which force us to agree with T. S. Eliot that 'the only wisdom we can hope to acquire is the wisdom of humility: Humility is endless'.[8] Let us look at some of the applications of the 'little way' as Thérèse worked it out in the details of her everyday life with those around her.

Mother Marie de Gonzague, the Prioress of Lisieux Carmel, was a strange, self-deluded, autocratic woman. She probably noticed the young novice's independence of mind and firmness of character and something within the older woman seems to have admired this and yet wanted to test it and even break it. Thérèse tells us that she came to be very thankful for the wisdom of Mother Gonzague that made sure she was not spoiled by soft treatment. In more ordinary language the all-powerful, ever-present Prioress gave the teenage novice 'one hell of a time'. Thérèse stood up to

---

8. *Four Quartets*, 'East Coker'.

this like a truly valiant woman and in time became Mother Gonzague's favourite confidante and firm support.

Sister St Peter was an old arthritic nun who had become very crotchety and set in her ways and was not quite able to get around on her own. Thérèse took on the difficult and entirely thankless job of steering Sister St Peter each day from the chapel to the refectory, full of complaints to the last, and then – the 'little way's' signature this – when it was all done gave Sister St Peter her most radiant smile. One does not understand Thérèse if one does not see that this smile was utterly genuine and yet laden with irony!

But it was in her relations with a certain younger very difficult Sister that we get the clearest glimpse of the 'little way' in its everyday realization. Here is how Thérèse tells the story:

> There is in the Community a Sister who has the faculty of displeasing me in everything, in her ways, her words, her character, everything seems *very disagreeable* to me. And still, she is a holy religious who must be very pleasing to God. Not wishing to give in to the natural antipathy I was experiencing, I told myself that charity must not consist in feelings but in works; then I set myself to doing for this Sister what I would do for the person I loved the most. Each time I met her I prayed to God for her, offering Him all her virtues and merits. I felt this was pleasing to Jesus, for there is no artist who doesn't love to receive praise for his works, and Jesus, the Artist of souls, is happy when we don't stop at the exterior, but, penetrating into the inner sanctuary where He chooses to dwell, we admire its beauty. I wasn't content simply with praying very much for this Sister who gave me so many struggles, but I took care to render her all the services possible, and when I was tempted to answer her back in a disagreeable manner, I was content with giving her my most friendly smile, and with changing the subject of the conversation, for the Imitation says: *'It is better to leave each one in his own opinion than to enter into arguments.'*
>
> Frequently, when I was not at recreation (I mean during the work periods) and had occasion to work with this Sister, I used to run away like a deserter whenever my struggles became too violent. As she was absolutely unaware of my feelings for her, never did she suspect the motives for my conduct and she remained convinced

that her character was very pleasing to me. One day at recreation she asked in almost these words: 'Would you tell me, Sister Thérèse of the Child Jesus, what attracts you so much towards me; everytime you look at me, I see you smile?' Ah! what attracted me was Jesus hidden in the depths of her soul; Jesus who makes sweet what is most bitter. I answered that I was smiling because I was happy to see her (it is understood that I did not add that this was from a spiritual standpoint).[9]

Most communities, whether religious or secular, contain at least one such person, and we could almost define a saint as the person (the only one usually) who manages to put up with them. But we must be careful here. Thérèse does not really pass judgement on this difficult Sister, rather does she look beneath the surface to what without irony she calls this Sister's 'virtues and merits', and she tells us that when it all became too much for her she simply fled.

This little story has a strange ending. The Sister in question read the *Story of a Soul* without having the least suspicion that she was the Sister in question. At last a priest pushed further than he could bear by this Sister's arrogance and self-satisfaction told her what everybody knew, that *she* was the Sister who so egregiously tested the patience of Thérèse, and everybody else. The Sister then, coming to the reality of the situation, asked pardon of the whole community, in a typical Thérèsian transformation. In all this we may perhaps begin to see, as John Bate saw, that neither Thérèse nor any great spiritual light can be said to stand alone. 'We live in each others shadow' says a Gaelic proverb, and Thérèse, for all her greatness, does not stand alone in isolation from the prayers and griefs of her companions. That is one reason why the 'little way' is for everybody as a calling and a vision among men and women everywhere. To realize it in practice however and in the detail of everyday living involves indeed a 'lifetime's death in love'.[10]

---

9. Clarke, *Story of a Soul*, pp. 222–3.

10. T. S. Eliot, *Four Quartets*, 'The Dry Salvages', *Collected Poems of T. S. Eliot* (London: Faber and Fabe, 1980).

The Little Way as a Mystical Way

At the centre of the spirituality of the two great sixteenth-century Carmelite mystics, Teresa of Avila and John of the Cross, was the distinction between two kinds of prayer, active prayer on the one hand, connected with meditation and the recitation of the Divine Office, and passive or receptive prayer, on the other hand, in which the Divine Other takes over in subtle, wonderful and sometimes paradoxical ways, and where very often the ordinary exercises of meditation become almost impossible. I have said that it is only within this context that the word 'mystical' has meaning, in this tradition, though both Teresa and John preferred the word 'supernatural', as connoting something coming from the uncreated living Source to the human heart and mind.

All this has been said more than once, yet it is so central to the whole adventure in prayer, in its active and receptive dimensions, that we must pause and reflect on it once more. The theme of mystical or receptive prayer runs like a silver stream through the whole of the New Testament, a somewhat hidden stream that shines forth brilliantly now and then. It issues forth, for instance, in a famous passage that accompanies the two presentations of the Lord's Prayer in Matthew, chapters 6 and 7, and in Luke, chapter 11. The passage reads at Luke 11.9, 'And I tell you, Ask and it will be given you; seek, and you will find; knock, and it will be opened to you' (RSV).

Staying with the text as it is presented by St Luke, whose whole Gospel is centred on prayer (though the theme is central in all four evangelists and in St Paul), let us note two important points. In the first place there is the parable of the grumbling householder and the importunate borrower, which seems to say: Keep on praying beyond all reason, beyond all commonsense; you must keep at it. Secondly, and even more importantly, what you get in receptive prayer, is not necessarily what you have been asking for in active prayer but rather that which alone is totally precious: the Holy Spirit (11.13). This is the rain which is the Fourth Watering of Teresa, and the living flame of love of John of the Cross.

The question that arises for us here is: where, if at all, is this flowing, this receptive mystical flowing in Thérèse of Lisieux. Is she not rather the perfect Martha serving and doing, rather than the receptive Mary sitting at the feet of the Lord?

Those who have studied the Carmelite way of prayer and the distinction made by the sixteenth-century Carmelites between active or ordinary prayer and receptive or mystical prayer, in which it seems to the supplicant that God takes over, have sometimes come to distinguish and contrast Thérèse of Lisieux with Teresa of Avila and John of the Cross. *They* were taken into the mystical way; *she* remained at the level of ordinary active prayer. Over against this, other students of Carmelite mysticism are quite convinced that Thérèse in her short life was brought into the heights and depths of mystical prayer and so lived and died in a deep state of receptivity. Yet she tells us that her habitual state was one of distressing aridity.

In order to understand the range and depth of receptive or mystical prayer in the prayer-experience of Thérèse it is necessary not only to distinguish carefully between ordinary prayer, by way of meditation, and that receptive prayer in which one is made as it were mute and helpless in 'waiting on God', but also between the impact or reception of the mystical divine flowing into the *emotional* level on the one hand, and on the other its presence and power at the level of the *will,* at a level far deeper and more lasting than all emotion. The transforming and purifying fire at the level of the heart (i.e. the emotions) percolates or descends to the level of the will as the power of decision and the ground of the virtues of heroic fortitude and steadfast loyalty to the Divine Lover and Beloved. This is the pure gold of prayer, and we find this in marvellous abundance in the story of Thérèse of Lisieux.

What is common to Teresa, John and Thérèse is the greatest of all the adventures in prayer, which they variously describe as Spiritual Marriage, union of all the faculties, and total dedication to merciful love. In all cases there is a deep conflagration expressed as light and fire at the affective or emotional level – the level of the heart – but this experience of fire and light is rooted in the will and shines forth in the great virtues of faith, hope and charity, in charity especially as the total service of God and neighbour. It is in this last, especially in its everyday practicality, that Thérèse is truly glorious in her patient uncomplaining service of her most difficult and demanding companions. This, above all, is the flower and fruit of that union with God as merciful love that is at the deep centre of her mystical prayer. No mere asceticism could achieve that in its living, everyday glow and graciousness. The encounter with the Supreme Being of purity and love has at its centre a strong missionary impetus to share this love with everybody, what Thérèse and some other mystics call 'a thirst for souls'. This missionary élan or impetus is not something added on; it is at the very centre of this Spiritual Marriage of the seeking soul or spirit and the all-giving, all-loving Source that it encounters receptively.

The spiritual union variously written about by all three Carmelite mystics, and indeed common to all mystics of every tradition, non-Christian as well as Christian, brings with it a kind of seal or signature which is universal and unmistakable to those who have any deep understanding of mystical prayer. I call this *substantial joy* and I tend to link it with what has been called the perfect joy of St Francis of Assisi. The story goes that Francis and a companion were trudging wearily along a winter road at evening, buffeted by wind and rain, and very hungry, when suddenly the companion asked Francis, 'Brother Francis what is this perfect joy of which you sometimes speak?' And Francis said '*This* is nearly perfect joy, but it would be indeed perfect joy if we were refused shelter tonight and cast out of doors even by those whom we think of as our friends. That, Brother, would be perfect joy in its acceptance.'[11]

This perfect joy is always present, no matter how hidden and unfelt, in those who have received that inner flowing of the Holy Spirit which is mystical prayer. It tends to break into song and dance and sometimes expresses itself in poetry and we know that Thérèse wrote poems of great fervour and exaltation even when her spirit was plunged in darkness.

---

11. See T. Okey, tr., *The 'Little Flowers, Life and 'Mirror' of St Francis* (London: J. M. Dent & Sons), pp. 15–16.

The poetry of Thérèse of Lisieux is not taken seriously by historians and critics of French literature, as is that of John of the Cross, who stands at the very summit of Spanish poetry, being declared patron of Spanish poets in 1952. Yet some very intelligent and erudite French writers such as Guy Gaucher and Jean Guitton do take her seriously as a poet. There is in fact a *hidden voice* in her poems, some of the later ones especially, which, like the blinded nightingale, sound all the more triumphantly beautiful for their captive pain and loneliness. The poetry shows how triumphantly that 'perfect joy' of St Francis was fulfilled in her, and for all of us who make even the least contact with Thérèse, a little of this anointing adheres to us.

The Oblation to Merciful Love

St Thérèse of the Child Jesus, who died at age 24 and is now being hailed as a Doctor of the Universal Church, awakened in her early years to the 'infinitely gentle, infinitely suffering' Being,[12] whom she knew as the 'good God' and the suffering Christ and, finally as Merciful Love. All very easy, it might seem, yet Thérèse, born into a military tradition, had to fight and to suffer every inch of the way, and she took Joan of Arc, the virgin soldier, as her inspiration and sister-in-arms. To understand or at least approach to an understanding of this campaign and its victorious outcome we must ponder on the way in which *knowing* reaches towards that assimilation in which the being who knows has to be united with the Being that is known. In order that the infinitely gentle Being that is the hidden God can come out of concealment as the *Logos* that shows itself as glory in the human world, it must find a receptivity that is always opening towards infinity, emerging from its natural finitude to an infinity that is beyond the natural level.

The genius of Thérèse Martin consisted in this: that she saw and felt to her depths that this infinity is at once an infinity of

---

12. T. S. Eliot, 'Preludes', iv.

greatness and an infinity of littleness. It seems that this realization (though not in those words of course), came to Thérèse like an Archimedean Eureka, a thunderbolt from the skies of meditation on, or near, the 9th of June, 1895, when as she left the choir (the place of communal meditation) she pulled her sister Céline along by the hand to share with her a great secret. The sharing came in the form of a request that her sister join with her in making an Oblation of herself as a victim to the Merciful Love of God.

The notion of victimhood is close to the notion of sacrifice. Sacrifice as a central notion in the relationship between humanity and its divine Source goes back to the origins of Judaeo-Christian religious consciousness; the same or a similar notion is the one found in all or most ancient and primal religions. The Hebrew Scriptures adopted by Christianity as the old or pre-Christian agreement, Covenant or Testament between the Creator God and the human race created by God are full of the presence of sacrifice and sacrifices, and of the need for the *purification* of sacrifice, away from the materialistic multiplication of animal victims to the spirituality of prayer and praise. There is, moreover, the crucial appearance of Melchizedek, the King of Peace, who is the archetypal priest offering the 'clean oblation' of bread and wine. Then in the fullness of time the anointed, the Christed One comes, not of human seed yet born of a human mother. The man is at once the Lamb of God, the true lamb of sacrifice and the true bread that came down from heaven to take on himself all human iniquity ('the iniquity of us all', said Isaiah) and undo 'the twist in the cosmos', in the words of the Fourth Gospel usually translated as 'take away the sin of the world' (*he hamartia tou kosmou*: John 1.29) Man has freely connived with an evil power that holds the world captive; and only the human prayer of sacrificial love can release mankind. That was and is the work of the Saviour-Christ.

We are here in the outskirts of a great mystery and there are two ways of proceeding from here into the vital centre of the mystery: there is, firstly, the way of the theologian, which works through intelligence and understanding, and this demands a great deal of reading and reflection; there is, secondly, and alternatively, the way of the mystic, which works through feeling, insight and intimation, and goes forward through prayer and meditation. The theologian must analyse very carefully in Scripture and in the ongoing meditation and self-understanding of the people of God as it tries to find 'space' and 'place' for the call to transformation and divinization. We are in the world of depth theology and those theological 'tomes' which Thérèse felt she had to avoid.

In place of these 'tomes' Thérèse relied on her personal, instinctual discovery of the love of God and the God of love. She constantly, deeply and poignantly experienced this love around her in her own family, especially in her very present father, who because of her much-loved mother's death, became at one and the same time father and mother even when her quite remarkable elder sisters took in turn the role of mother. In these circumstances the young Thérèse could have become selfish and thoroughly spoiled. But the father's hand was, for all its gentleness, firm as a rock and always pointing beyond to the all-fathering Source. The older sisters followed suit in a very feminine way that the father readily obeyed, so that, for instance, Louis Martin could take his little daughter for a walk only when her elder sisters allowed it. This sometimes involved disappointment for an eager lively little girl of four or five years, but she knew that her father was disappointed also; thus the connection between love and suffering was established and was sown as a seed that would grow with the years. Thus, a place, a receptive human centre, was being prepared for that 'infinitely gentle, infinitely suffering' Being.

So gradually, as she grew in the understanding of life, Thérèse began to glimpse the vital link between love and suffering, between the infinitely gentle Presence all around her to be received, taken in, loved beyond all else, somehow calling at times for the sacrifice of those joys and comforts to which her childhood will tended to attach itself. She loved the natural world in all its variety of colours and forms, in all its amplitude of earth and sky and sea, but she felt no less constantly and insistently the call of a great Presence *through* all this and somehow *beyond* all this. As she grew towards womanhood and began to develop a lively imagination and a love of words and rhythms, Thérèse began to 'sing along' with the beauty of life, but a beauty always opening up to eternal horizons. This making of songs was to stay with her all through her short life lived in an enclosed contemplative convent.

In a sense these poems were the verses of an imaginative schoolgirl, mere 'prentice' piece. But in another sense they were the 'extempore effusions' (to use Wordsworth's term, describing one of his finest poems) of a completely mature woman. For, as we have seen, total womanhood – wise, caring, coping, mothering the world around and the world beyond, had descended on Thérèse like a thunderbolt just prior to her fourteenth birthday. And whoever has really studied the matter carefully can only exclaim, 'What a woman!' Coping serenely with a superior acting day in day out like an unbalanced prima donna, coping so well, so lightly, obediently, joyfully, even hilariously that the same superior became her fervent admirer in time; surviving no less serenely the fire-tipped arrows of her fellow novices, who had been placed quite unfairly and irregularly in her charge who was the youngest of them, yet who very, very gently told them the truth about themselves quite fearlessly; dying at age 24 in great agony of body and darkness of mind, yet 'carrying' with total poise and granite patience, the whole community that clustered round her, making sure that her last look was directed towards the Mother Superior *as* Mother Superior; then beyond that last look an ecstatic upwards glow as she turned towards the Being she loved with her whole bridal heart. From being an immature girl full of tears and fears Thérèse had suddenly become the human bride and consort of divinity become man.

Thérèse had discovered love and had begun to have glimpses of the unity of love and suffering: it was by the light of this insight that, not yet 16 years of age, she entered the bleak and demanding world of an enclosed Carmelite convent. The Carmelite convent in Lisieux was every bit as bleak and demanding as Thérèse expected, though the community was rather more than she could have expected: the presence there of her two older sisters, whom she dearly loved, made the situation more rather than less difficult, for she felt that she should absolutely refuse to give or be given any special treatment. But, as the poet John Bate says: 'What no one/had reckoned was how much she could suffer,/nor the sheer size of her capacity/to look back cheerfully at torturers.' Her course in Carmel is a mystery and must remain a mystery, though the present Carmel of Lisieux has published eight large brilliantly edited and beautifully produced volumes of her 'works'.[13] But perhaps we can make a first connection with this mystery by looking at a little paragraph from the testimony of one of Thérèse's novices given to the process that preceded her beatification. It reads as follows:

> One day when I was in her room she said to me in a tone of voice which I cannot reproduce: 'God is not loved enough! And yet he is so good and kind . . . Oh, I wish I could die!' And she began to sob. Not understanding what it was to love God so vehemently, I looked on in amazement and wondered what kind of an extraordinary creature I was standing in front of.[14]

Sister Thérèse of the Child Jesus was indeed an extraordinary being but – and this paradox has become rather a cliché – most of all extraordinary in her ordinariness, within which she was to become almost invisible, so much so that some of her companions said that there was nothing to be said of her by way of obituary. Yes she had kept the Rule and lived her life but had she really *done* anything? What she had done was to transform radically the Christian mystical horizon, so quietly that she made no noise, no stir at all.

In her discovery of the 'little way' *La petite voie*, Thérèse had glimpsed or awakened towards the first of three insights that for her illuminated the mystical horizon. The other two were not long in coming: the little way of spiritual childhood meant for Thérèse,

---

13. *Editions Critique des Oeuvres Complètes* (Paris: Editions du Cerf – Desclee de Brouwer, 1992).

14. Christopher O'Mahoney, ed. and tr., *St Thérèse of Lisieux by those who knew her: Testimonies from the process of beatification* (Dublin: Veritas, 1975) p. 261.

towards the end of the nineteenth century, the rediscovery in all its freshness and newness of St Paul's discovery at the dawn of Christianity, of the central paradox of strength in weakness and weakness in strength. This discovery is most clearly and powerfully expressed in the twelfth chapter of the Second Letter to the Corinthians which culminates in the statement at verse 10: 'When I am weak then I am strong.' But it is one thing to *grasp* this statement; it is another thing to *live* it. For the human spirit on the road towards the mystical horizon of transformation has to contend most of all with Satan, the Adversary whose main weapon is accusation, and who indeed is often called the Accuser by the spiritual masters. This situation is not simply an unhappy accident; it is the divinely ordained way of purification and ultimate divinization. For the 'endless' humility of the human spirit becoming more and more receptive and emptied of vain self-assertiveness, must, and this is really and truly a 'must', be balanced and steadied on its course, *sicut gigas ad currendam viam,* by that true, unbreakable self-esteem of the child of God *as* child *of God,* God who is infinite in all things. To *live* this for Thérèse meant everyday rejoicing at her own inadequacy and everyday rejoicing in the great Presence become intimately present within Thérèse herself. So it was that those who knew her best in the everyday found that she was particularly lively and cheerful after somebody had especially humiliated her.

The third and culminating insight that illumined the mystical horizon of Thérèse was what she called the Act of Oblation as a victim to Merciful Love. At that time, under the influence of that Jansenism that emphasized human depravity in a measure not unlike Calvinism, some dedicated contemplatives offered themselves heroically to be victims of Divine Justice, thus carrying, after the example of Christ, the sins of the world on their shoulders. This sometimes entailed a kind of joyless and censorious righteousness which Thérèse and her family, her father especially, rejected and set themselves against. It was primarily because she did not strive after this high and heroic asceticism of self-denial that most of her community entirely overlooked Thérèse as a candidate for sanctity. But, as Thérèse realized in a moment of profound insight, it was possible to offer oneself as a victim to the *merciful love* of God as truly – indeed more truly! – than to the justice of God. For she saw the Source is *all-giving*, is, as it were, in the pain of giving, and to open oneself to this excess of giving is to accept total transformation into the fire of divine love.

An incident from Thérèse's childhood sheds light on this. Leonie, one of the elder Martin sisters, was leaving childhood behind and was offering Thérèse a box of scraps to pick and choose from. Thérèse said 'I choose the whole lot!' She goes on to say,

> Only a childish trait, perhaps, but in a sense it's been the key to my whole life. Later on, when the idea of religious perfection came within my horizon, I realised at once that there was no reaching sanctity unless you were prepared to suffer a great deal, to be always on the look-out for something higher still, and to forget yourself. There were plenty of degrees in spiritual advancement, and every soul was free to answer our Lord's invitation by doing a little for him, or by doing a lot for him; in fact, he gave it a *choice* between various kinds of self-sacrifice he wanted it to offer. And then, as in babyhood, I found myself crying out: 'My God, I choose the whole lot. No point in becoming a Saint by halves. I'm not afraid of suffering for your sake; the only thing I'm afraid of is clinging to my own will. Take it, I want the whole lot, everything whatsoever that is your will for me."[15]

'My God, I choose the whole lot.' But this choice is also a choice to *receive* the whole lot. Yet Thérèse knew well, as Luther knew well, that all is grace, all is gift; but she also understood, that a gift is not truly given until it is received, and that this involved suffering, great and constant suffering, the suffering of the creature being transformed into the creator, the suffering of the sacrifice of nature to open up the receptive space for supernature. Luther's Tower experience, which is the hinge of all that is best in Reformation theology, was an experience of God's all-giving goodness breaking

---

15. *Autobiography of a Saint*, ed. R. Knox (London: Harvill Press, 1958), p. 51.

through all conditionalities, legalities and human mediations, a vision of divine goodness already expressed by St Paul in the letter to the Galatians and the letter to the Romans. Luther's vision of God's free gift (*sola gratia*) and total givingness needs completion by Thérèse's understanding of *receptivity*, total childlike receptivity. From the beginning Thérèse understood that this receptivity involved suffering and that the measure of suffering is the measure of receptivity. All that she needed to 'choose all' was the *will* to suffer all. So she decided to hand her will over to God. But already God is the God not of justice but of love. She stands with enormous trembling courage right in the path of the mighty waves of divine love. Her will stands firm but only through her total offering of that same will to the divine will supporting her in the suffering of total transformation. This is indeed the way of Eliot's 'wisdom of humility' which Luther could not quite reach but which Thérèse reached knowing that 'humility is endless'.

This was the kind of victimhood Thérèse could understand; this was the kind of victimhood that her rather endearing elder sister Marie of the Sacred Heart could understand, even though the idea of victimhood appalled Marie and she said so in her customary honest way. Thérèse succeeded in persuading her otherwise, and she did in fact make the oblation though she stipulated that a reference to the divine heart should be included. We are in a world of symbols not uncommon in the world of Catholic devotion, ancient and modern. What is special to Thérèse is the extent, unique in modern times, to which these symbols of fire and transformation become realized in the mode of total receptivity, joyful in the midst of suffering.

The French philosopher, Jean Guitton defines Thérèse's special genius as a mystic and teacher of mysticism by what he calls 'effortless effort'.[16] It is that total receptivity which is to be carefully distinguished from both pure activity and pure passivity, being at once active and passive. Pure activity would be possessive and selfish;

---

16. See Jean Guitton, *The Spiritual Genius of Saint Thérèse of Lisieux,* tr. F. Leng (Burns & Oates, 1997), p. 44–51.

pure passivity would be that Quietism that refuses to accept the 'infinitely suffering' Being that Thérèse received fully into her own life, so that she shone forth both as infinitely gentle and as infinitely suffering. She became a living mirror of the holy countenance described in Isaiah 53, being not only Thérèse of the *Child Jesus* but also Thérèse of the *Holy Face*.

If we are to make any attempt at grasping the vast dimensions, the infinity of the mystical horizons of this receptivity, we must try to envisage the horizons of Christian virginity in which the human as receptive dares to equal the divine, the eternal, the inconceivable as grace and giving.

The Adventure of Cosmic Motherhood

We have seen that the 'Christmas Grace' of 1886, when Thérèse was on the eve of her fourteenth birthday (2 January, 1887) was of crucial importance in her development. She had passed in a single moment from rather weepy and distressing girlhood to the full maturity of womanhood, becoming a centre of mothering love and care. Typically, she, who already understood the redemption and the fatherhood-motherhood of Christ, took for the first child of her cosmic motherhood a hardened and angry murderer. In the wake of this first mothering, Thérèse found herself mothering her whole family and especially the religious family which she joined at the age of 15. In taking the name of Thérèse of the Child Jesus, it was understood that she had given her life to the total virginal contemplation of the divine childhood – indeed, in this kind of statement 'total' means 'virginal' and 'virginal' means total, and does not exclude marriage, though it does exclude all cheapening of the holy force of sexuality.

It is not easy to take hold of all this, not only because of her youth but more especially because we live in a time in which celibacy-virginity, little understood at the best of times, is hardly understood at all, and seen as barren and unnatural. The topic has come up already, when we looked at St Teresa, but since it is of central importance it will be helpful to look at it again and this time with special reference to Thérèse of Lisieux. For Thérèse not only chose the way of celibate virginity for herself but in fact was one of five sisters who all made this choice.

Moreover it is clear that for Thérèse at least this choice was not made through a lack of understanding of the laws of life and of human procreation. She told her sister Pauline that she had come to understand human procreation 'from watching the flowers and the birds'. And she added that all this matter of procreation was chosen by God and very good. 'Marriage,' she added 'is a very fine thing for those whom God has called to it.'[17]

Among those 'called' to marriage through the Christian sacrament of marriage as a channel of divine grace were Zélie Guerin and Louis Martin, Thérèse's mother and father, both of whom separately had sought to be celibates in religious orders. After marriage Zélie and Louis remained celibate for several years until a priest advised them otherwise. It is quite clear that for the Martins, intercourse was for procreation alone, as in the Book of Tobias accepted by the Catholic Church as part of the Bible. It would seem that their whole relationship was held towards God in a constant movement of prayer and that each in different yet similar ways accepted the cross of Christ in ways both daunting and terrifying. We are looking in on a situation where we are almost forced to tread very delicately. There is no reason to suppose that the marriage relationship between Louis and Zélie Martin was lacking in human tenderness, yet it seems certain that tenderness as well as the deep joys of motherhood and fatherhood, as also the deep griefs, were held within the God-centred vows that constituted for them the graced sacrament of marriage. That first dedication to the Source which led them towards a monastery and a convent became fulfilled in a marriage full of prayer, dedication and sacrifice.

All this upward streaming of the whole instinctual-emotional level in her parents' marriage flowed through the marvellously fruitful

---

17. O'Mahoney, *St Thérèse*, p. 58.

virginity of Thérèse in her 'espousals' and 'marriage' with the crucified and glorified Jesus Christ. Through this dedicated virginity Thérèse became in her first maturity a cosmic mother. This was sealed by her profession as a Carmelite, yet at that stage some of her children were already around her, notably the penitent Pranzini and the prodigal son, Hyacinthe Loyson, for so she saw him motherwise. She soon took within her womb all who came her way seeking spiritual mothering near and far. Being 'a mother of souls' was no mere metaphor for her, nor did she, brave woman that she was, underestimate the cost of such birthing and such nurturing.

In all this Thérèse is the Bride and Christ is the Bridegroom and the love between Bride and Bridegroom is as fruitful as it is deep: the metaphor is made to work and passes into analogy, that is to say a deeper reality at a higher level; the analogy is made to work so much that there is not only the question of its reflecting the best of human physical mothering but rather is there the question of the best of human physical mothering reflecting *it* in the *terribili quotidiano* of the 'little way'.

Thérèse was a woman deeply and wonderfully open to the masculine and here it is necessary to look closely at her relationship with her father. He was indeed a very holy man, a very monkish and dedicated man, yet he was a very real man, as much a soldier as a monk, an explorer who loved travel and journeys, quite fearless, it would seem and with that rare courage by which one faces one's own confusion and mental dissolution. For Thérèse he was her 'king' and she was his 'queen', a playful relationship to be sure, but with that playfulness that, Plato tells us, best goes hand in hand with deep seriousness.

But to understand her feminine as relational, as indeed defined by this relationship, as the true masculine is related to the feminine and defined by this relationship, we have to look at Thérèse's letters to her two missionary brothers as she called them. Here we find an unexpected tenderness reaching toward the 'holy touch' the *hagion philema* of St Paul (1 Cor. 16.20). Very delicately, almost invisible in its delicacy, this woman gives to the man that glory which only a woman can give and without which a man normally cannot really reflect the glory of God, the *'doxa theou'* in which, as in Genesis 1.27, man and woman *together* image forth the pulse of creation, increasing and multiplying to fill the whole cosmos.

Two men especially gave Thérèse that seminal spark which her whole feminine receptivity yearned for in the mode of psychic or spiritual receptivity. These were the Franciscan, Fr. Alexis Prou, whom she encountered at her all-important retreat at the age of 18, on the threshold of full womanhood, and the Carmelite long dead but very present to all Carmelites as the holy father John of the Cross. It was in her last Gethsemane phase especially that she, in the depths of her dark night, came closest to his dauntless loving spirit.

Her single encounter with Fr. Alexis was clearly an encounter with a presence that she desperately needed. It seems to have depended more on what he was than what he said, and it entered seminally into her very depths. 'I felt disposed to say nothing of my interior dispositions', she tells us, 'since I didn't know how to express them, but I had hardly entered the confessional when I felt my soul expand.' She felt launched on 'waves of confidence and love', and after that she never looked back to the way of fear.

Fr. Alexis was wise enough to realize that, in the perfect love that animated Thérèse, there was no place for the way of fear, for he saw that she had never departed from or betrayed that perfect love which casts out fear (1 John 4.18). But the world is for many people ruled by fear because they connive with Satan, the lord of fear. Ignatius and the Jesuits were right in realizing that this servile and negative fear had to be dissolved into that filial fear of the Lord whereby there is an end of connivance with the lord of fear and annihilation. Thérèse went even further and had the terrifying courage to take her sacrificial love into the dark world of the absence of love and so try to cast out fear even there. And in this her companion could be nobody else but John of the Cross, fathering that new world that she strove to mother.

Here the limitless horizons of the cosmic all-mothering love begin to appear. Like every true mother she is not only ready to suffer the birthpangs of this motherhood but also its nurturing humility and constancy. Thus it is that those who come close to Thérèse need not feel overawed by her perfection but rather drawn into the radiance of her presence.

The Mysticism of Virginity

Seen thus, in relation to these mystical horizons, virginity is no mere side issue nor is it a kind of optional extra nor, and this is especially to be noted, is it a kind of asceticism like abstension from meat or alcohol. It is supremely positive, *centring* the life of prayer and the seasons of liturgical observance. It opens up to the fullness of the ascending eros, yet without losing touch with human joyfulness and tenderness.

It is in the consecrated virgin-celibate that most of all, both in reality and symbol, the fullness of divine giving is met by the fullness of human receptivity. This is why in her fullest maturity, as in the 'Oblation to Merciful Love', Thérèse dares to use the word infinite to describe her desire for total union with God. On the advice of a theologian she agreed to change 'infinite' into 'immense' because, one supposes, the theologian felt that, strictly speaking, nothing human can be named infinite. With her usual ready obedience she made the change, but one can question whether the word infinite may not have been quite correct from the point of view of the traditional theology of the soul as *capax dei* and *capax infiniti*. In fact there was from the early centuries a hidden dimension within the ancient theology of *theiosis* or divinization that has been left to a new Doctor of the Church to discover or recover on the threshold of the third millennium. For detachment from desiring particular things or persons need not be seen so much as a going beyond desire, as an opening towards the fullness of desire, so much so that Thérèse of Lisieux could talk of her 'infinite' desires and desiring which only God could fulfil. Only that kind of nuptials, only that kind of marriage can fulfil the deeply hidden desires of the virgin-celibate in the Christian tradition, a tradition that sees itself as going back to the celibate Christ and his virgin mother.

There is thus a true sense in which virginity-celibacy takes up into itself and gives their full eternal supernatural dimension to marriage and family as in another sense marriage and family produce and alone produce virgins and celibates. For this reason Thérèse must be seen in her familial setting to be understood. The Martin sisters, all five of them, were not sacrificed to a life-denying puritanism but to the fullness of motherhood and fruitfulness. Nor did Thérèse see the virginity option as a condition to following her *all the way* into total dedication to Merciful Love. Her 'little way' was not for people vowed to virginity-celibacy only, it was not for dedicated religious only. It was, and is, for everybody who looks up from the depths, the deeper the better, towards the God of Merciful Love who is in *pain of giving*.

Virginity has its vital centre not in the body of woman or man, but in the human *will* that dares, in fear and trembling, to open to the infinity of God's giving. This can only fully come through death and a totally new kind of living beyond death. In the tradition of Christian asceticism, virginity-celibacy is not an option for barrenness but for the fullness of life. It is the ascending eros fulfilled in glory.

Mystical virginity-celibacy is not cold and withdrawn but rather warm and friendly. It is not selfishly sentimental, nor attention-seeking. It is an expression of that charity that 'seeketh not its own' but 'is patient and kind' (1 Cor. 13). For Thérèse entering an enclosed contemplative community as a bright, lively intelligent 15-year old there was very real danger of what has been called 'infantilism' which is supremely selfish and self-centred, and is the polar opposite of that 'spiritual childhood' which Thérèse saw as the royal road to sanctity. She could have been patronized by her two elder sisters, already full members of the community, but she kept clear of this from the outset. More dangerously, she could have been taken into the rather voracious possessiveness of her prioress, Mother Gonzague. It seems probable that the young Thérèse drew very firm boundaries from the outset, and that this was resented by Mother Gonzague especially, who proceeded to make life very hard for Thérèse; for this Thérèse very genuinely thanked her later on with an irony so subtle that it was almost totally invisible. But it must be said that Mother Gonzague for all her faults, and they were glaring, had the intelligence to see that Thérèse was first and last *une vraie comédienne*. It was this that kept her sanctity at once invisible and fresh as the first breeze of spring, the metaphor is Thérèse's own, and might be used to describe her whole spiritual atmosphere.

We now come to the celebrated and often totally misunderstood 'smile of Thérèse' around which sometimes gather a whole cluster of misunderstandings, as if this woman of infinite desires and unbreakable patience were simply a smiling child with golden curls and angelic expression, who never really grew up and who died in a kind of glow of innocence. Thérèse's smile had in fact nothing of the superficial about it; it was neither an ingratiating nor a political, nor yet a photographic smile. Neither was it the smile of 'chintzy chintzy cheeriness' of John Betjeman's nurse,[18] nor was it *un certain sourire* of disillusioned experience. It was a smile from the depths of that charity that is always patient and kind and never seeks its own, a smile from the depths, of a kind of substantial joy that can only grow in the world of the mystical horizons of infinite gentleness and infinite suffering. Let us look again at Thérèse's relationship with Sister St Peter. The following passage, in Thérèse's own words, shows quite unconsciously on her side, the power of a smile rising from the depths of charity. I am following the Knox translation.

> I can remember one act of charity God inspired me to do while I was still a novice; it was a very trifling thing, but our Father who sees what is done in secret doesn't care about the importance of what you do, as long as you do it in the right spirit, and he has rewarded me already, without waiting to do it in the next life! It was when Sister St Peter still went into choir and refectory. I used to kneel just behind her at evening prayers, and I knew that at ten minutes to six trouble was coming to somebody, because she had got to be piloted into the refectory and the infirmarian sisters had their hands too full to deal with her. A trifling service, but it cost

18. John Betjeman, 'Death in Leamington'.

me something to make the offer, because I knew poor Sister St Peter
wasn't easy to please; she was very ill, and didn't like having a change
of guides. But it seemed too good an opportunity to be missed; what
did our Lord say about charity? He told us that if we did anything
for the most insignificant of his brethren, we should be doing it for
him. So I swallowed my pride and offered my services; I had quite
a lot of trouble in getting her to accept them. Well, as it turned
out, when I got down to the job it was a complete success. Every
evening, the moment I saw Sister St Peter shaking her hour-glass
at me, I knew that meant: 'Let's go.'

You wouldn't believe how much I minded being disturbed in this
way, at first anyhow. But I lost no time in making a start, and we
had to make a real ceremony of it. I had to move the bench and
carry it away just so, without any sign of hurry – that was important
– and then the procession began. The thing was to walk behind the
poor invalid holding her up by her girdle; I did this as gently as I
could manage, but if by some piece of bad luck she stumbled, she
was down on me at once – I wasn't holding her properly, and she
might easily fall; 'Heavens, girl, you're going too fast; I shall do myself
an injury.' Then, if I tried to walk still slower it was: 'Here, why
aren't you keeping up with me? Where's your hand? I can't feel it,
you must have let go. I shall fall, I know I shall. How right I was
when I told them you were too young to look after me!'

We would get to the refectory at last, without accidents. There
were more obstacles to be got over; Sister St Peter had to be steered
into a sitting position, with the greatest possible care, so as not to
hurt her. Then her sleeves had to be turned up, again in a particular
way; then I could take myself off. But I noticed before long the
difficulty she had, with her poor cripppled hands, about arranging
the bread in her bowl; so that was another little thing to do before
I left her. She hadn't asked me to do it, so she was greatly touched
by having this attention paid to her; and it was this action (on which
I'd bestowed no thought at all) that established me firmly in her
favour. There was something even more important, though I only
heard about it later; When I'd finished cutting her bread I gave her,
before I left, my best smile.[19]

---

19. Knox, *Autobiography*, pp. 295–7.

Mon plus beau sourire: as usual Knox gets it just right, *not* 'my most beautiful smile', not 'my most special smile', but, with the faintest touch of gentle irony, 'my *best* smile'. For the whole passage is gently lightened and decompressed by what can only be called God's own irony as mediated by the exquisite gentleness of a great lover who is nevertheless all the way *une vraie comédienne.*

We shall return to this passage from the *Story of a Soul* again, for it had a further and deeper importance for Thérèse, and the smile appears only in passing, but, there is more to be said about the smile of Thérèse that is relevant to the mysticism of virginity.

In the first place it is clear that as far as Sister St Peter was concerned her whole situation of being helped on her way had become perfunctory and impersonal, a job to be done which might well be seen and felt as tedious and tiresome. This new novice probably had her own little scheme of gaining points of charity in this world and the next; she was one of these Martin girls who were all brought up in comfort and ease. Well, she, Sister St Peter, would keep this novice in her place etc, etc. But it had to be admitted that this youngster was gentle and patient. And there she was, cutting up her bread so neatly and quietly. And, finally, turning the whole thing into a kind of joyful event by smiling brightly!

What Thérèse was doing was *personalizing* the whole transaction. Her smile was not dismissive but rather a kind of invitation, an invitation to open to the depths and heights of bridal receptivity. It is clear that Thérèse saw this possibility and this invitation as open to every human being, every 'soul' to use her own language, and that she saw her little community of sisters in all their fragilities and inadequacies as in a sense calling forth her welcoming and personalizing and individualizing smile of intimacy. This smile for all that it was individual and personal made no demands, contained no least seed of that cancer of community life traditionally named 'particular friendship'. Thérèse made a special and in some cases totally heroic effort to connect with those in the community who were most difficult and negative. It seems that, as in her smile for old Sister St Peter, Thérèse's smile was the kind of gift of herself that could not be lightly turned on and off. It was somehow deeply connected with that healing smile that seemed to shine on her from a statue of the Virgin Mary. Every true smile has a heavenly dimension, and is a message from another world, however fleetingly given and received. The smile of Thérèse came from a heavenly presence fully and deeply realized in our incarnate everyday world.

Thérèse concludes the account of her relationship with Sister St Peter with a hint of this heavenly dimension:

> Dear Mother, it must seem very strange to you that I should be writing about this tiny act of charity, long since over and done with. Well, I have a reason for it – I feel it's my duty to record, in his own honour, the mercies the Lord has shewn me, and this is one of them; he's allowed this incident to remain in my mind like a scent in the nostrils – a scent which lures me on to perform fresh acts of charity. There are details in connexion with it which still have, for me, the freshness of a spring breeze. Here is one that comes back to my memory; a winter evening when I was doing my bit as usual – the cold – the darkness . . . All of a sudden I heard, far away, lovely music being played. And I constructed a picture in my imagination of a drawing-room splendidly lit up, with gilded furniture; of young fashionably dressed girls exchanging compliments and the polite small-talk of society. Then I looked back at the poor invalid I was helping along; there was no music here, only a piteous groan every now and then; there was no gilding, only the plain brick of our bare convent walls, faintly visible in the flickering light.
>
> Of the inner experience I had, I can tell you nothing; I only know that God enlightened my soul with rays of truth, which so outshone the tawdry brilliance of our earthly festivities as to fill me with unbelievable happiness. I tell you that I wouldn't have exchanged those ten minutes of charitable drudgery for a thousand years of worldly enjoyment . . . Here we are struggling on painfully, in the thick of the fight, and even so the thought that God has taken us out of the world can give us, for the moment, this feeling of happiness above all earthly happiness, so what will heaven be like? All will be lightness of heart there, all repose; and we shall see what an inestimable grace the Lord has bestowed on us in choosing

us out to live in this earthly home of his – the anteroom, did we but know it, of heaven itself.[20]

Here we see Thérèse meeting marvellously well the supreme challenge of the mystical writer, which is that of describing clearly and simply the normally indescribable. She says rightly that she can tell us nothing of this experience, nothing, that is to say, by way of direct description. She goes straight to the world beyond the physical which ever since the time of Aristotle has been called the *meta*physical, and she speaks of the light (*rayons*) of truth. She is using the metaphor of light, having made clear that it is only a metaphor and yet at the same time the *only* metaphor that is suitable, brilliantly framing and focusing it by recalling the merely earthly brightness of the ballroom with its gilt and glamour of fashionably dressed and politely conversing beautiful young people. Most important of all is the fact that the true light which shows the tawdriness of mere earthly glamour is something not imagined but *given,* not the conclusion of an effort of thinking but a sudden uncalled for, unasked for, illumination, a *misericorde du seigneur.*

---

20. Ibid., pp. 297–8.

CHAPTER 8

THÉRÈSE AS A WORK OF GOD

Gratia Praeveniens

Thérèse was, is, a work of God, perfect or almost perfect. Her life shows forth the wonders of God not through the miraculous and extraordinary as with Peter, Francis, Catherine; not through special graces and visions as with Paul, Augustine, Bernadette; not through miraculous writings full of the pure light of truth as with Bonaventure, Aquinas, Teresa of Avila; not at all, not primarily in any of these ways that break in on our deafness and flash in on our blindness. No, in the glorious company of these great, these especially chosen ones, Thérèse is something entirely new, coming towards the end of the nineteenth century (most evil, most miserable of centuries; says John Beevers[1]) gradually becoming manifest in the twentieth century and set up by the all-fathering Source, to enlighten the third Christian millennium.

If we are to see Thérèse clearly, or in a gradual clarification, as a work of God, we must begin by seeing her as set within the surrounds of her family: her mother, her father (importantly), her sisters, each in a different place, her second family, the Guerins, who led the Martin family to Lisieux and its hitherto unknown Carmelite convent.

Thérèse's first visit to that quiet secluded convent that she was to make famous is recalled very quietly in the narrative of her early years:

---

1. See John Beevers, *Storm of Glory*, (London: Sheed & Word, 1952), pp. 203 ff.

Each afternoon I took a walk with Papa. We made our visit to the Blessed Sacrament together, going to a different church each day, and it was in this way we entered the Carmelite chapel for the first time. Papa showed me the choir grille and told me there were nuns behind it. I was far from thinking at the time that nine years later I would be in their midst![2]

Nine years later: Thérèse entered the Lisieux Carmel on 9 April 1888; so this first visit was in 1879 when Thérèse was in her sixth year, and still under the comforting shadow of her much-loved father.

Already even then the young girl is being deeply called to open to another fatherhood, and this will expand and deepen over the following decade before she enters the narrow confines of the Carmelite convent. Her journey to Rome through the Alpine mountains and valleys will fill her heart and imagination in a way that will remain with her in Carmel. Prior to this great experience she was, as it were, being prepared for it by the large expanses of the Normandy countryside around Alençon. 'Already I was in love with the *wide-open spaces*. Space and the gigantic fir trees, the branches sweeping down to the ground, left in my heart an impression similar to the one I experience still today at the sight of nature.'[3] She is writing in 1895, already seven years in the convent, having passed through the transforming trial of her father's mental illness and death. Her beloved father is safely at home in the Father's house. And it is only after fourteen years, a year before the time of writing, that Thérèse understood the 'extraordinary vision' she saw when she was still a little girl of six or seven years of age, 'an age', she tells us, 'when illusions are not to be feared'.[4]

From the standpoint of the understanding of Thérèse of Lisieux as a work of God, this fore-vision of her father's illness is of the highest importance. She herself gives us the clue to this, though

---

2. J. Clarke, OCD, tr., *Story of a Soul: The Autobiography of St Thérèse of Lisieux* (Washington, DC: Institute of Carmelite Studies, 1975), p. 36.
3. Ibid., pp. 29–30.
4. Ibid., pp. 45–7.

we may be tempted to let it slip by us as a mere 'pious thought', not realizing that there is no such thing in the *Story of a Soul* as a 'mere pious thought', that when she speaks of this or that divine gift or grace she means just that.

In this present case of the prevision of her father's trial she tells us that there were two gifts and two giftings; one direct from her *heavenly* father, the other mediated by her *earthly* father now in heavenly glory. The gift direct from her heavenly Father was the vision itself, given with the utmost delicacy so that Thérèse could experience it as a *mere foreshadowing*, which was all that she could bear just then, preparing her in a deep, semi-conscious way for the great trial that was to come, 'a thing which, if she had understood, would have made her die of grief'.[5]

It was about a year before she penned the first part of her 'Story' that, in conversation with her eldest sister Marie, when she was describing this strange experience, its meaning became simultaneously and with dramatic suddenness clear to both of them – to their great consolation. This consolation was a divine gift which their human father in glory obtained for them both.[6] It may be added that even today there are those among the devotees of Thérèse who are conscious of the special intercessory power of Louis Martin. It is as if Thérèse in glory were fulfilling her promise to 'come down', but somehow wished to stand back and let her human father's glory shine, as if he were still her beloved king, as she was his queen, and as if the great God of all goodness were thus showing forth the *homeliness* of heaven as a revelation of glory.

Louis Martin is no mere background presence in the story of St Thérèse. He enters with her, indeed leads her, into the holy of holies of that total sacrifice in which the seed dies in producing fruit a hundredfold. There is a sense, a very real sense, in which *his* sacrifice was deeper, more total, more piercing than hers, for he was asked to offer that which for most *men* (indeed for all men, as Teresa of Avila noted) is hardest of all and acts as a barrier to

---

5. Ibid., p. 44.
6. Ibid.

the deeper flowings of mystical prayer: their *honra*, their place in the world of men and women, all of which has to be immolated to make room for the most precious graces of transformation which otherwise cannot flow in. No less terrifying, perhaps even more terrifying, is that total letting go into the hands of others, which is announced by the first onset or premonitions of mental disease. This became distressingly clear in various ways, including total 'blackouts' of memory in one of which he totally forgot to care for a favourite bird that died of neglect.[7] This total dying of the seed that will produce fruit a hundredfold was accomplished in Louis Martin *before* it was accomplished in his beloved daughter, Thérèse: there was a real sense in which she, his 'queen', found support in his strong soldierly presence. The story of Thérèse, of her marvellous life and Christ-like death, is indeed the story of a family. She is indeed the morning star of the third Christian millennium that shines steadily within a constellation for those who have eyes to see it.

St Thérèse of Lisieux, great beyond all superlatives in her littleness, is forever connected with Normandy, but she is also, through her much-loved father, connected with Brittany and with the Breton culture that connects with that marvellous submerged Celtic world. This has begun to surface in our times like the living coals of a new Easter fire long hidden beneath the ashes of its smooring. There is much in the writings of Thérèse and in what is sometimes identified as 'Lexovian Spirituality' which seems to echo Alexander Carmichael's *Carmina Gadelica* and Douglas Hyde's *Religious Songs of Connaught*.

There is one aspect of the *genius* of Thérèse of Lisieux (the word is that of Jean Guitton), which has been made little of, unjustly it seems to me, and this is that aspect of her that shows her as the poet of her community, a poet that like the greatest poets sings because she wants to sing, because she *has* to sign, like a blackbird or thrush among the trees. This gift of song is almost untouched

---

7. See Joyce Emert, *Louis Martin, Father of a Saint* (New York: Society of St Paul, 1983), p. 104.

by any kind of sophistication, and it is all the purer and more melodious for that. It is to the credit of Dr Joyce Emert, professional academic in the field of literature, that she, however tentatively, takes this gift seriously, as she takes seriously Louis Martin's tendency to break into song. This almost irrepressible gaiety of father and daughter, both gifted mimics who never descended to mockery, is an essential ingredient of Lexovian Spirituality, the salt that preserves its freshness: Thérèse was seen by the formidable Mother Gonzague as *'une vraie comédienne'*. Even in the dark night at the end of her life Thérèse never lost her gaiety. Even in his darkest 'end-time' Louis Martin could be moved to a kind of ecstasy by the singing of a nightingale.[8] The ancient, eternal springs of that ascetical lift and liveliness that vibrated within the ancient Celtic monasteries are always present in the poems and letters of Thérèse and in the three manuscripts which go to form the *Story of a Soul*. One does not have to trace this connection historically to recognize that it is present spiritually in the eternal symphonies of faith, hope and love. These God-centred attitudes or 'theological virtues' were deepened and purified in Thérèse in a most wonderful way that was rooted in the soil of a deep and deeply purified affectivity that had truly become a 'flame of living love', the *'llama de amor viva'* of John of the Cross whose *way* she understood and lived in a new way that was a way of marvellous simplicity.

Thérèse was surrounded from her birth with the most constant and tender affections: from her mother as long as her mother lived, from her four older sisters, above all from her father. He was her king and she was his queen, and one is reminded of the lovers of the Song of Songs, though it is abundantly clear that this father-daughter affection was never in the slightest danger of becoming jealously possessive or sliding into eroticism. It was totally in the mode of the holy touch and the sacred kiss, the *hagion philema* of the first Christians who with St Paul lived in the glow of the Risen Christ.

---

8. Ibid., p. 152.

If we have almost to strain language to speak of this, as we have to speak of Thérèse's sisterly surround of tenderness all through her life in the convent, we have really no language at all to speak of Thérèse's relationship with her two 'brother' missionaries. Yet it was in this relation especially that Thérèse's holy feminine showed itself in the full maturity of holiness and the full maturity of femininity. So it is really necessary to try to say something about it even though language in which to say it with any clarity hasn't yet been fashioned.

Thérèse was, is, one of the great lovers. Some commentators follow Anders Nygren, the Swedish Lutheran theologian, in interpreting Christian love as defined by a radical distinction between eros-love and agape-love, the first being self-regarding and closely connected with sexuality, the other being other-regarding and closely connected with obedience to God and the adoration of God in righteousness and self-transcendence: this is Christian agape, and it is untainted by the selfishness and softness of eros as sexual and procreative. Eros love has its place, even its necessary and rightful place, in human life but in itself it has nothing in common with that agape by which Christ is activated, which St Paul places at the centre of Christian life in 1 Corinthians 13.

Reform theology on the whole tends to accept Nygren's distinction; Catholic theology on the whole tends to reject it, in accordance with the general thesis that grace (the gift from above) does not replace or destroy nature, but rather purifies and perfects it.

Thérèse does not theorize about this, but she stands consistently and practically within the Catholic tradition of an acceptable continuity between human love and divine love. Her human love, that for her father especially, is constantly being purified and transmuted into divine love by deep and deepening sacrifice. The face of her father, noble and even kingly in quite natural human terms passes over into the face of Christ as described by Isaiah, bruised and broken, dishonoured, without human beauty or nobility in the natural sense. A new beauty, a new glory is born and she is ready to accept this. This she felt deeply, affectively, tremblingly, was the *truth;* and it was only by this truth she could live; it was only in this truth she could be finally happy. So it is that if we look carefully at the letters that Thérèse wrote during her father's terrible final 'breakdown' of body and mind we notice a kind of serenity takes over, not a stoic serenity of 'making the best of it', but the serenity of a deep joy gradually shining through the suffering, the joy of *meaning:* that this is how it must be if the best is to be.

Nowhere is the protective preventive grace of the Divine Lover, the *gratia praeveniens* of Christ, more clear and clearly paradoxical than in the account Thérèse gives of her experiences as a timid, overly sensitive schoolgirl seeking affection from her peers and teachers and not finding it. This account is written by the young woman of 22, now in her first maturity and able to lighten her narrative with the salt of comedy that only serves to enhance its seriousness in the growth of a wisdom of the heart that opened up to a most precious understanding of the divine prevenient protectiveness.[9] Like St Mary Magdalen she loved much, but where Magdalen had followed the false light of human loves and could only be brought back to the truth by repentance, Thérèse was *prevented* from going this way by the prevenient care and love of God and therefore should be more, not less, thankful than Mary Magdalen. On this point she is warmly and uncharacteristically emphatic. It is, after all, crucial to the understanding of the 'little way'. She, who in her own nature and by her own deep tendency to give her heart away to wordly vanities even more surely than Mary Magdalen, was preserved only by God's grace. She, the littlest of all, most of all totally dependent on merciful love, was chosen to lead the way for a great army of 'little souls', – the way that was the littlest way of trust in the infinity of God's merciful love. Hence her fascination with Joan of Arc; hence those extraordinary paragraphs of Manuscript B,[10] which mark the apex of Thérèse's spiritual writing. To miss this is to miss the whole mission of Thérèse. All those who see her as 'too perfect' do indeed, however understandably, miss this.

9. See Clarke, *Story of a Soul*, pp. 30–4.
10. Ibid., p. 200.

Among the many philosophers and theologians of the highest competence, from André Combes in 1945 to René Laurentin, Hans Urs von Balthasar and a whole constellation of scholars in recent times, there is one that may be said to stand out and to deserve special attention. That is the editor of the facsimile edition of the *Manuscrits Autobiographiques* published in 1956: Fr. François de Sainte-Marie, Discalced Carmelite. In the course of Chapter 3 of Volume I entitled *Introduction*, he deals with what he calls the *Themes Fondamentaux* of the Manuscripts and he looks for the *key*, the 'golden key' which opens to us the mystery of Thérèse. He finds this in the following passage: 'The theme of the divine mercy is for me the supreme principle of intelligibility of the autobiographical manuscripts, and at one and the same time the golden key which opens to us the soul of Thérèse.'[11]

This is certainly true, and this must stand. But it cannot be left to stand alone. In fact it can stand at all only as an essential part or unit of two pillars supporting the triumphal arch of the spirit and spirituality of Thérèse. The other pillar is freedom, the inviolable, virginal, purified (how terribly and marvellously purified!) freedom of Thérèse herself. It is Thérèse's total response to a total invitation to bridal love, the fiat of the virgin-bride to the Divine Bridegroom. It is this virgintity of choice and this choice of virginity that is especially preserved by the prevenient grace, *gratia praeveniens*, of the Divine Lover, spouse of virgins. Thérèse was a soldier after the model of St Joan, the daughter of a line of soldiers, crusaders for Christ, and nowhere is her martial spirit more evident than in her courageous and lucid defence of 'the other half of the soul', Céline, where she has to battle against the admirable good sense of her beloved cousin Jeanne and that cousin's admirable husband, Dr La Neele, a good sense that, for Thérèse, did not quite reach the heavenly good sense that had its roots in the childhood of Thérèse and Céline.

---

11. François de Sainte-Marie, ed. *Manuscrits Autobiographiques de Sainte Thérèse* (Office Central de Lisieux, 1956), p. 61.

Both Céline and Thérèse were free and that freedom was God's very special gift. But it was a gift of freedom freely given to be freely used. So, too, those who follow the 'little way' can do so only in freedom, freely responding to the call of merciful love as Thérèse responded freely. Here there is that coincidence of opposites beloved of Cardinal Nicholas of Cusa, a coincidence in which the opposites do not destroy one another but open up to that divine mystery which combines them both in a unity and harmony beyond all analytical understanding. But love understands, and Thérèse – for whom at the end love is everything – Thérèse, the Lover transformed into the Beloved, understands. All is gift and all is giving. In the bonding of love the Lover does all that the Beloved does, in full freedom, and the Beloved does all that the Lover does also in the service of total freedom.

We have here the union of the highest attraction of the good and the true with the deepest freedom of the will to release itself from everything that would pull against this attraction. The Christmas grace, the great gift from above, from the beloved in the eucharistic communion of love, released Thérèse from the unfreedom of childishness to the true freedom of maturity. Within this freedom she could reach back to the light-heartedness of the little girl whose slippers have been filled with childish gifts. She was given the strength to *play* at still being the child so as to please her father and her sister, being now totally in command of the situation and of her own future.

Woman of Desires

If we look at the *Table des Citations* which forms the third volume of the *Manuscrits Autobiographiques*, we find that the word *désir* occurs 93 times and *désirer* 58 times. A few of these, very few, are non-significant; most of them express a deep orientation of soul towards the divine Source directly or indirectly. They manifest a very significant interweaving of activity and receptivity. Some of these desires are somehow born within Thérèse herself; some come from

God, are somehow *given* by God. But this division is not absolute, but rather do they flow freely together. They are part of that deep bonding of love which is the deepest meaning of the *Story of a Soul*. This meaning is indeed very simple, and it addresses itself in the first place to the simple and humble of heart, and nobody who misses this point can ever hope to understand or to *take in* the message of Thérèse. But it is also very profound and it opens up to the widest and deepest borizons of Christian theology as André Combes was perhaps the first to see, fifty years after the death of Thérèse. The real danger in the understanding of Thérèse is to miss its profundity, thus enclosing its simplicity within narrow pietistic and self-indulgent horizons. It is true that Thérèse turned away from what she called the 'Great Tomes', but this was because she was turning towards the unfathomable profundity and inexhaustible treasury of Scripture, and she brought to the study of Scripture not only a sensitive heart but also a mind always open to the most expansive and releasing insights. Where Teresa of Avila was lighted on her way towards and into what she named the Seventh Mansions by 'intellectual visions', as she called them, Thérèse, shy and distrustful of 'visions', found her way by insights usually arising from texts of Scripture.

But it would be false to see Thérèse as independent of and somehow standing outside of the Christian tradition mediated by the Fathers of the Church and the medieval schools, mediated on its ascetical and mystical side by *The Imitation of Christ*, by Teresa of Avail and especially by John of the Cross, mediated also by Cardinal Bérulle and Fr. Arminjon. This she would have variously encountered through Fr. Pichon and the various great masters who 'preached' the annual retreats that she was obliged to attend. These would almost certainly have included the topic of the human desire for God which could find fulfilment in God alone. What was perhaps special to Thérèse was the realism and amplitude of her appropriation of this mystical doctrine. This is most powerfully expressed in Manuscript B, the letter to Sr. Marie of the Sacred Heart, although or perhaps because, at the time she wrote it she was experiencing what is usually called the dark night of faith, though in the language

of St John of the Cross it may be called the passive dark night of
spirit.

A careful reading of the *Story of a Soul* makes it clear that
Thérèse, in her short life, had already passed through the nights
of sense in what she called her customary aridity, and what John
termed the active night of spirit, in which her faith in the rewards
of heaven became independent of all the consolations of certainty
and an inner vision of heavenly joy; but this later experience was
much deeper and more terrifying than this, being a purifying
darkness in which it seemed as if God had ceased to exist and she
was forced to sit at the table of unbelievers and sinners, so that
all that was left to her was love without the least light or assurance.
Yet her desires, her immense desires remained as a kind of inner
fire in the heart without the least comforting light in the mind.
She had read and pondered on John of the Cross and she must
have realized deep down that she was being led along that way in
which the fire in the heart becomes the sole light of the mind. But
it seems clear that none of those around her, not even her sisters,
could understand this.

But what is clear, from Manuscript B especially, is that the final
darkness, lasting from Easter 1896 until her death at the end of
September 1897, and therefore including the writing of both
Manuscript B and Manuscript C, increased rather than diminished,
clarified rather than obscured, her immense desires. It is especially
in Manuscript B, where she is writing in full freedom, for her sister
Marie, that these immense desires attain their full dimensions, so
that we have to remind ourselves that Thérèse, for all her liveliness
and spontaneity, never indulges in rhetorical exaggeration but
speaks straight from her heart. It is as if the darkness at the level
of the rational, reasonable, measuring intellect, had left her free
to give full rein to her desires at the level of will and desire. The
same is true of some of the poems she wrote during this last
period. When she told one of the sisters of her great darkness within
her by which all thoughts of heaven and eternal life were totally
negated the sister protested that the poems she had been writing
gave the lie to what she was saying. Thérèse said simply: 'I write

what I want to believe.' This reply cannot be seen in terms of 'wishful thinking'. What Thérèse 'wants to believe' connects with a life-time of immense desires which in the order of her relationship to the good will be fulfilled by the good God who is now being sought and loved as the hidden God. It is only in the glory of this hiddenness that the immense desires can be fulfilled, will be liberated into the infinity of merciful love.

The liberation of desire. . . from a certain perspective this may be said to be the story-line of the *Story of a Soul*, that logical chain (*chaîne logique*) which the graphologist Raymond Trillat sees as the dynamism that pulses through the original script of the Manuscripts of St Thérèse. It is perhaps best expressed by Fr. Sebastian Moore. He writes,

> Desire, whereby alone a person lives, is the trusting relationship that binds the person to all being, becoming actual. Desire is 'stretching' in the reality I am in . . . what is happening is that the relationship that I am in with the mystery of being is becoming alive and inviting. Desire is love trying to happen. Always the mystery is prior and all-embracing. In the heightened consciousness of the mystic, the all-embracing mystery is known as the spouse.[12]

We are back to the language of Thérèse and her heavenly simplicity, but our brief detour through mystical theology has reminded us how firmly and beautifully Thérèse steps out of the Great Tradition which unites Hellenism and Judaeo-Christianity, and which shines with the light of the Transcendentals and glows with the warmth of the living flame of love that is the Holy Spirit of God.

The Transcendentals

'The light of the Transcendentals': this is for many a mysterious phrase, and it sounds somewhat grandiose and indeed unsuitable

---

12. *Jesus the Liberator of Desire*, (New York: Crossroad, 1989) pp. 10–11.

to the holy simplicity of Thérèse's spirituality, which centres on
the 'little way'. But if we are to have some vision of the Thérèse
phenomenon in its rudiments and as a superb work of God we
must be on our guard not only against analytic complexity but,
even more, against false simplification, especially the self-satisfied
simplification of those superficial guides and preachers who try
to persuade themselves and others that there is a way to God outwith
the way of the cross. For one person who has been prevented from
understanding Thérèse by philosophical and theological complexity,
ten and more have been side-tracked into the kind of spiritual
kindergarten which Thérèse went beyond, far beyond, in the
moment of enlightenment and strengthening which she named her
'Christmas Grace' on the eve of her fourteenth birthday.

But perhaps rather than the light of the Transcendentals one
should speak of 'the light (or lights) above the mind' and read, or
read again, Book 7, Chapter 10 of the *Confessions*.[13] Here we have
one of the great masters of the spoken word putting words to the
human experience (the philosopher's dower and birthright) of the
discovery of Truth *as* Truth, as 'the master-light of all our seeing'
(in William Wordsworth's genial phrase), as that light which first
and last the lover of God must follow, which first and last, Thérèse
followed. On her death bed, near the very end, she said: 'I never
looked for anything but the truth.'[14]

'Eternal Truth, true Love, beloved Eternity', so spoke St
Augustine, so by her life and death spoke St Thérèse. Even more
than Augustine, though since comparisons are out of place, let us
say: as deeply as Augustine or any of the great lovers of Christ and
God, Thérèse allowed the source of all Truth and all Goodness
and all Beauty to transform her being into Itself. Looking at this
final immolation, this final victimhood we can only gaze in wonder
and awe. We can only gaze in great fear and trepidation, for we all
fail at this point or near it. We all fail, but in realizing, in accepting
that failure we are at once borne up on wings by the 'little way' of

13. *op. cit.*, pp. 146–7.
14. *St Thérèse of Lisieux: Her Last Conversations*, tr. J. Clarke, OCD. (Washington
    DC: *Institute of Carmelite Studies*, 1977), p. 205.

trust and total surrender. *Confortamini, confortamini*: Be ye comforted. This is the place of letting go into the great God of total Truth, total Goodness, total Humility.

'Purity of heart,' says Soren Kierkegaard, 'is to seek one thing'. This unity of seeking, of desiring was the central line of force in Thérèse. That one thing was the Ultimate Thing, the Totality, the Totally Real, that, passionately sought, shed its own reality, its own realism, over every least thing that Thérèse did and said.

So we can add Reality (*ens*) and Unity (*unum*) to Truth (*verum*) and Goodness (*bonum*), and we begin to complete the portrait of Thérèse as the seeker, the woman of desires, the lover of that all-holy light above the mind (*lux supra mentem*) that Augustine found and adored as the very creator of his being.

But traditionally there is a fifth luminosity that must be sought after and loved, and even adored as divine, if we are to complete that vision of glory, which is the heritage of every human being as it issues from the Source. This is the light, the vision, the transcendental idea of *Beauty*, and this was with Thérèse from the beginning of her short life right to the end when she passed from pain into ecstasy.

The words *beau, belle* come readily to Thérèse, especially in her relationship with the physical world all around her. She loved flowers and the varied beauty of the natural scene, all the more as she was leaving it behind to enter the narrow world of a Carmelite convent. She carried with her always (she never left it behind) the inner *idea* or *illumination* of the Beautiful which is beyond all definition and can only be saluted, and admired within the heart. Thérèse never lost this flow of love and admiration for the beauty of flowers and birds and the freshness of nature in all its moods and changes. Yet what may be called the Platonic ascent, from physical to spiritual beauty, was second nature to her; so much so that the beauty of the suffering face of Christ as depicted in Isaiah, and the beauty of the noble countenance of her father humiliated by his 'descent' into senility, were somehow one and continuous as a manifestation of that higher Beauty that Plato could only aim at or guess at in his upwards journey towards *to kalon*, the Beautiful Itself.

Strangely, we catch this ascent, almost in the very act of its ascension, best of all in Thérèse's account of her dream encounter with the Venerable Anne of Jesus who links the Spanish and the French Carmels historically in that instantaneity of heavenly life so dear to Thérèse. In the dream she comes near Thérèse in a kind of Mother-daughter embrace across the centuries, 'Her face was beautiful,' Thérèse writes, 'but with an immaterial beauty.'[15] This immaterial beauty radiates love and kindness, so much so that Thérèse, writing several months later can still *feel* the tenderness of the experience. There is here a strange interpenetration of dream and reality, that is all the more remarkable because of Thérèse's strict and almost fierce separation of the two, and her refusal to place her trust other than in the common everyday world of reality and truth. All higher reality had to come through faith and in the darkness of faith, purged not only of all the comforts of pious feeling, through what she termed her customary aridity, but also of all intellectual light and satisfaction through the terrible passive night of spirit in the final 18 months of her life. It was during this period, after one whole month into it, that she had her visionary dream (only a dream, it must be repeated) of the Venerable Anne of Jesus and felt the special kind of consolation it brought, a consolation, it seems, quite compatible not only with her customary aridity but with the terrible desolation passive night of spirit (though she does not in telling of it, use the terminology of John of the Cross.) We have here that 'doubling' of the soul which is experienced by many of the great mystics.

Thérèse's journey from the beauties of nature to Beauty Itself, God Himself, the journey into the Infinite, into mystery was essentially the Platonic journey towards the one light above the mind, of which Augustine speaks. But in the case of St Thérèse of Lisieux, the discovery of the fifth 'light above the mind', the Transcendental Beauty Itself, involved a special journey which casts its light on every human journey. Her discovery of the deeps

---

15. Clarke, *Story of a Soul*, p. 191.

of the Beautiful came through the way of pathos, along the sacred, almost indescribable, almost unsayable pathway of pathos.

Here the way forward in this meditation on Thérèse as a work of God is by going back to what is said in the book, *Heaven in Ordinarie,*[16] originally published in 1979, and written during the sixties and seventies. This contains two chapters on *pathos*, each an exploration of a central dimension of human experience and the God–man encounter hitherto left almost totally unexplored by theology. Left unexplored also by philosophy, yet from the beginning a central theme if not *the* central theme of poetry and drama.

Once Jesus had wept over Jerusalem and once this fact had been reported by the witnesses, it would have seemed inevitable that pathos as the holy space left behind after the vanishing of significance, should find its place at the centre of Christian theology.

'And when he drew near and saw the city [of Jerusalem] he wept over it, saying, "Would that even today, you knew the things that make for peace! But now they are hid from your eyes"' (Luke 19.41). This is the Holy Face, the eyes that weep, the face of goodness, kindness, love that has been rejected by the vulgarity and coarseness and narrow selfishness of the world, the world that has been seduced by the Adversary. It confronts this endless cruelty of the Adversary, confronts it in steadfast love, in unbreakable tenderness, in patience beyond all reasonable hope – it suffers all this, endures beyond all human capacity for endurance in the desperation of a prayer that is the cry of the *Lamma Sabacthani* (Why, oh why hast thou forsaken me?). It is in this final ecstasy of love beyond all support except itself that a new world is being brought to birth within this virgin-mother, as she makes it her prayer in the depths of the dark night and in her death. Somewhere, at some point along this terrifying embrace of the *Lamma Sabacthani*, the virgin-bride has been taken over the threshold between earth and heaven by the Christ-bridegroom whose name is Pathos, 'the

16. N.D. O'Donoghue, *Heaven in Ordinare* 2nd edn. (Edinburg: T & T Clarke, 1996).

Suffering Servant' of the Father. It is he, only he, that this woman, already transformed into charity, will accept as she has already accepted her father's countenance, veiled, deeply veiled in the shame-veil of a broken mind. That vision of the Source, the all-holy one, as Pathos and poignancy, which long ago broke through a lowering political skyscape upon the astonished gaze of Isaiah, finds its place of reception and human realization in this virgin-bride of the great mystery. This mystery manifests itself as Merciful Love. By comparison with this revelation of pathos, all power, all glory, all 'divinity' is tinged with vulgarity. It is from within these wounds of divine pathos that Thérèse will sing her songs in words that can indeed *seem* commonplace but are truly new-born, new-minted, fresh from the transforming fires of the divine heart.

The vision or pre-vision of her father with his face veiled in shame and suffering is explained by Thérèse as providing a certain comfort when this terrible event declared itself. This was surely true, but it seems likely that the pre-vision had a deeper significance as well. It was a vision of Christ, the Bridegroom, the Beloved whose lineaments as the Suffering Servant it was the great work of Thérèse's whole life to *create*, so that at the end, when the dark night hid from her all the glory of the divine countenance, and she could barely manage an act of faith in the existence of a beyond and a creator God, she saw this countenance with a strange clarity *in creating it*. In this final act of creation, in this final act of love, she died.

Theogony

In her death Thérèse is bringing to life and realization the astonishing words of the great mystical philosopher Maurice Blondel who was to write:

> God, in order to create free beings, has as it were withdrawn himself
> partially from his sovereign domain, he has as it were, exiled himself
> or committed suicide; and then it is up to us to turn over to Him

his empire, to make room for Him in us, and if we owe this power to Him he owes it to us to recover his own being in us.[17]

These are, let me repeat, astonishing words, but for all their depth and urgency they are the words of a scholar, a thinker, an academic, words searched for and written in the austere calm and comfort of a philosopher's study, a theologian's sanctum. More astonishing still, though easily missed in the fevered atmosphere of a sickroom that then became a death-room, is the impression that Thérèse as she cries out 'O my Good God', in her agony is not only calling on God but somehow creating God as Goodness. Do we not have the impression, as we ponder on the precious accounts given to us by her sisters, that in some way beyond our understanding *the Good God is being born* of this virgin mother of 24 years of age?[18] But of course we can at this point, in the precincts of this holy of holies, only speak in whispers, only share our intimations. But the philosopher's study, the theologian's sanctum is not far, only a step or two, from this holy of holies.

---

17. Exigences philosophiques 129, see James le Grys, Blondel's Idea of Assimilation to God through Mortification of Self, *Gregorianum* 77, 2 (1996) pp. 319–20.

18. There is a sense in which human beings may be said to *create* God. This is called by some authors, such as Maurice Blondel, *theogony* or the bringing to be or to appear of God (from *theiosis*, God, and *gonos*, birthing or engendering). More completely it means the 'allowing' of God to appear, 'to come out of concealment' or *alétheia*. The idea is that the Divine can *show* itself only to the extent that human beings can *receive* it. Thus we might say that the Divine can show itself as Merciful Love only in so far as human beings are open to receive it as Merciful Love. This receptivity is quite distinct from passivity for it comes from the co-operation of man and God. It is the *glory* that shines forth from the sacred marriage of divinity and humanity. We can, as it were, see this happening in the life and death of Thérèse of Lisieux, though it is present in some way in every deeply religious life and death; it can be seen as the birthright of every human being who opens to the fullness of life.

Of course when Blondel speaks of the suicide of God and of turning over to Him his empire he is using words in a rather special way. We are, as it were, striving for a new vision of the deep things of God. Perhaps this is possible only through such pain of transformation that we are unable to bear it unless we are specially upheld by God. Yet if God does it all then human beings are mere puppets and human life is no more than games played by the Gods. Here we have the abyss of Quietism which Thérèse very deliberately turned away from.

That there was no danger of quietistic passivity in the spiritual development of Thérèse herself becomes clear as soon as we look at her positive approach to suffering as the central exercise of loving. Thérèse makes it quite clear that this desire to suffer for love came to her as a grace, a gift which she gratefully received. It seems that her eldest sister Marie prepared her not only for her First Communion but also for the Communions that followed at short intervals. 'Marie took me on her knees and prepared me as she did for my First Communion.' And Thérèse continues: 'I remember how once she was speaking to me about suffering and she told me that I would probably not walk that way, that God would always carry me as a child.' This was indeed a critical moment, for Marie's concern was misguided, though Thérèse does not say this. But she goes on: 'The day after my Communion, the words of Marie came to my mind. I felt born within my heart a *great desire to suffer,* and at the same time the interior assurance (*l'intime assurance*) that Jesus reserved a great number of crosses for me. I felt myself flooded with consolations so *great* that I look upon them as one of the *greatest* graces of my life.'[19]

In the milieu in which Thérèse was writing this first, longest section of the *Story of a Soul,* written directly for her sister Pauline, it was common to speak easily, lightly even, of 'graces' and 'great graces'. Thérèse used this language, but she used it with a difference. Wherever in these manuscripts she uses the word 'grace', the word is loaded with significance. A grace is something *given* directly by

---

19. Clarke, *Story of a Soul,* p. 79.

God as Father, Son or Holy Spirit, by the three person Trinity in fact. Here that strange joyful attraction to suffering is not seen as a passing ripple on the surface of consciousness but rather as a seed deeply digged in and deeply sown. It is sown directly by the great husbandman in the graden of the soul in the most delicate and tender intercourse of the Bridegroom God and the Bridal Soul. This is the great theme that is at once veiled and revealed in the mystical underflow of the Song of Songs. It is the theme that is at once the foundation and the binding cement of the *Story of a Soul*, being always not the work or achievement of Thérèse herself, but the work that is *done* in Thérèse, which she fully and thankfully accepts and receives. *Fiat mihi: Be it done unto me:* this accepting word of the Virgin of Virgins, that falls gently into the Lucan account of the coming of salvation, is at the very centre of the mystery of fruitful virginity in Thérèse as in Mary. It sounds the keynote of the marvellous life of Thérèse and of that which was done in her by that love which she knew from the dawn of consciousness as the spouse of Virgins.

The freedom of the human will must be preserved at all costs; here the Pelagian or Pelagianizing way and tendency of a certain Celtic Christianity, that somehow reached Thérèse through her saintly father, enters the story not to take over from the Augustinian emphasis on 'grace alone', but rather to balance it and steady it on the solid human earth. Céline is right to see her sister as *debout*, standing before the Son of Man in accordance with Luke 22.46. It is essential to preserve the delicate balance of divine activity and human receptivity. St Thérèse's *Story of a Soul*, like St Teresa's *Life* is the story of the divine activity, the divine mercies all the way through, but in each case it is a *human* story, lived out in constant prayer and constantly passing from active prayer to receptive prayer, that is never purely passive. All is grace, yes; but all is grace gratefully received.

It is only when this is understood that we can speak freely of the life of St Thérèse as the work of God. But we *can* speak freely and let the glory of the Source shine through. We can then admire the way Thérèse's short life was at every moment *overlighted*. It would be an interesting and fruitful study to prove this, or rather illustrate this, by going through the *Story of a Soul* chapter by chapter, but it is really enough to indicate this as a subject for a year's meditation; a prayerful attentive focus will produce not only the fulfilment of this expectation but some genuine surprises, for the divine work is wonderful beyond all human skill and genius.

All that has been said already about that 'prevenient grace' by which Thérèse saw herself as it were forelighted by the loving care of the great Lover fits in here. When Father Pichon in his rather ponderous way, assured her that she had 'never committed a single mortal sin', he added: 'You must thank God for the mercy he has shown you; if he left you to yourself you wouldn't be a little angel any longer; you'd be a little demon.'[20] Typically, Thérèse took this rather obvious piece of Father Confessor rhetoric and transmuted it into one of the golden hinges of her 'little way', insisting that for all her purity of life she was essentially a 'little soul' and that her way was truly open to every least and last and littlest 'little soul'. One is left wondering how far the great director of souls heard this call to the glory of humility in the depths of his own soul. Perhaps, after all, Fr. Hyacinthe Loyson was nearer to that glory at the end . . . But, quite firmly, Thérèse will not allow us to judge any of the priests who entered her life, nor for that matter anybody else. Least of all will she allow one to judge oneself except in the totally purifying, totally gentle light of Merciful Love.

20. *Autobiography of a Saint*, ed. R. Knox (London: Harill Press, 1958), p. 185.

CHAPTER 9

PRAYER AS PARTNERSHIP: THE RECEPTIVE DIMENSION

The Martyrdom of Desire

The mystical union towards which all Christian prayer reaches is a creative union of activity and passivity, which is best named receptivity or active receptivity or even active passivity. This journey of prayer involves a partnership between God and man in which God is all-goodness and all-giving, is as it were, in pain of giving, but *there is no real giving without receiving*, nor is there any real receiving without free consent. The best metaphor for this, at once metaphor and analogy, is the full, fully loving and fully responsible, union of man and woman in marriage. It is therefore named the 'Mystical Marriage' and expressed symbolically at the most sacred centre of revelation in the Song of Songs. It is God's gift, freely given, unconditionally given, as St Augustine and his followers emphasize, but it is also man's work as free receptivity, and this is what Pelagius and his followers emphasize.

We can watch this as it works itself out in practice in Manuscript B of the *Story of a Soul* of St Thérèse, and especially in the letter she wrote to her elder sister Marie of the Sacred Heart on 17 September 1896 (LT 197). This is of course connected with Manuscript B, a letter also written to Marie, in response to her request that Thérèse share with her some of the secrets that Jesus had confided in 'His little priviledged Spouse'¹. This letter, this manuscript, represents one of the summits of Christian mysticism. It was and is so powerful

---

1. *Letters of St Thérèse of Lisieux*, tr. J. Clarke, OCD. (Washington, DC: Institute of Carmelite Studies, 1988), Vol. II, p. 991.

in its expression of love of God that it left Marie convinced that this kind of love of God was totally outside her reach. Our present text is Thérèse's reply to this, a reply penned in a few minutes of free time before the nine o' clock office of Compline. It is worth quoting in full.

Dear Sister, I am not embarrassed in answering you . . . How can you ask me if it is possible for you to love God as I love Him? . . .

If you had understood the story of my little bird, you would not have asked me this question. My desires of martyrdom *are nothing*; they are not what give me the unlimited confidence that I feel in my heart. They are, to tell the truth, the spiritual riches that *render one unjust*, when one rests in them with complacence and when one believes they are *something great* . . . These desires are a *consolation* that Jesus grants at times to weak souls like mine (and these souls are numerous), but when He does not give this *consolation*, it is a grace of *privilege*. Recall those words of Father: 'The martyrs suffered with joy, and the King of Martyrs suffered with sadness.' Yes, Jesus said: 'Father, let this chalice pass away from me.' Dear Sister, how can you say after this that my desires are the sign of my love? . . . Ah! I really feel that it is not this at all that pleases God in my little soul; what pleases Him is *that He sees me loving my littleness* and my *poverty, the blind hope that I have in His mercy*. That is my only treasure, dear Godmother, why would this treasure not be yours?

Are you not ready to suffer all that God will desire? I really know that you are ready; therefore, if you want to feel joy, to have an attraction for suffering, it is your consolation that you are seeking, since when we love a thing the pain disappears. I assure you, if we were to go to martyrdom together in the dispositions we are in now, you would have great merit, and I would have none at all, unless Jesus was pleased to change my dispositions.

Oh, dear Sister, I beg you, understand your little girl, understand that to love Jesus, to be His *victim of love*, the weaker one is, without desires or virtues, the more suited one is for the workings of this consuming and transforming Love . . . The *desire* alone to be a victim suffices, but we must consent to remain always poor and without strength, and this is the difficulty, for: 'The truly poor in spirit, where do we find him? You must look for him from afar,' said the psalmist . . . He does not say that you must look for him among great souls, but 'from afar,' that is to say in *lowliness*, in *nothingness* . . . Ah! let us remain then *very far* from all that sparkles, let us love our littleness, let us love to feel nothing, then we shall be poor in spirit, and Jesus will come to look for us, and *however far* we may be, He will transform us in flames of love.

Oh! how I would like to be able to make you understand what I feel! . . . It is confidence and nothing but confidence that must lead us to Love . . . Does not fear lead to Justice (1)? . . . Since we see the *way*, let us run together. Yes, I feel it, Jesus wills to give us the same graces, He wills to give us His heaven *gratuitously*,

Oh, dear little Sister, if you do not understand me, it is because you are too great a soul . . . or rather it is because I am explaining myself poorly, for I am sure that God would not give you the desire to be *possessed by Him* by His *Merciful Love* if He were not reserving this favour for you . . . or rather He has already given it to you, since you have given yourself to *Him*, since you *desire* to be consumed by *Him*, and since God never gives desires that He cannot realize . . .

Nine O'Clock is ringing, and I am obliged to leave you, Ah, how I would like to tell you things, but Jesus is going to make you feel all that I cannot write . . .

I love you with all the tenderness of my *grateful little childlike heart*.

(1) To *strict justice* as it is portrayed for sinners, but not this *Justice* that Jesus will have toward those who love Him.

If one looks closely at the key third paragraph through the lenses of analytical understanding, one is soon rebuffed by an inner contradiction between the unconditionality of 'the desire alone suffices', and the strong conditionality of 'but we must consent', and as long as we work in this cold clear light of the mind the contradiction remains. It is only when, going behind the words, we begin to connect with the strong pure feeling out of which the words are so painfully penned that a warmer light begins very gently to reveal to us another kind of reality, that can only be *seen* as it is *felt* in 'the deep heart's core'. For ultimately, as St Augustine saw, the light of truth shines not only on the mind but on the heart as well. It is not only 'the light above the mind' but also 'the light that charity knows' (*Confessions* Bk 7, ch. 10). St Thérèse was no philosopher, but all this she understood intuitively. Blondel was not a mystic but a philosopher with a rare understanding of Christian mysticism, and he was one of those who, in the wake of the great Pascal, brought into his philosophy the wisdom of the heart. This, he knew, can only be trusted when the heart has been purified by prayer and sacrifice.

The balancing of head and heart, of intellect and feeling is one of the great challenges for every human being and there is little doubt but that Thérèse achieved this balance with unexampled finesse and consistency. But a far more difficult challenge, only achievable if at all, at the highest level of wisdom and experience, is that of balancing intellect and feeling *as ways of knowing* and understanding. It is not only that, in Pascal's words, 'the heart has its reasons which reason does not know', but that, at the mystical level, which is the level of the fullest truth, reason must find room for the insights of the heart. There is a level of mystical knowing which must take account of the contributions of feeling, where we must feel our way *willingly* and painfully into the truth. Not only has the Truth, *veritas (talēthes)* to be seen in order to be lived (for it is also the Real, *to on*) but it must be lived *and felt* to be truly seen. That is why one can speak of a 'moral logic' which unites heart and head, which unites meditation and prayer. It is armed with this moral or mystical logic that we must focus on the writings of St Thérèse of Lisieux.

Let us look more closely at the letter cited above. The first part of the first paragraph has to do with desire. In Manuscript B Thérèse had given free rein to her desire or desires for martyrdom, not in itself or in its negativity, but simply as an expression of love: etymologically, martyrdom means witness or testimony; it bears witness to the total seriousness of one's commitment to God, as enshrined in that ancient Mosaic commandment which Jesus summed up in the one commandment of love of God and love of the neighbour. Those who seek the fullness of life and being, desire this total commitment to God as source and fulfilment, indeed as the 'pearl of great price' of which the gospels speak. According to the Christian mystical tradition, which Thérèse and her sister have chosen freely, yet with the help of the gracious drawing of God's love, this love and the desire for it, is at one and the same time a gift of God and a free human choice, thus at once a gift received and a gift freely accepted and freely preferred to everything else, even to life itself. It is the 'pearl of great price' for which a man or woman gives up all he or she has.

In this first paragraph of LT 197, Thérèse makes it quite clear that, as she sees it, her desires for martyrdom are a free gift from God, which indeed can be seen as a kind of consolation that God gives to weak souls because they are weak. There is, she adds, in paragraph 2, no 'merit' in this, that is to say no special claim on God. Reform theology would tend to say that there never is any human claim on God and that it is quite wrong to speak of merit in this sense. Thérèse would agree that everything between God and humankind is grace and gift and that this is true even of our desires. In her mystical receptivity she is very happy indeed to see everything coming down from heaven to meet human need and littleness as its proper receptacle. Indeed her great discovery as a spiritual genius is that the more we accept our littleness and nothingness, like children who depend for everything on their parents, the more truly we are following the way of Christ, which is the way of spiritual childhood.

This she tells us in the third paragraph of LT 197, is the way to be what she calls a *victim of love*. Being a victim of love for Thérèse, who in a real sense invented the phrase, means letting the merciful love of God so transform us that our whole nature is, as it were, sacrificed to this as in ancient times the gifts offered up to God were totally consumed in the sacrificial fire. So, being a victim of love implies a total consecration and immolation of one's whole natural self to God's invitation to be one with him in Spiritual Marriage. But, and this is all-important, marriage is not marriage unless the bride *consents* to it. Not only this, but the matter is so important, the free consent of the bride is so necessary, that the divine bridegroom has, as it were, to test the bride, to discover if she is truly receptive, truly open to all he has to give. So, four small words in paragraph 3 are so central that everything hangs on them.

These words are *but we must consent* (mais il faut consentir); and of course this consent must be truly free.

It may seem a small thing, and Thérèse is adept at uttering the whisper laden with eternal meaning. But there is no doubt about it: she will have nothing to do with Quietism nor with that understanding of grace in which the divine unconditional giving is so emphasized that it sweeps all before it, in which the divine decree of predestination carries with it as logical companion a divine decree of reprobation. The God Thérèse discovered, mediated by her father, mediated by the Suffering Servant of Isaiah, was and is the God who is Merciful Love. It is this God that she is, strangely, bringing into being for the whole modern world. And just as it is clear from St Luke's account of the Annunciation that the free consent of Mary (the *fiat mihi,* the *genoito moi,* Luke 1.38) is *essential* to the narrative, so here in this account of the birthing of God in Thérèse and those who follow her 'little way', free consent is essential to this sacred marriage (*hieros gamos*) of the soul and God. This in its turn gives its proper dignity, in joy and sacrifice, to human marriage as a great 'mystery' and a sacrament.

Thérèse was a woman of desires: this is the whole burden, the central theme of Manuscript B and we have already noted how often this theme appears in her writings. Indeed in the *Table of Citations* which forms the third volume of the *Manuscrits Autobiographiques de Sainte Thérèse* we find that *désir* and *désirer* together run to five columns of references. This indicates, but does not by any means measure, the importance, at once central and profound, of the desiring will which is both the pulse beat and the limitless horizon of the heart-world of Thérèse, whose aspiration was to be love at the heart of the mystical body. Here we are looking at a place, an ambience, where measurement is no longer valid. Thérèse is indeed willing to change her phrase 'infinite desires' to 'immense desires' in obedience to theologians, but one feels strongly that in changing the word Thérèse was in no way changing the sentiment and that human desires could be, indeed had to be, the full bridal echo of the heart of the Bridegroom.

It is in Manuscript B especially that Thérèse feels she can give full expression to her boundless desires and she tells her sister Marie, though she is by a kind of open subterfuge directly addressing Jesus Christ, that these desires are a veritable martyrdom. This 'martyrdom' was surely the pain of transformation as the divine infinity touches and unites with human finitude but this touch, this meeting of finitude and infinitude would be simply impossible were it not that there was a real *capacity* for it both ways, that is to say, for human deification and for divine humanization. The patristic theologians used to state as a kind of principle that God became man in order that man should become God.

When Marie of the Sacred Heart very naturally felt discouraged on reading about these desires (quite unexampled in mystical writing, it must be admitted), Thérèse is moved to protest in a tone of (for her) quite unusual urgency. 'My desires of martyrdom *are nothing*; they are not what gives me the unlimited confidence that I feel in my heart. They are to tell the truth the (spiritual) riches that *render one unjust*.' And Thérèse refers to Luke 16.11 which contrasts true and false riches: if one sees these desires as somehow one's own possession (as Marie seems to want) they become a barrier to God's grace as do the riches of 'the sinful mammon'. These desires she saw as *given*, as graces, as a kind of riches which had to be received in humility. So the desires are really a divine gift and as such they carry an implicit promise of fulfilment. But the same proviso always holds: provided we open up in blind hope to the divine merciful givingness. 'Blind hope', that is hope blindly willed, for at this time, September 1896, Thérèse is within that total darkness of feeling and understanding which came to her at Easter 1896, and lasted right up to her death on 30 September 1897. As the desires are in the *will*, so too is the blind hope (*l'espérance aveugle*), for the light of intellect has totally vanished into the 'impenetrable darkness' that surrounds her.

Here some of the purest springs of mystical wisdom flow together. The 'blind hope' of Thérèse unites with the light within the darkness of the *noche oscura* of St John of the Cross, for this light is also that which, in the deep darkness of intellect, burns within the heart (*en el corazón ardía*), that is to say within the affective will. As far as this point the human self, the soul has walked in the daylight of a reasonable faith, a faith seeking and finding understanding, a faith secure in its own light, a faith not indeed arrogant but self-sufficient. But what is the soul to do when this light goes out and with it all security and sufficiency? Here in this dark tunnel, in this 'impenetrable darkness' there is neither God nor heaven nor any life beyond death. Yes, but, for Thérèse there are still her desires, her immense desires, her infinite desires. 'Do not say infinite', says the theologian, 'for nothing merely human is infinite, say "immense" and this Act of Oblation to Merciful Love, can stand.' Thérèse obeys but she knows that she is now in a world beyond ordinary theology and she will continue to speak of 'infinite desires'. For though God has hidden his face and all comforting images of heaven and a life beyond have vanished, yet Thérèse still believes, all the more purely and firmly believes, in merciful love, and more than ever she is creating the human receptacle for merciful love. This is the act beyond all acts within all human action that Maurice Blondel came to envisage at the highest point of the meditation on *Action*.

We are here at the highest and deepest point of Catholic mystical theology; at this point the theorizing of this century's greatest philosophical theologian, Maurice Blondel, coincides with the lived experience of her who is arguably the century's greatest mystic, Thérèse of Lisieux. This is indeed a very French achievement but it is not really thus confined in space and time. For it is clear that Maurice Blondel in his vision of theogony was deeply influenced by that mighty human vision of the ultimate known as post-Kantian German Idealism. On the other hand, Thérèse was helped and supported by the hand of St Francis of Assisi, stretched across the centuries; moreover, in her rediscovery of the God of Merciful Love she was returning to the spirit of the Spanish Carmelites: one feels that her unconscious, or her highest vision, was assuring her of this in her dream of the Venerable Anne of Jesus which introduces Manuscript B. Something of universal significance for the third millennium was emerging from the burning heart of Christian Europe.

The Time of Trial

Let us look again in detail at Thérèse's experience of the 'impenetrable darkness' that descended on her with varying degrees of intensity for the last eighteen months of her life, opening up various mystical horizons. Thérèse referred to this firmly and not infrequently as the time of her trial (*épreuve*) and the most complete account of this is to be found in Manuscript C of the *Story of a Soul*. This account begins with the incident on the night of Good Friday, 1896, which Thérèse sees as 'the first call' (*premier appel*) of her only beloved, Jesus, the Divine Bridegroom, to come to him. This was, medically speaking, haemoptysis (or the spitting of blood) and for Thérèse it foretold her death as coming soon. At this point, heaven and all it meant of joy and gladness was so clear and certain for her, that she was filled with joy (*une grande consolation*) and she noted that this call came on the anniversary of the death of the one she loved above everybody and everything: this though she did not usually attach much importance to what may be called 'the piety of anniversaries'. She told Mother Gonzague that she then received a great grace, or at least what on consideration she had come to see as a great grace; *Je la considère comme une grande grâce*. With that mixture of astonishing magnanimity and breath-taking humility so characteristic of Thérèse, she sees it as an important event in Mother Gonzague's term as prioress. As much as to say: 'You are truly honoured by this event that has set the seal on *my* nothingness.'

Up until this point, Thérèse had felt safe and secure within a Roman Catholic style of belief accepted in its totality and in detail. In other words her *will* was firmly supported by a belief system which only strict Roman Catholics could accept then, and can barely accept today. So strongly, so totally *alive* was her faith that she simply could not understand or imagine how anybody could really and truly and honestly disagree with this watertight system. Yet, immediately after that Good Friday–Holy Saturday call and the 'great consolation' that accompanied it, at Easter that is to say, when that liturgy by which a Carmelite lives and breathes is full of joy, Thérèse suddenly awakened as it were, to find eveything changed, for she had somehow been plunged into darkness. The way Thérèse introduces this is significant. She introduces it as a God-given or God-permitted state coming directly after a strong statement telling of the clear and living faith that filled her whole mind; so much so, she adds with, it seems, conscious irony, that she could not accept that anybody who denied the reality of heaven was not speaking against his inner convictions. It is thus, somewhat indirectly, that she develops her description of the darkness that has come upon her, telling us that it is such that *now* she understands the inner state of unbelievers, and that she has been asked 'to eat at their table'. Here is her experience in her own words:

> I should explain that at this time I had a faith so living and so lucid that the thought of heaven was the sum of all my happiness. I couldn't believe that there really were godless people who had no faith at all; it was only by being false to his own inner convictions that a man could deny the existence of heaven. What, no beautiful heaven, where God himself would be our eternal reward?
>
> But there are souls which haven't got any faith, which lose, through misuse of grace, this precious treasure, fountain of all pure and true happiness. And now, in those happy days of Easter-tide, Jesus taught me to realise that. He allowed my soul to be overrun by an impenetrable darkness, which made the thought of heaven, hitherto so welcome, a subject of nothing but conflict and torment. And this trial was not to be a matter of a few days or a few weeks; it was to last until the moment when God should see fit to remove it. And that moment hasn't come yet.
>
> I wish I could put down what I feel about it, but unfortunately that isn't possible; to appreciate the darkness of this tunnel, you have to have been through it. Perhaps, though, I might try to explain it by a comparison. You must imagine that I've been born in a country entirely overspread with a thick mist; I have never seen nature in her smiling mood, all bathed and transfigured in the sunlight. But I've heard of these wonderful experiences, ever since I was a child; and I know that the country in which I live is not my native country; *that* lies elsewhere, and it must always be the centre of my longings. Mightn't that, you suggest, be simply a fable, invented by some dweller

in the mist? Oh no, the fact is certain; the King of that sunlit country has come and lived in the darkness, lived there for thirty-three years.

Poor darkness, that could not recognise him for what he was, the King of light! But here am I, Lord, one of your own children, to whom your divine light has made itself known; and, by way of asking pardon for these brothers of mine, I am ready to live on starvation diet as long as you will have it so – not for me to rise from this unappetising meal I share with poor sinners until the appointed time comes. Meanwhile, I can only pray in my own name, and in the name of these brothers of mine: 'Lord, have mercy on us, we are sinners! Send us home restored to your favour. May all those who have no torch of faith to guide them catch sight, at least, of its rays. And, Jesus, if the table they have defiled must be cleansed by the sacrifice of a soul that still loves you, let me go on there alone, taking my fill of trials, until you are ready to receive me into your bright kingdom. All I ask is that no sin of mine may offend you.' . . .

What I was saying was that the sure prospect of escaping from this dark world of exile had been granted me from childhood upwards; and it wasn't simply that I accepted it on the authority of people who knew more of the matter than I did – I felt, in the very depths of my heart, aspirations which could only be satisfied by a world more beautiful than this. Just as Christopher Columbus divined, by instinct, the existence of a New World which nobody had hitherto dreamt of, so I had this feeling that a better country was to be, one day, my abiding home. And now, all of a sudden, the mists around me have become denser than ever; they sink deep into my soul and wrap it round so that I can't recover the dear image of my native country any more – everything has disappeared.

I get tired of the darkness all around me, and try to refresh my jaded spirits with the thoughts of that bright country where my hopes lie; and what happens? It is worse torment than ever; the darkness itself seems to borrow, from the sinners who live in it, the gift of speech. I hear its mocking accents; 'It's all a dream, this talk of a heavenly country, bathed in light, scented with delicious perfumes, and of a God who made it all, who is to be your possession in eternity! You really believe, do you, that the mist which hangs about you will clear away later on? All right, all right, go on longing for death! But death will make nonsense of your hopes; it will only mean a night darker than ever, the night of mere non-existence.[2]

We know that Thérèse already possessed her faith in deep and constant aridity.[3] Aridity was a state of the soul recognized by all the writers on the spiritual life then as now: it means that the understanding of prayer and the will to pray were unaccompanied by any *feelings* of joy or comfort. In other words, the whole world of sense as perception and feeling was in a kind of dryness and deadness, even though at another level that was not affected by sense-perception or sense feelings, there was light in the understanding and a strong adhesion to God in the will, as conviction and as love. All self-related feelings of comfort and consolation had vanished to be replaced by a firm adhesion to the truths of reason and revelation already deeply and securely held, as accepted and understood. Thus the virtue of faith flourished having been as it were watered by the insights and 'imaginations' of the Illuminative way: asceticism and purification had already been assimilated and put in place in the Purgative way.

Thérèse never used this kind of language any more than Shakespeare spoke of catharsis or quoted Longinus *On The Sublime*. She did not have the education for this in the way that John of the Cross had or Edith Stein. She was grateful to God that she did not have to spend time over 'spiritual tomes', yet she did very happily and fruitfully study the spiritual tomes of St Teresa and St John of the Cross and found inspiration in recalling both, St John of the Cross especially, right up to the end.

Thérèse gives no indication that she linked her trial and its 'impenetrable darkness' with the 'dark night' of the most celebrated of the great mystical poems of St John of the Cross, or with the treatise on the *Dark Night of the Soul* in which John 'explains' these

---

2. *Autobiography of a Saint*, ed. R. Knox (London: Harvill Press, 1958), pp. 253–6.
3. Sister Geneviève of the Holy Face, *A Memoir of My Sister St. Thérèse*, (Dublin: M. H. Gill & Son, 1959), p. 103.

stanzas, this although it seems clear that Thérèse had read and studied John's writings. Commentators are divided on this issue, and it seems best to take Thérèse's experience in its own terms, while keeping in mind that Thérèse admitted her debt to John, yet as subordinate to her debt to the New Testament. She would certainly be more constantly conscious of the *Lamma Sabacthani* of Jesus than of the dark night of St John of the Cross, and it is in this especially that she would have found that higher light within the darkness of which she was to speak as giving something of perfect joy, so much so that at times she even wonders whether heaven can hold or could hold, any greater joy. These moments, like the moment of meeting Fr. Alexis Prou in the confessional, were precious moments and they link Thérèse with St Francis of Assisi and 'the perfect joy of St Francis', but they were all the same fleeting moments and the passage in Manuscript C must stand as Thérèse's own considered statement, given under obedience, of her trial, sometimes called, but not by Thérèse, her 'trial of faith'.

At the time of her trial Thérèse had long gone beyond all reliance on pious feeling and consolations. Her state, she tells us, was one of habitual aridity. But she had come to a firm intellectual acceptance of God; we must remember that every Carmelite had a retreat of eight days every year as well as days of silence from time to time, and thus acquired a rather specialized knowledge of Christian theology, a full exploration of the faith in its Roman Catholic mediation with a strong emphasis on ascetical and mystical theology. But Roman Catholic theology, whatever its limitations, will have nothing to do with blind fideism. Faith has to be a 'reasonable service' and the common attacks on the faith and the misunderstandings of such doctrines as Mariology and Papal Infallibility are explored. Normally the retreat father was a Jesuit, and it was not forgotten that the great Teresa of Avila preferred a truly 'learned' man (i.e. theologian) to a merely pious man, though she hoped for a combination of learning and piety. From this point of view the Franciscan, Fr. Alexis Prou, was regarded as not quite up to standard, though ironically he turned out to be just what Thérèse needed at that time.

So Thérèse, after eight or nine years in Carmel was not at all, especially given her natural sharpness of mind and deep love of the truth, a woman of simple unquestioning faith. She was in fact very given to reflection and intellectual exploration. Nor had she, as one might be tempted to suppose, a naive 'childish' conception of heaven. Rather hers was a faith always 'seeking understanding'.

This 'impenetrable darkness', this 'wall up to the sky' was not simply a question seeking an intellectual solution, a challenge to deeper understanding, not even a feeling of confusion such as can be reasonably postponed for a quiet time or for the help of some 'learned man'. Thérèse had had plenty of experience of this, and was in a distress of this kind when she was rescued by Alexis Prou. No, this great trial at the end of her short life was of a different quality altogether. The night of mere non-existence, *la nuit de néant*: it is a chilling phrase and the chill (*amertume*) was to stay with Thérèse during all the remaining eighteen months of her life. At its worst it left her alone in the dark with a mind once so full of light now totally devoid of light. Yet this closing off, it would seem, of all *intellectual* light forced Thérèse to travel in the dark by the light of the *will*. It forced her, as it were, to *create* the God she could not see, to bring the God of love to birth in a place where only love remained.

It is at this point that it is, I think, necessary to supplement the *ipsissima verba* of Thérèse as we find them in Manuscript C of the *Story of a Soul* with what may be called the *fioretti* of the Carmelite mystic, not quite the *ipsissima verba*, but yet rather more well attested than the *fioretti* of St Francis. I am thinking principally of the *Last Conversations* and the *Memoir* of Sister Geneviève, Thérèse's sister Céline.

Two things especially emerge from these documents. Firstly, more and more Thérèse is moving from a vision of God as love to a vision of love as God. God as Father, as Son and as Holy Spirit has hidden himself, but all the more does love follow him, all the more does she affirm that 'love alone counts'.[4] This love by which

---

4. *St Thérèse of Lisieux: Her Last Conversations*, tr. J. Clark, OCD (Washington, DC: Institute of Carmelite Studies, 1977), p. 261.

Thérèse lives and breathes is only deepened by the pain of the absence of God, and so, in typical Thérèsian fashion loss is turned into gain, the God who hides himself is all the more truly found by sacrificial love. Secondly, the goodness of God is strongly affirmed against the absence of God. 'Oh, my *good* God', Thérèse prays again and again, as if she is affirming the truth of God's goodness against all the forces of evil. It is as if the pain of absence of God is being turned to the gold of the presence of God won in that very pain and thus distilling perfect joy. Here we see the precious transformative effect of that prayer that is rooted and grounded in the human will, what *The Cloud of Unknowing* names the 'naked intent of the will'. Thérèse knows she is dying but in her feelings and in her thoughts all this means is total eternal annihilation in 'the night of nothingness' as she names her state of total darkness. All feeling and all thought of God's presence is gone; all that remains – and this nevertheless is everything in the order of love and desire – all that remains is that 'naked intent of the will'. It is here, though she cannot *feel* or even *think* this, that the final union of the soul and God, the final spiritual marriage is achieved.

Thus it is alone and at the level of the will that Thérèse accomplishes the great work of theogony, as it were creating the God who has hidden himself, withdrawn himself. She is finding that face of God that has been hidden and could only show itself in so far as it found a human receptivity, a human heart on which to imprint itself. There is a sense in which Thérèse crying 'O my *good* God' is providing the human receptacle for that goodness, is in a sense creating that goodness.

The will of Thérèse was, is, a great work of God, yet the works of God are all partial works unless they are also works of man, of manwomanhood, marked deeply with the signature of the *humanum* in its full freedom as divine consort. In full freedom the human will opens up the space for receptivity which the eternal divine love and 'givingness' is yearning to fill and simply cannot fill unless the human open freely to receive it. Anything else would be a kind of rape, violence rather than gentleness. That 'infinitely gentle' Being can only come into total gentleness and the human will must 'bend low and low' to receive this gentleness. To know is to possess but it can be to possess in the mode of having and attachment, so for the consummation of this spiritual marriage all having, all possessiveness, all dogmatic certainty must go. As John of the Cross saw clearly, the fire burning in the heart must take the place of the light in the mind. This involves a liberation from dogma in the possessive and arrogant sense. It is the way of pure receptivity, opening ever more deeply to the inner horizons of the prayer 'out of the depths' – *De Profundis*. Thérèse *lived* this in the drama of her death in a kind of total purity of receptive suffering, which had to be illuminated by the glow of the fire of love in the deepest darkness of understanding.

Thus, it would seem that once the mystic has lost all sense of the companionship and presence of God then he or she, because life consisted in total absorption in God, has lost everything. Surely Thérèse, living day and night in 'impenetrable darkness', would have little or nothing to say about the God so totally in hiding, or about that total security of faith that had, as it were, flown away. But almost the opposite is true. Not only is she constantly cheerful and constantly supporting those around her, but the salty gleam of irony is more lively than ever. It was during this time that she wrote Manuscript B and Manuscript C of the *Story of a Soul*, it was during this time also that she wrote some of her most vibrant and transcendent poems; it was to this period that most of her *Last Conversations* belong.

Thérèse herself tried to explain the poems by saying simply: '*Je chante simplement ce que je veux croire.*' Knox does his best with this phrase, at once as light as a snowflake and as heavy as the whole of human destiny; he translates: 'I'm simply talking about what I'm determined to believe.' A good shot and worthy of Knox. But does he realize that here the bride is veiled, even veiled from her own eyes? That in Thérèse which consummated the spiritual marriage is that which emerges, alone and beautiful beyond all earthly beauty, from the cleansing alchemy of the 'impenetrable darkness'. It is that human *will* which alone consummates the transformation of the spiritual marriage and which is the true story of Thérèse's nine years of preparation and suffering in the convent. In order that her bridal will should be finally transformed into charity, the light of the intellect had to be taken away and with it all sense of a heaven that would appeal to the merely natural, to the senses and the imagination. What remained, stronger than ever, was the will and the way of love which only the divinized soul could appreciate. What we must try to understand is that through the years of heroic sisterly charity, Thérèse had become established in the full willing acceptance of this. This could only arise from the marriage of the human will with the divine will beyond all human understanding, beyond all mere human rejoicing. We are in the 'beyond' region, facing the horizons of mystery and the mystical. Here Thérèse can give us light born of darkness.

The Liberation of Dogma

The 'impenetrable darkness' was not only a dark night of purification, but also a precious gift and divine grace of *liberation* from the swaddling clothes of Catholic and Christian dogma. This is at once a liberation *from* dogma and a liberation *of* dogma: it releases or extricates the mystical kernel of dogma from the containing shell. The mystical kernel is variously named as love, goodness, greatness of soul, holiness, purity of soul: this one thing has many names. Maurice Blondel, the great Christian philosopher names it, in New Testament terms, as the *unum necessarium* or the 'pearl of great price'.

In the great religions there has been a constant dialectic or to-and-fro tension between the people of the kernel, the mystics, and the people of the shell, the theologians. The shell of dogma is necessary to preserve the kernel. But of itself the shell is useless: 'like a sounding brass or a tinkling cymbal', says St Paul who names the kernel as agape or love-charity. (1 Cor. 13). Normally the shell is necessary to preserve the kernel, and it can be disastrous to throw away the shell for the sake of the kernel. Only the divinity present in the kernel can do this.

If we look back at the passage cited above (p. 229) from the point of view of the metaphor of the kernel and the nutshell, we can say that Thérèse woke up one morning to find that the much cherished nutshell of dogma or dogmatic faith had disappeared into broken fragments and it almost seemed at first as if the kernel had disappeared with it. But the kernel had not disappeared and Thérèse could sing along with it more tunefully than ever and could still radiate its power and joy to all around her. We must therefore be very careful with the phrase, *Je chante simplement ce que je veux croire*, though, as has been said above it must be admitted that Knox made a good shot at it when he translates 'I'm simply talking about what I'm determined to believe', for in fact her imagination is opening to the hidden beauty and radiance of the 'pearl of great price' in its pure heavenly beauty. It is, in St Paul's words, the agape, the charity that 'never fails', even if all its external concomitants ('prophecies', 'speaking in tongues', even 'knowledge', *gnōsis*) should disappear. This spiritual beauty of charity had shone forth for a few minutes as Thérèse guided the faltering steps of the suffering old Sister along the bare Carmelite cloister in the cold light of evening. It was to shine forth again, this time steadily and without the least ray of halfway radiance, in the last comfortless period of Thérèse's life towards that death which is 'precious in the sight of the lord' in ever purer heavenly radiance.

The Holy Face

At this point a further horizon begins to appear. Thérèse's way of littleness, as she lived it to the full in her following of Christ, led her deep into the Garden of Gethsemane and on to the final dereliction of the cross as expressed in that ancient song that goes beyond all religious comfort: *My God, my God, why hast thou forsaken me*. It would seem that Jesus, the Anointed One, was identifying with the forsakeness of a world that had so forsaken God, so connived with the enemy of God, that its deep (ontological) state of being was that of *being forsaken by God*.

As Thérèse deepened her understanding of her call to contemplation, she entered more and more into what has been called the dark ikon, that is the picture of the face of the suffering Christ as portrayed by Second Isaiah ch. 53, vv. 2–3, the image of a face bruised and battered, a once beautiful face now darkened, dishonoured, spat upon, despised. Joining hands across the millennia with that great prophet and mystic, Thérèse added a new contemplative image to her name and was thereafter to be known as Sister Thérèse of the Child Jesus and the *Holy Face*. This was no simple pious addition, for in choosing the contemplation of the suffering countenance of Jesus as the full statement of her vocation, Thérèse knew that she was entering into the depths of spiritual and psychic dereliction, the test or *peirasmos* which is named as the great affliction in the Lord's prayer, in the face of which this prayer protects the Christian, indeed protects all who, in any religious tradition, are called into the depths of sacrifice. For the Lord's Prayer opens up to the all-fathering, all-mothering source of all being and goodness and calls out for protection against two dark terrors, the terror of the great test, the crucible, the *peirasmos*, and the terror of the evil power, of Satan, the Adversary, the *Ponaeros*

Lead us not into *temptation*
But deliver us from *evil*

If we read Luke's account of the Prayer of Jesus on the Mount or Garden of Olives, we find him praying desperately to the Father, which is the Divine Source of his Being to remove from him the cup of what Hopkins calls 'the dark and driven passion', and when he comes out of this terrible place and finds his disciples asleep he says 'Rise up and pray that you may not enter into temptation' (Luke 22.46). It is as if they had come to the fringes of something unbelievably terrible and needed to ward it off by prayer. Indeed for those who do not trivialize it, the Lord's Prayer is a constant daily call for protection from the terror of darkness and undoing. Yet the Lord's Prayer does not quite say *this*, as it prays to ward off Satan. The great test, the *peirasmos* is not just pushed away; rather does it seem that we are being led into it by the Source Itself, by the all-holy, all fathering, all-mothering God, so that what the prayer does is to ask that we should not be brought too deep into this ultimate terror; 'Do not lead us too far into this terror': that is our prayer.

Now Thérèse knew all this and she prayed this prayer. But she was also totally dedicated to the sacrifice of all that she had and all that she was, like a rose unpetalled leaf by leaf under the bleeding feet of the Beloved: the image is her own and she wrote a poem about it, shortly before she died. Thérèse was a fair versifier, and there is a deep-lived sincerity about the image of the unpetalled rose which gives the poem its own beauty in the original French.

And so, Thérèse of the Child Jesus and the Holy Face followed her Beloved right into the Garden of the Agony. So great of heart and soul was she that she set out to scale that ultimate pinnacle of the total sacrifice of the Lamb of God. Let us see the way of this, how it happened and why.

In its relation to the central figure of Jesus Christ, the Son of God, who is also the human son of man, Christian theology in the Western world tends to take one of two forms: the substitutional form and the imitational form. We find both forms on either side of the great divide of the Reformation but on the whole Reform theology tends to be substitutional and Catholic theology (Roman or Anglican) tends to be imitational. In substitutional theology, Christ has 'done it all' for us, that is to say, all and more than all that is necessary for salvation, for shaking off the bonds and bondage of sin and becoming bright and shining in God's sight. Christ lifts us up, reaching down for us, not because of any merit or justification of our own, but through free grace and graciousness. To try to do anything of ourselves by way of pilgrimage or fasting or monastic observances or 'indulgences', or the so-called sacrifice of the Mass is to put on our own moth-eaten garments when we could be freely clothed by Christ through faith. Over against this there are the various theologies of imitation which focus on those texts in the New Testament in which Jesus asks people to follow him, to take up the cross daily, to leave all and thus be fully his disciples. This approach has been central to that traditional Catholic theology and piety in which Thérèse grew up from her earliest years and which is at the back of the decision that gradually took hold of her to follow Jesus all the way to Gethsemane and Calvary, to share all its total dereliction and terror. It was within this that Thérèse lived in the last eighteen months of her life until she died on 30 September 1897.

Thérèse lived and died half a century before the advent of existentialism with its emphasis on the paradoxes of being and nothingness, yet in trying to express her state of mind and soul she comes up with a phrase that has the authentic note of existentialist *angst*. She finds herself she says, in the 'night of nothingness' *la nuit de néant*. It must be understood that this night of nothingness as Thérèse experienced it, as perhaps Jesus experienced it in the *Lamma Sabacthani*, is not itself negative in the sense that it is a cessation of consciousness; quite the contrary, it is a positive, totally shattering, totally annihilating experience of being annihilated, a living, lived annihilation, a deep nightmare from which one cannot awaken, for the reason that it is experienced in the total lucidity of wakefulness. It may be said that Thérèse is upheld by faith, but this experience is far beyond all faith.

But why should all this be? One can, of course, speak of the passive dark night of spirit as vividly explored in the second book of the *Dark Night of the Soul* of St John of the Cross, a text that Thérèse knew almost by heart. But to understand Thérèse one has to bring forward something in the background in John of the Cross, perhaps too securely taken for granted in both Teresa of Avila and John of the Cross. It is this. The place in which Thérèse found herself was that 'hell' in which those people found themselves who had not simply lost touch with the Divine Source, but had become by various forms of connivance held in total bondage by another force, by Satan, the terrible *Ponaeros* or Adversary. Satan had gained a certain 'rightful' hold over such people and that hold could only be broken by a fellow human being who could suffer and survive through this terror and despair that sealed it and, so to speak, cemented it into the soul that had given away its freedom. Again here Luther will say that Christ had already done this and done it far more perfectly than any human being could do it.

Indeed for Luther it is to diminish Christ and deconstruct his work to see any need for another intermediary.

This controversay goes deep and it must be treated with respect and understanding. Both attitudes have their roots in the New Testament, St Paul especially, but it may be claimed that a careful understanding of the sense and scope of the scriptural evidence allows us, and indeed invites us, to reconcile the two. Luther is not denying the force of the imitational texts, but only saying in the wake of St Augustine, that nobody can follow Christ without the constant present help of the grace of Christ. Neither is the theology which Thérèse represents saying that one can go the whole way or even one step of the way in the following of Christ without the grace of Christ helping, sanctifying and transforming. But the theology which Thérèse followed made much of certain texts which Luther tended to overlook or explain away, especially St Paul's statement in Colossians 1.24, where Paul tells us that he rejoices in his suffering in order to 'complete what is lacking in Christ's afflictions'. Thérèse felt an insistent call to do just this by, as she puts it, sitting at the table of sinners in a great and terrible darkness so that her prayer and presence could as it were provide a space for Christ to enter, for nothing can be given that is not received; thus Thérèse, by making common cause with these held fast through their own weakness and connivance in that hell which is the very ambience of Satan, is able to receive within that place the presence and fragrance of Christ. This is vicariousness at a very deep and terrifying level, and in the last 18 months of her life Thérèse, having accepted this great 'total experience' of the *peirasmos*, was totally broken and seemingly destroyed. Yet she was on the way to Resurrection for all of us.

Before she died, Thérèse spoke of her belief that she would 'spend her heaven doing good upon earth'. She concealed, as she tended to do, a phrase of cosmic scope and daring within the language of conventional piety. Deep down, albeit inarticulately, she felt that out of the total misery and pain and dereliction of the Cross of Christ renewed in her, and the face of Christ reflected in her, the whole fabric and face of creation was being transformed.

The Ultimate Horizon

St Thérèse died on 30 September 1897 at 7.20 in the evening. Here, as close as we can come to it, is the Carmelite account of her death:

> Hardly had the community knelt at her bedside when Thérèse pronounced very distinctly, while gazing at her crucifix. 'Oh! I love Him!' And a moment later: 'My God, I love you!'
>
> Suddenly her eyes came to life and were fixed on a spot just a little above the statue of the Blessed Virgin. Her face took on the appearance it had when Thérèse enjoyed good health. She seemed to be in ecstasy. This look lasted for the space of a 'Credo'. Then she closed her eyes and expired. It was 7.20 in the evening.
>
> Her head was leaning to the right. A mysterious smile was on her lips. She appeared very beautiful; and this is evident in the photograph taken by Céline after her sister's death.[5]

It seems, then, that Thérèse died in an ecstasy of love passing out of deep and terrible suffering into a kind of fullness of joy, a joy not only held within the 'naked intent' of the will, but a joy flowing freely and abundantly into her affectivity or feeling level and somehow overflowing into her worn and ravaged body, restoring it to youth and beauty. This transformation was not sudden and fleeting but lasted for the space of a *Credo*, which is a relatively long time even if one is thinking of a *Credo* recited rather than sung. This transformation, moreover, was but the first of many miraculous or at least wonderful events connected with the heavenly birth and continuing presence of Thérèse in our human world. 'I am not dying; I am entering into life!' Thérèse wrote shortly before she died. She has been with us since; she is with us still; she will surely continue to be with us into the third Christian millennium.

Thérèse was a Catholic and a Carmelite and it is only right and just that the Catholic Church and the Carmelite Order should celebrate her life and spirituality. Few will resent this. Yet there is a real

---

5. *Story of a Soul: The Autobiography of St. Thérèse of Lisieux* tr. J. Clarke, OCD (Washington, DC: Institute of Carmelite Studies, 1975), p. 271.

danger that a truly cosmic being might become imprisoned within the world of the Carmelite mediation of Christian mysticism, or the rather wider world of the Roman Catholic mediation of Christian mysticism; or even for all its riches and glory, the Christian mediation of the universal sacred marriage of divinity and humanity. It is this universal sacred marriage that appears like the first delicate luminosity of dawn in Eliot's 'notion of an infinitely gentle, infinitely suffering' Being, it is this marriage that moves on towards full union in Thérèse's Act of Oblation to the Merciful Love of God in Christ.

Those who have studied the matter tell us of the presence of Thérèse among the soldiers in the two world wars that have ravaged planet earth since her death, and that this presence was wider than Catholicism or even Christianity. There is a church dedicated to Thérèse in Cairo which, it seems, is much visited by Muslim women. When I was there I was told that these women found acceptance and identity which they otherwise lacked. I think rather that she represented a link with their own very rich mystical Sufi tradition, which has always stressed the merciful love of the creator. So also the Hindu Bhakti tradition and Buddhism in its various forms echo the Thérèse phenomenon within Christianty. The love of God is not something held as a possession but something expansive and outgoing; it is this that is so powerfully expressed in Manuscript B of the *Story of a Soul*. This missionary élan is central to Christian mysticism.

Thus it would seem that, in some mysterious way, Thérèse became a cosmic presence not only for Catholics, not only for Christians, but for all who could contact this presence in any way. For she loved everybody everywhere and she had prayed earnestly that, as she put it, she would spend her heaven on earth to help all who would somehow make contact with her. In accordance with the traditional term which we find echoed in Shakespeare's *Hamlet* she had become a 'ministering angel', thus realizing in a new dimension that greatness that she sought by way of littleness.

CONCLUSION: *CARITAS NOVIT EAM*

Caritas novit eam: charity knows this light. This phrase comes from the Latin original of Book 7, Chapter 10 of the *Confessions* of St Augustine. This passage has to do with the light, the unchanging light, *lux incommutabilis*, which Augustine saw within him, with the inner eye of the soul (*occulus animae meae*). This light is not, it would seem, either physical light or any imagined extension or deepening or brightening of this physical light but a light quite, quite other (*aliud, aliud, valde*) than all such things. There is obviously some kind of similarity or analogy with ordinary physical light, dismissed as *vulgaris* and *conspicuus omni carni*, that is clear to animals as well as human beings. Augustine just manages to keep a hold on physical light by a slender thread of analogy. Even as *above* the mind (*supra mentem*) this height is not at all spatial or measurable even metaphorically. It is above the mind in a very special, a unique sense. It is above the mind as having created that very mind on which it shines (*superior, quia ipsa fecit me*). Thus, at once, is expressed infinite distance and infinite closeness, with that kind of power and clarity special to Augustine, the master of rhetoric.

All this is pulled strongly 'upwards' into the double illumination or luminosity of the Platonic–Plotinian 'lamps of the mind', on the one hand and the 'metaphysics of Exodus' (Gilson's phrase) on the other, in which 'far off' Augustine hears the voice of God saying in the words of Exodus 3. 14: I am the God who is (*ego sum qui sum*). The light is somehow *seen*, the voice is somehow *heard*. The voice is heard in the heart (*in corde*) in such a way that all doubt vanishes.

But already, in the heart, a voice has spoken, a very gentle voice that brings all this lofty intellectual speculation within the glow of the 'fire in the heart'. In one short phrase the whole experience of 'the light above the mind' takes on a human countenance, *caritas novit eam*: charity *knows* this light. But surely charity does not *know*? The heart seeks, desires, loves. But does it know? Not only does

CONCLUSION: CARITAS NOVIT EAM

it know this light but in knowing this light 'it knows eternity'. There is, it would seem, a way through from charity as it warms the heart, softens the feelings, opens out to all human beings, and perhaps beyond, in universal compassion – there is a way through from the deep flowing of the heart to that light that shines in on the mind, a way that is according to the way of charity of 1 Corinthians 13.

From this viewpoint it is not so much 'faith that looks through death', in Wordsworth's phrase. It is charity that looks through death. It is charity in its fullness that flows, very gently, grounded in humility, into the awakening to eternity. Charity has its treasures within itself, within the heart's love and tears and does not rest on prophecies or vision; it becomes itself a vision of eternal life. It does not pass away. It gives life and in giving life awakens to that eternal life it gives.

The way then is to a vision, *some* vision, a realization, *some* realization, of the existence of eternal life. This vision for human beings subject to death, is *through* the heart, the heart that awakens, that is softened through that humility that looks upwards and becomes receptive and open to the light.

Nevertheless, although Augustine has a glimpse of this horizon of charity as knowing the light above the mind it does not seem that he is really passing from an intellectual vision of the light to a vision that has its centre in the heart; rather does the heart, as love and humility, share in this vision. When we go on to John of the Cross and the Franciscan – Carmelite approach to God as source and creator we find that the vision of God as love takes over from the vision of God as light and illumination. This is at the centre of the transforming experience that is achieved in the mode of mystical receptivity through the dark night of spirit. Here the light of the intellect is, as it were 'put on hold', so that the heart 'kindled in love with fire of yearnings keen' (*con ansias, en amores inflamada*) (DN st. 1) enters, in deep darkness of the intellect, on the path of spiritual transformation 'with no other light or guide than the one that burns in the heart' (DN st. 3).

Here the journey begun as a journey in the light of intellect, and aided by the feelings, becomes a journey made in inner intellectual darkness. It is within this darkness that the lover God transforms the lover-soul into Himself (Itself, Herself). At this point all knowledge of God is by way of the love of God in the heart. The way of light and truth has become the way of love. It is not that the light of intellect has been in any way negatived or superseded or contradicted, but the fire of love has become the light that guides the lover 'more surely than the light of noon' (DN st. 4). This night-light has been thoroughly purified by the healing darknesses and tribulations, first of the dark night of sense, and then by the dark night of spirit.

Here is charity at its highest, the same charity that St Paul describes in its practical everyday applications in 1 Corinthians 13. Here there is no place for pride or 'seeking one's own' or even for unbelief, for this charity, 'believes all things', as it also 'hopes all things', and 'endures all things'. The heart is fortified by this vision of charity that it follows.

What is surprising and even disconcerting about the later stanzas of the *Noche Oscura* (stanzas 6, 7 and 8), is the extremely tender physical imagery and tone of these stanzas; indeed some have found them erotic in the sense that we are in the atmosphere of a refined and delicate physical relationship of lover and beloved. We are a thousand miles away, it seems from Kant, Luther and Kierkegaard. Yet all this has come out of the bleak asceticism of the dark night at both levels, of sense and spirit. It would seem that for John, now that love has been purified and healed, by its deep immersion in the dark nights, it can show forth frankly and innocently a very human face. It can do this only because John has insisted, more than any Christian writer, on *asceticism*, on the centrality of the cross. It is because of this purification of the *will* that this pure, flowering tenderness is freed from all intrusions of self-indulgent eros at the level of feeling, so much so that the world of feeling has become entirely free and entirely unalloyed by self-indulgence at the physical level of the holy touch and the holy kiss. This is a kind of crowning of the transformation of eros achieved by the first dark night, the dark night of sense. That it should thus emerge and blossom at the purely spiritual level seems to imply and affirm the Resurrection of the Body, so that we have moved far away from the Platonic world of a transformation that is purely spiritual and intellectual, within the intelligible world of the Ideas. The fire in the heart has become the light in the mind, even it may be said the light *above* the mind that 'knows eternity'. It is no wonder that some of John's contemporaries and earliest critics were scandalized by this doctrine and dismissed it as a kind of 'animality'.

It is important at this point to bear in mind that John of the Cross underwent, in the celebrated theological school of Salamanca, a full training in Catholic theology, and that he is at pains to make it clear at the very beginning of his treatise on the *Ascent of Mount Carmel*, and he repeated this in all his great mystical writings, that he submitted all he wrote to the judgement of the Roman Catholic Church, as did also Teresa of Avila. John arose within this tradition and he never deviated from it. This meant that he carried with him a strong and clear intellectual mind-set and that when his experience and doctrine of the dark night took hold of him he remained true to his intellectual training and never put it in question in whole or in part. The great Christian doctrines of the Trinity, the Incarnation, the Resurrection of the Body and the rest were constantly present in his system giving it a firm intellectual ground and horizon. When the will took over and the intellect was left in darkness, this always implied the presence of an implicit intellectual light which he never relinquished for a moment. This traditional light gave him a clear direction, but it did not form the substance of his prayer, which acquired depth and warmth and a new level of illumination by the way of the heart 'kindled with love in fire of yearnings keen'. This journey of illumination and union with the Divine Lover is made in deep darkness of sense and spirit, yet it is made in total security because the senses are at rest and at the end of the journey, 'He was awaiting me: him I *knew* well (*quien yo bien me sabía*)' (DN st. 4). Long meditation on Christ's presence in Scripture had made him securely present to the understanding, who was now to be met in a union of love. This union filled the heart to overflowing and flooded 'the deep caverns of sense' (LF st. 3): this flooding is lyrically expressed in the three concluding stanzas of the poem.

But this flowing and overflowing is also a kind of *knowing*; it is a knowing of God as the great lover, and this is the highest, purest and deepest knowledge of God that the human mind can reach. It is the fulfilment and liberation of the deepest desire of the human being. Jesus Christ as the true Bridegroom of the soul 'kindled with love in yearnings keen' is in Sebastian Moore's phrase 'the liberator of desire', though it can be asked how far Moore is able to fulfil the promise implicit in the phrase without making use of the ancient mystical category of the spiritual senses.

Knowledge and love are indeed distinct as intellect and will are distinct and open towards different objects and objectives: all kinds of disasters large and small come from confusing them. But at a certain pure and exalted level they travel together. Around the summit of 'Mount Carmel', in his famous drawing of the Mount of Perfection, John himself writes: 'Here there is no longer any way because for the just man there is no law; he is a law unto himself.' If there is no longer any way, there is no longer any need to discern or see the way with the eye of the intellect. But it must be kept firmly in mind that 'the just man' is the person who has passed through the narrow gate of the *nadas* and lived by those daunting sayings set down at the foot of the drawing and repeated in Chapter 13 of Book One of the *Ascent*. Any kind of facile 'follow the ecstasy' or 'x easy lessons on mysticism' approach is totally opposed to the way of John of the Cross. This is not a matter of choice, not a matter of willing and feeling, but a matter of strict logic and clear thinking. It is only *when this intellectual work has been done* and is fully established that the way of the heart can take over and that love can be said to 'see the way'. It is only then that charity may be said to 'know'.

Not only does the way of charity, the way of love, come in at this point to supplement the way of the intelligence and philosophical speculation: rather does it bring a new kind of illumination which floods the whole landscape of the soul and spirit. Indeed this is the central insight of all spiritual genius, from the genius of Paul at the gate of Christian experience, through Teresa and John of the Cross, right down to Thérèse of Lisieux at the gateway of the twentieth century.

Again and again we read St Paul's hymn to charity in 1 Corinthians 13, again and again we hear it read without letting it burst upon us like sheet lightning. St Paul we must understand, is here dealing with *ways*, with different *understandings* of the Christian *way*, all within the light-world of intelligence. Then like a thunderclap the text breaks apart in a great rhetorical explosion of charisms, heroisms, almsgiving, martyrdom, all of which ways are left in tatters and fragments. Not this, not that, not that other, though they are in each case great heroisms, *admirabilia*, it would seem, of godliness and greatness of soul. Not only are they not the better, the super-excellent way; they are without *it* absolutely false and worthless. One is left wondering at the gateway of the third millennium, whether Christians who so marvellously over the centuries have filled a thousand academies and a million pulpits have ever really awakened to this heart-knowledge, that does not go ahead of, but presupposes and transcends intellectual knowledge, and at a certain point or threshold takes up the whole space occupied by intellectual knowledge.

The great temptation at this point is to sharpen, widen, deepen our intellectual analysis of the text of St Paul, weighing ever more carefully the words of the original Greek text, comparing it with other texts, variously opening up horizons, consulting various commentaries. In all this we are still in the world of the ordinary ways. We have not found the *kath hyperbolen hodon*, the alternative way, that is an alternative to all understandable ways, that is not a way of understanding at all, but a way of living, a way of praying, a way of suffering, a way of being human.

Above all it is a way of humility 'the only wisdom we can hope to acquire.' (T. S. Eliot). It is a way of *listening*; it is the way of the heart that listens to something that is all around us. As I listen I may feel I am being judged, that the Accuser, the Adversary, is wrenching the text away from me. Instead of being humanized and softened by these heavenly words of St Paul I am perhaps being forced to harden myself into self-defence. 'Love does not insist on its own way,' but I do constantly insist on my own way as do all the people around me. Already I am hearing the text in a mental, analytical way, and already I am beginning to feel the chill, and I am shutting out the healing warmth of the vision behind the words. To connect with this warmth I must leave aside the way of analysis and open up to the way of intimation. Yes, perhaps it is true that as a general rule I do insist on my own way, but perhaps this once I may manage to insist less insistently, or perhaps I may at least *wish* to do so, and by this wish I am already taking a first step towards the wisdom of the heart. I am beginning to open to a warm vision rather than subjecting myself to the cold eye of self-judgement and self-rejection.

In this paradox of warmth and cold we are touching the fringes or curtains of mystery, and our intimational explorations must rest in prayer on the human side of mystery, accepting in the warmth of humility the opening horizons of the divine glory. Somehow, somewhere – perhaps when he was taken up into the third heaven (2 Cor. 12.2) – Paul had a vision or glimpse of this divine glory of love-agape, and it is this vision that he is striving to convey to the troubled hearts and confused minds of his Corinthian Christians. He knows that there is no way of clarifying their minds – this would be simply to add another *ism* to their confusion – except by first softening and deepening their hearts. He is giving them warmth rather than light, the kind of warmth that brings *its own kind of light*. *Cor ad cor loquitur*: heart speaks to heart. The whole text must be *felt*, and it will be understood only according as it is felt. It can only be felt if there is a shift of attitude, a change of heart, a *metanoia*; and without this all knowledge is vain and all heroism is vain. It is at this point that the warmth of agape flows into knowledge and completes it *as* knowledge, and that the truth begins to live in the human soul, in 'the deep heart's core'.

This is not a trivial point, nor is it merely a question of a balance between head and heart, intellect and will. Rather, there is question of the kind of balance which can be lost imperceptively so that the link with the Source of vitalizing goodness can be lost. It is the kind of balance that is achieved not by subtraction but by addition, not by diminishing intellectual clarity to suit an undeveloped heart, the half-light of feelings half realized, but by prayerful and sacrificial cleansing and strengthening of the intellect as the servant of the light. The profoundest wisdom of the intellect is that of putting the heart's fire ahead of the mind's light; by its own best light the mind sees it must accept a kind of transfiguration into fire, that holy fire from which all light comes: 'the same heart's fire He came to light them by' (Thérèse, poem 23).[1] This is the message of all apophatic mysticism from Denis to the *Cloud*, to John of the Cross, to Thérèse of Lisieux; for the apophatic is literally what cannot be said because it cannot be thought. It shines by its own fire-light in the deep heart's core. To 'see' it demands not less of visioning but more, and that more comes only as a gift to the heart of man from the heart of God, once the heart of man is readied and ready to receive it.

Three precious testimonies have emerged from the final tremendous period of Thérèse's short life, and it is from these especially that we may hope to understand the 'little way' which has marked a revolution in the Christian understanding of God as Father and Lover.

There is in the first place, and most important, the third manuscript of the *Story of a Soul* (Manuscript C); secondly, the so-called 'Yellow Notebook' of Pauline (Mother Agnes) published under the title *St Thérèse of Lisieux: Her Last Conversations*; and thirdly, Céline's book, '*A Memoir of My Sister St Thérèse*', less important than the other two but interesting from a pedagogical point of view, as showing how Thérèse's 'little way,' seemingly so easy to grasp, only gradually and painfully dawned on her first pupil. It gradually 'dawned' on Céline not because it is difficult to grasp or because Céline was lacking in intelligence, but because it is not something that can be grasped or understood by the mind, but rather very gradually assimilated by the heart: *caritas novit eam.*

But, of course, neither the *Story of a Soul* nor the *Last Conversations*

1. *Poems of St Thérèse of Lisieux*, tr. A. Bancroft (London: HarperCollins, 1996), p. 90.

is a book simply to read and pass on. Each book is an invitation to share an experience of unique depth and purity, expressed with disconcerting bareness and simplicity, expressed one might be tempted to say in clichés, until one realizes (on second or third reading perhaps) that these clichés are all new coin fresh from the original royal mint. And, especially in the *Last Conversations*, the material being used is the pure gold of sacrificial love.

This metaphor slips in easily: the material is pure gold, yes. But how pure is pure? And how is one to judge, to estimate purity? The truth is that there is here the question of a purity that vanishes from view, that vanishes into the clouds, that vanishes into the sun. It hurts normal eyes, normal vision. Here the theologian is dazzled as the philosopher is dazzled. The mystic whose essential work as mystic is in the order of the receptive heart rather than the controlling mind, the mystic who is also a poet, can alone face this vision, 'being guided by the light that burns in the heart', to use John's words in his great poem *The Dark Night*. This light is not so much light as fire; it does not illuminate unless and in so far as it is first *felt* 'in the deep heart's core'.

For what Thérèse has to say about the great love that has 'stolen' her heart is not descriptive or evocative but intimational. It calls us to share an experience, to enter an inner sanctuary, a place of the shedding of sandals and of half-experienced whispers. One cannot enter in booted and spurred in readiness for a theological gallop. One can only enter on tiptoe; one can only enter through the doorway of wonder, bending low and low like a child. This is all implied in the pedagogy of the 'little way' of Thérèse.

Caritas novit eam: charity knows this light. At the beginning of chapter eleven, the final chapter of her story, Thérèse tells us that Jesus granted her the grace (i.e. the heavenly God-given gift) of 'penetrating into the mysterious depths of charity'.[2] In this final chapter Thérèse does not talk about merciful love, but it fills the whole chapter

---

2. J. Clarke, OCD, tr. *Story of a Soul: The Autobiography of St Thérèse of Lisieux* (Washington, DC: Institute of Carmelite Studies, 1975), p. 233.

like a perfume and it completes what she has already written about her 'little way' of merciful love. For here her whole life shows this merciful love flowing out to those around her and flowing back from others into her own life and death. For, as Fr. François de Sainte-Marie saw, this is the 'golden key that opens for us the soul of Thérèse'.

For merciful love is not only God's love as it flows into each of us, but also that same love as it flows through us and from us and towards us from others. I can only open my heart to this love to the extent that I show it forth to those around me. Charity does not seek its own according to the measure of justice; it flows forth in abundance according to the divine flowing of mercy that is part of the mysterious depths of charity that Thérèse, the great mystic, has received as a *grace*. This is abundantly expressed in her life and death.

What is also abundantly expressed in her life and death, emerging very clearly in the additional chapter of the *Story of a Soul*, not written by Thérèse but added, it seems, by her sister Pauline and continuous with the *Last Conversations*, is that Thérèse looked for support in her terribly testing journey into death, not only to her sisters, but also to her superior, Mother Gonzague, that heroic and formidable and all-too-human woman who stayed with her all the time. This above all is the trial and test of merciful love as mediated by others to us in sickness and old age. It makes the most absolute demands on that childlike humility which is the foundation for all of us of that 'little way', which in the end is the only way to self - knowledge and the deep knowledge of the Source of our being as merciful love received in total trust, humility and prayer.

INDEX